MEMOS
OF A
WEST POINT
CADET

MEMOS OF A WEST POINT CADET

Jaime Mardis

David McKay Company, Inc.
New York

Library of Congress Cataloging in Publication Data

Mardis, Jaime.
  Memos of a West Point cadet.

  1. United States.   Military Academy, West Point.
2. Mardis, Jaime.   I.   Title.
U410.P1M37   355'.007'1174731   76-17295
ISBN 0-679-50602-0

To Selwyn,
a Southern Belle
in the grand tradition

I wish to acknowledge the steadfastness and the acumen of my editor, David Currier.

Disclaimer

Memos of a West Point Cadet is based on the year I spent at the United States Military Academy. With the exception of myself, the characters in this story are fictional. Each character is a composite—whether officer, cadet, or civilian—representing a "type" rather than a particular individual.

Any resemblance to any person is entirely coincidental.

Most of the events in this story are based on fact. However, as in any account transformed for dramatic purposes, chronology and context and relations of characters to events have in some instances been altered or distilled from several sources and combined.

I have spent three years and written over 2,500 pages of material to faithfully reproduce my impressions of the human condition at the United States Military Academy in the troubled years 1969-70.

JAIME MARDIS

Introduction

**HEADQUARTERS NEW CADET BATTALION
UNITED STATES CORPS OF CADETS**
West Point, New York 10996

ADMINISTRATIVE MEMORANDUM   1 July 1969
NUMBER   1

FOURTH CLASS SYSTEM

1. The Fourth Class System operates to support the missions of the United States Military Academy and New Cadet Barracks. It is a process of converting a young man from a civilian into a professional soldier. Its purpose is to develop in the Fourth Classmen:

  a. Discipline.
  b. Poise and confidence in his abilities.
  c. Pride in himself, his unit, and his profession.
  d. A knowledge of his profession and his unit.
  e. An unyielding sense of duty.
  f. Military bearing and attention to personal appearance.
  g. Physical and mental toughness.
  h. An ability to work with other people.

2. New cadets will be required to adhere to the highest standards of military decorum at all times. They will salute all cadets and officers.

3. New cadets are not authorized to escort prior to granting of New Cadet Privileges.

4. Fourth Classmen have the duty to answer all reasonable questions in a direct and unequivocal manner.

1

5. New cadets are expected to maintain the Fourth Class position of attention except in the following places:

a. In Thayer Hall.

b. On the Plain.

c. When outside the area of barracks on privileges.

d. From Taps to First Call for Reveille.

e. When in a new cadet room unless in the presence of a detail member.

f. In specified latrine areas.

g. In the Mess Hall from the command "Take Seats" to the command "Battalion Rise."

6. *In Barracks.* New cadets will adhere to the following policies when in barracks:

a. In halls, sinks, orderly rooms, and upperclass rooms, new cadets will:

(1) Be at the Fourth Class position of attention from first call for Reveille until Taps.

(2) Talk only when addressed by an upperclassman or in the conduct of official business.

(3) Not smoke, eat, or consume beverages.

(4) Not use vending machines.

(5) Walk at the quick time on the wall side of the hallway in all halls, except that new cadets will double-time, but not run, or skip steps, when going up and down stairs.

(6) Be required to yield the right of way in the halls and stairways.

(7) Square all corners in halls.

(8) Remove caps when entering barracks except when under arms or on official business.

(9) Remove all outer garments when entering upperclass rooms, except on official business.

(10) Report on special inspection in the uniform for the next formation, unless directed to do otherwise.

(11) Not read the bulletin boards from ten minutes before, until ten minutes after a formation, unless directed to do otherwise.

(12) Not use the latrine area as a thoroughfare.

(13) Be at ease in the latrines.

b. In new cadet rooms, new cadets will:

(1) Call the room to attention when an upperclassman or officer enters.

(2) Keep their doors closed at all times from Reveille to Taps, except when otherwise directed; and will keep their doors open at all times from Taps to Reveille except when otherwise directed.

(3) Not lie down until Taps unless given specific authority to do so.

(4) Keep their rooms in proper order at all times as prescribed by New Cadet Barracks Regulations.

7. *On the Apron.* The Apron is defined to be the cement area adjacent to "C" and "D" wings from Thayer Road to Scott's place. When on the Apron, new cadets will:

a. Be at the Fourth Class position of attention at all times unless otherwise directed.

b. Talk to classmates concerning official business *only* with the permission of an upperclassman in the vicinity.

c. Confine their movement to that area on the inside of the imaginary line formed by the inner row of elm trees.

d. Move at the double-time with arms parallel to the ground unless otherwise directed.

e. Not pass through nor watch any formations.

f. Be in ranks by the initial sound of the first call bell at all formations.

8. *In the Dining Hall.* New cadets will adhere to the following policies when in the dining hall:

a. When entering the dining hall and when at their seats before "Battalion Attention", new cadets will:

(1) Remove their caps at the foot of the steps as they enter the dining hall, except when it is raining. When it is raining, they will remove their caps at the top of the steps. They will replace their caps similarly upon leaving the dining hall.

(2) Double-time, but not run, from the bottom step to their seat, except when wearing overshoes. They will confine themselves to the center of the aisles and will give upperclassmen the right of way.

(3) Not use the outer two aisles nearest each wall.

(4) Keep head erect and eyes downward except when addressed by an upperclassman, in which case they will face and look at the upperclassman.

(5) Upon reaching the table, stand at the Fourth Class position of attention behind their seats with their caps in their left hand.

b. When seated at the table, new cadets will:

(1) Sit erect on all of the chair at a normal position of attention with their back not resting against the chair.

(2) Keep their head erect and eyes directed on the plate, except when performing duties or addressed by an upperclassman.

(3) Take a normal size bite.

(4) Take only one swallow of liquid at a time.

(5) Not begin to chew their food until their utensils have been properly placed on their plate, and will not pick up another portion of food until they have completely chewed and swallowed their previous bite: a similar policy applies to liquids.

c. New cadets will perform the following duties:

(1) Each new cadet will know the beverage preferences of the upperclassmen sitting at their table.

(2) Each new cadet will know the waiter's first name and will treat waiters courteously.

(3) One new cadet will be detailed as "Hot Beverage Corporal" and will sit adjacent to the hot beverages. He will keep the table supplied with the hot beverage being served.

(4) One new cadet will be detailed as "Cold Beverage Corporal" and will sit at the foot of the table. He will keep the table supplied with the cold beverage being served.

(5) One new cadet will be detailed as "Gunner" and will sit opposite the Hot Beverage Corporal.

(6) One new cadet will be detailed as "Dessert Cutter"and will sit adjacent to the Gunner. He will see that all desserts that require cutting are cut in the appropriate number of pieces. He will ascertain the appropriate number of pieces by stating: "Sir, the dessert for this meal is ———. Is there anyone who would not care for ———?" At the completion of the cutting, he will announce: "Sir, the ——— has been cut. ——— to Mr. (*Table Commandant*) please sir."

4

(7) Before sending serving dishes to the kitchen to be refilled, the Gunner will announce: "Sir, there are ——— servings of ——— remaining at the table. Would anyone care for more ———, sir?"

(8) When the waiter's table is adjacent to the head of the table, the Gunner will announce: "Serving dish for the waiter's table please, sir," and will pass the dish by the most direct route.

(9) On receipt of all food and beverages, the recipient will thank waiter and announce: "Sir, the ——— is on the table." When the food is extra, the recipient will so state.

(10) New cadets will ask for additional food only after the upperclassmen at the table have been served, and will determine the foregoing by asking, "Sir, would anyone else care for more ———?" Following which he may request food be passed to him by saying: ——— please, sir."

9. *Limits.* Locations listed below are OFF LIMITS to new cadets:

a. At all times:
(1) Flirtation Walk
(2) Delafield Pond and Picnic Area.
(3) The Plain, except when training, on official business, or engaged in athletics as directed by OPE.
(4) Grant Hall except as authorized by Regulations (Supplement), New Cadet Barracks.
(5) Weapons Room.
(6) New Diagonal Walk, except when in formation or escorting.
(7) All other areas as outlined in Regulations (Supplement), New Cadet Barracks.

b. That portion of Brewerton Road between the steps leading to Building 720 near South Area and the 50th Division of Barracks is OFF LIMITS except as required to accomplish official business.

10. *Restrictions.* Listed below are specific restrictions which apply to new cadets. New cadets will:

a. Not talk or smoke in halls of academic buildings.
b. Have the opportunity, when privileges are in effect, to attend the motion picture individually only when escorting.

5

c. Not use steps adjacent to the Cadet Chapel nor the steps behind West Barracks.

d. Use barber shops from Monday through Friday. Members of Detail will have priority in the barber shops.

e. Not wear jewelry to include rings or identification bracelets. New cadets may wear a wrist watch and a religious medalion.

f. Not have alarm clocks.

g. Not play any sports except as directed by OPE.

h. Not watch upperclassmen in formation.

i. Not possess cameras.

11. *New Cadet Duties.*

a. New cadet duties will be performed by all new cadets.

b. Improper performance of new cadet duties will require corrective measures.

c. New cadet duties will include the following:

(1) Dining Hall duties as prescribed in paragraph 8.

(2) Company duties:

    a. Mail Carrier.

    b. Laundry Carrier.

    c. Other duties as prescribed by the Company Commander.

    d. Minute Caller.

    e. Assistant Cadet-in-Charge of Quarters may be detailed when New Cadet Privileges are in effect. New Cadets assigned this duty will be detailed by Company Duty Roster for one of the following periods:

        Saturday afternoon

        Saturday evening

        Sunday morning (must attend Chapel)

        Sunday afternoon

12. *Duty*: Laundry Carrier

a. Responsibilities: The laundry carrier is responsible for the prompt and correct delivery of all laundry and dry cleaning delivered to the company area, to include any staff attached to the company. In addition, laundry carriers are responsible to deliver clothing returned to the Orderly Room from the Cadet Store clothing repair section.

6

b. General:The laundry carrier is under the supervision and control of the Head Laundry Carrier and the Cadet-in-Charge of Quarters. The detailed new cadets bear the responsibility of delivery of laundry to their respective floor. However, it is the obligation and duty of all Fourth Classmen in the company to help the detailed Fourth Classmen in the delivery of dry cleaning and laundry. All laundry and dry cleaning will be delivered to the appropriate cadet by 1800 hours of the day it is placed in thecompany area.

13. *Mail Carrier*

a. Responsibilities: The mail carrier is responsible for the prompt and correct delivery of newspapers, mail and official distribution.

b. General: The mail carrier is under the supervision and control of the head mail carrier and the Cadet-in-Charge of Quarters. Before returning to his room, having completed his distribution, the mail carrier will report to the CCQ to insure that he has no more duties to perform at that time. The regular duty uniform will be worn at all times; the head gear will not be removed while performing his duties. The head mail carrier will report to the First Sergeant's room for distribution at 1145 and 1930 hours to pick up distribution. The head mail carrier is responsible for insuring that his company gets sufficient newspapers daily and that all newspaper scraps are policed. Insufficient newspapers should be reported immediately to Company Supply Sergeant.

c. Specific Duties:

Time	Duty
0550	Obtain enough newspapers for the assigned area from the company pickup point and distribute to the floor—one newspaper per room. If there are not enough newspapers, insure that upperclass rooms receive one. Mail carriers are *not* excused from reveille to perform their duties. They will attend reveille formation. Check the doors of all upperclass

rooms for mail and deposit it in the mailbox at the southwest corner of New South Area prior to reveille assembly. Police the area of newspaper scraps.

1155   Report to the Orderly Room to deliver mail and official distribution.

1520   Report to the Orderly Room to deliver mail.

1915   Report to the Orderly Room to deliver official distribution. On days before laundry goes out, deliver two (2) laundry slips to each individual in the company. On days prior to dry cleaning going out deliver dry cleaning or press only tags to all personnel. Give each individual only as many tags as he needs.

NOTE: Under no circumstances will mail carriers miss any scheduled formation to perform their duties. If they must delay completion of their duties, they will return any undelivered mail to the Orderly Room for distribution at a later time.

14. *Duty*: Minute Callers

a. Responsibilities: The minute caller is responsible for calling minutes on his floor for all formations which include more than half of the company.

b. General: The minute caller is under the supervision and control of the upperclassmen on the floor for which he is calling minutes.

(1) The minute caller will appear in the uniform which is to be worn to the formation.

(2) The minute caller will insure that he leaves his post

with enough time to arrive at the formation on time. There is no excuse for being late to the formation.

c. Specific Duties:

(1) For reveille, meal, and training formation, the minute caller will announce the minutes remaining at 10, 5, 4, 3 and 2 minutes until the formation.

(2) For Chapel, Parades, and Ceremonies, the minute caller will announce the minutes remaining at 20, 15, 10, 6, 5, 4, and 3 minutes until the formation.

(3) The minute caller will report to Special Inspection five (5) minutes early on days that he is to perform this duty.

(4) The following format will be used when calling minutes: SIR, THERE ARE —— MINUTES UNTIL AS-SEMBLY FOR —— FORMATION. THE UNIFORM IS ——. ——MINUTES, SIR!

(5) When calling minutes for all meal formations, the menu will be announced between the uniform and the repetition of the number of minutes remaining. The menu will include the main course, at least two (2) side dishes, the dessert, and the beverage. The following format will be used:

FOR —— WE ARE HAVING: ——, ——, —— AND ——.

The menu will be inserted at the 10, 6, and 4 minute calls.

(6) When calling the last minute for a formation, the following announcement will be inserted between the uniform and the final repetition of the minutes.

THIS IS THE LAST MINUTE TO BE CALLED FOR THIS FORMATION. DO NOT FORGET YOUR LIGHTS, SIR.

(7) When calling minutes for optional meals formations, the following announcement will be inserted just prior to the repetition of the minutes remaining: DO NOT FORGET YOUR MEAL TICKETS. . . . This announcement will be inserted at every minute called.

15. *New Cadet Knowledge*

a. The purpose of this section is to outline the traditional knowledge which the new cadet will know so that he will be prepared to join the Corps of Cadets.

b. The purpose of New Cadet Knowledge is to introduce the new cadet to the customs and traditions of West Point and the United States Army. The new cadet will not be required to learn trivia or material failing to contribute directly to this end.

c. The following knowledge will be learned by the end of the first detail.

(I) Verbatim knowledge.

First Week

a. Chain of Command—President to squad leader.

b. The days.

Second Week

a. Schofield's "Definition of Discipline".

b. Mission of the United States Military Academy.

Third Week

Alma Mater; The Corps (only those verses contained in Bugle Notes).

Fourth Week

a. The Code of Conduct.

b. Worth's "Battalion Orders".

c. Familiarization with "All Rights".

d. The following knowledge will be learned by the end of the seventh week:

(1) Verbatim knowledge:

a. Benny Havens and Army Blue.

b. Chairman of the Joint Chiefs of Staff, and Chief of Staff of each of the Armed Forces.

c. Insignia of rank of the Army, Air Force, Navy, and Marine Corps.

d. Insignia of Cadet Rank.

e. Branch insignia.

f. Corps Squad Captains.

g. Songs & Cheers.

(2) General knowledge:

a. Basic Military courtesies.

b. Basic principles of etiquette.

e. The following knowledge will be learned daily:

(1) The "Days" to include:

a. Movies and upperclass events for the week.

b. Special programs for the weekend.

c. Number of days until the Ring Hop, away football

10

games, Navy games, Christmas leave, 100th Night, Spring Leave, and Graduation.

 (2) The Officer-in-Charge.

 (3) The menu for the day only.

16. *Format: The Days*

 Sir, the Days. Today is Sun., 27 Jul 69. The events for the week are as follows: Today at —— hours in the S. Auditorium of Thayer Hall there will be a motion picture entitled, ———, starring Miss —— and Mr. —— ———.

 Monday at —— hours, "etc.". . . .

 Tuesday. . . .

 Wednesday. . . .

 Thursday. . . .

 Friday. . . .

 There are *5* and a butt days until the weekend and the following events:

 Saturday at —— hours, "etc.". . . .

 Sunday at—— hours, "etc.". . . .

 There are *61* and a butt days until the Ring Hop.

 There are *82* and a butt days until Army beats Vanderbilt University in Nashville, Tenn.

 There are *96* and a butt days until Army beats the University of Notre Dame at Yankee Stadium.

 There are *124* and a butt days until Army beats the University of Oregon in Eugene, Oregon.

 There are *145* and a butt days until Army beats the hell out of Navy at John Fitzgerald Kennedy Memorial Stadium in Philadelphia, Penn.

 There are *166* and a butt days until Christmas Leave for the United States Corps of Cadets.

 There are *231* and a butt days until 100th Night for the Class of 1970.

 There are *255* and a butt days until Spring Leave for the upper three classes.

 There are *331* and a butt days until Graduation and Graduation Leave for the Class of 1970, Sir.

17. *Reporting*

 a. When an officer enters a new cadet room, all new cadets

11

will come to the position of attention. The new cadet who is nearest to the officer will salute and report "Sir, New Cadet ——— reports." When the officer returns the salute, the new cadet will order arms. When the officer leaves the room, all new cadets will salute and report "Good Morning, Sir".

b. When an inspecting officer or cadet officer enters a new cadet room, during a scheduled room inspection, the room orderly will report "Sir, New Cadet ——— reports Room (118) is prepared for inspection." When the inspecting officer or cadet officer leaves the room, all new cadets will salute and report "(Good Morning) Sir".

c. When a new cadet reports to an officer or cadet, he will knock twice and wait for a response. If there is no reply he will open the door, enter and salute. He will report, "Sir, New Cadet ——— reports to Mr. (for special inspection) as ordered." When the new cadet leaves the room, he will face the officer or cadet, salute, and report, "Good Morning, Sir." He will then order arms, return the door to the position it was in when he entered, and depart.

FOR THE COMMANDER:

Cadet Captain
Adjutant

MEMO 1.

History knows by now that one of those first three men to land on the moon was a West Pointer. *God bless America!* is what I think he said as he plunged a conquering banner deep into the lunar sand. Then he grabbed a rock and waved it gaily before the camera eye. *Hi, Mom! This one's for you! Hi there, Mister President!* And a million miles below, the world gasped, *It's a rock!* . . .

"Quit daydreaming, Mardis, you beanhead. Wipe that look off your face. This is history."

That was Cadet Corporal Garth U. Tilson, my Squad Leader in New Cadet Training, or Beast Barracks as it's called. The date, July 1969, and the freshly arrived class of New Cadets had been corralled to the South Auditorium of Thayer Hall to witness the moon landing. I sat in an aisle seat, with Garth Tilson stooping over me in the darkness.

"I guess you know you'll never make it that far, don't you?" he hissed. "Well, let's have an answer, Mister."

"Yes, sir," I whispered.

"That's more like it," my squad leader told me. "But you know, you *bug* me, Mardis. I mean, you really bug me. And I think I know what it is with you, too. You wanta know what it is? I'll tell you. It's not that you're just a lousy cadet. You make a *lousy* human being, too."

Cadet Corporal Garth U. Tilson leered at me. He had a nervous nose and a fatso belly flanked by two oddly skinny arms, like a pregnant fashion model. But in his

13

tight khaki uniform and midnight-blue helmet, Garth U. Tilson looked like a god. He said, "Just watching you giggle in the presence of those astronauts up there gives me a bad case of the bad ass, buddy. But now I know what kind of stuff you're made of, all right."

A grand cheer went up in the auditorium as the astronauts held up a virtual boulder for everyone to see. Tilson cast a glance to the moon men bobbing back and forth across the gray screen, and then he turned on me viciously, some six inches away. "Your kind make me sick, Mister. Plenty sick," he said with piercing breath. "Now you watch those astronauts, Mister Beanhead, and you watch 'em good, and if you can't appreciate your betters, you better make it look like you do. West Point is for men, beanhead, for *great* men, and you don't even qualify as a boy scout."

It was true; I never was a boy scout. I went to St. Francis's Preparatory School, where we'd been taught to behave like young gentlemen and to look upon the follies of boyhood as something crass. We were taught to conform to an elite social order. Nevertheless, a social disorder in the form of peace marching, flower children, LSD, and long hair emerged uninvited at St. Francis's Preparatory in my second year of high school.

Our glee club had been the most responsible, or irresponsible, for staging the disturbances and demonstrations in our sacred St. Frankie quadrangle. And those radical glee club boys, in their hooliganism, did succeed in affecting the rest of us. We felt old-fashioned, and left out, and, at the very least, sheltered. As for me, I began to feel that I too wanted to be unconventional—to be different! I was, after all, a nonconformist in my own way, and when I informed Mr. Murray, the dean, of my college decision, he was astonished.

14

"Why . . . you'll never make it, lad," he told me in his Harvard way. "Not a chance in heaven! Don't you realize what time cadets have to wake up in the morning?" Mr. Murray was unconvinced that the class leader in tardy arrivals would fare well in a military setting—and he only agreed to endorse me after I promised never to be late for his classes again. "My son," the silvery-haired gentleman addressed me, "if you claim to be capable of turning over a new leaf, I see no reason why you shouldn't start tomorrow morning. Eight fifteen, shall we say?"

But it was unlikely that I'd be on time because I had other priorities on my prep school schedule—namely, dreaming late into the night along with the late movies. *Captains Courageous, The Charge of the Bengal Lancers,* how I longed to follow in the footsteps of those grand cavaliers, swashbuckling and fencing my way forth, hopping on my steed and galloping onward past the drab monotony of a pedestrian society. I had even imagined that I'd return to St. Francis's some day with my dashing staff, and stage a Robin Hood orgy in the cafeteria. But I knew from my studies that this would be an act of *iconoclasm.*

At the suggestion of an Academy memorandum, I had stayed at New York City's Hotel Biltmore on the night of June 30th, the night before the day of report for New Cadet Training. Specially chartered buses would pick us up at the hotel early the next morning and make the trip sixty miles north along the Hudson River to West Point. There were three other "unescorted" appointees in the hotel room, and they mostly sat around and drank milk shakes and discussed football heros. But I was on the other side of the room, intently absorbed by a movie on television called *The Brave Die Young.* The fellows weren't interested in it in the least, because, after taking a

15

look, they all agreed that the deaths weren't very authentic.

When morning came I was gentlemanly enough to let everyone go ahead of me in the bathroom, and this act of kindness was responsible for my being on the last bus leaving for the Point. The last bus took its time going there too, and once we did arrive, our group was way at the back of the line for "in-processing." And when I finally reported to Fifth New Cadet Company in New Washington Hall with my two duffle bags of cadet-issue equipment, the basic marching formations had already ended. The immediate order of business for the upper-class chain of command was to have us properly dressed for the Official Oath Taking Ceremony, which would be attended by the Vice-President of the United States.

Garth Tilson had frowned when he met me, but he was too busy verifying that I had a correctly fitting and complete uniform for the Oath Taking Parade to bother asking whether I knew how to march. He just said, "Get pinging, smack! We got a Full Dress Parade with the Veep at 1530!"

By 1525 hours, we new men of the Corps were lined up handsomely along the parade plain, standing ready for our benediction march. A plumed upperclassman drew and pointed his saber toward the distant speakers' platform. "Number Two is up there!" someone cried. Then the band struck up the Official West Point March, commands were given, and I took my first step on the wrong foot—the right foot, not the official left foot. I was out of step the whole way, causing a ripple to shoot across the field of soldiers like a runner in a new stocking.

Tilson was ripping off his gloves and wrinkling his nose as he charged into Room 3242 after the Oath Ceremony. Room 3242 was the new home I shared with two other New Cadets, and not a very private one. My room-mates hit the wall in terror at the sight of our furious squad leader. Fortunately his rank didn't entitle him to a

16

saber; he might well have diced me up where I knelt tying a shoe lace.

"You made half this company out of step in front of the Veep, you filthy bozo!" raged Tilson. "I should have spotted you for a bozo, all right!" He seemed stupified for a moment. "Mister! You stand at attention when addressed by an upperclassman!"

I finished the lace and stood, tensing up into a position of attention. "What's a bozo, sir?"

"You're a bozo, Mister—and don't use contractions! And you *jump* when an upperclassman comes into the room. Get that chin in! Get those shoulders back! You don't speak unless spoken to, get it? Now let's have your four regulation answers," he snorted.

One of the roommates had to fill me in, at Tilson's request. "Sir, my four regulation answers are *Yes, sir; No, sir; No excuse, sir; and Sir, I do not understand!*"

"Which one do you want, ya bozo?" he asked.

"Sir, I do not understand."

"Try again, Mister Mardis."

"No excuse, sir."

"That's right, Mardis. There is no excuse. And I doubt you'll ever find one. Now let me tell you something, you lowly beanhead. We don't like your type around here, get it? So you better shape ship and shit sharp, get it? *Now why were you out of step?*"

It was soon obvious that Garth Tilson was not my friend. Nor was he alone in his belligerent attitude; all the upperclassmen were enemies of the New Cadet. And they all seemed to speak the same language, tough-guy threats uttered with an incoherent, Cro-Magnon fervor. Sometimes when the upperclassmen were hazing us, they threw in some brotherly concern just to make us feel at home—"You *like* this, don't you Mister?" they'd pant. "If you don't like it, Mister, then what the hell are you doing here? Mister! You better tell me you *like* it!"

Cat Man, who jumped out of a third-story window and

17

landed on his feet, didn't like it. The River Rat, who bolted from our third parade and swam the Hudson River to freedom, also reneged. But Brasso Man, who voluntarily drank a can of brass polish to spite his squad leader, stayed on. He had guts of steel and, like the majority, could adjust to the incarceration, the memorization, the backbreaking regimen, endless formations, corrections, and relentless harassment of Beast Barracks.

In the Darwinian style, the eight weeks of training made us fit, bold, and proud. When we saw the blister squad hobbling to a lecture or to meals, we in ranks felt just a little bit better because we had tougher feet. When a fellow New Cadet was braced against the wall and hazed because he couldn't recite his Plebe Knowledge, we'd feel that much better than him since your poop was "pat and packaged." The thrill of being more adaptable reached a peak however, when a failed cadet would be seen in escort to the Boarders Ward—quitters' prison—where he'd be processed back to the civilian world COD! We had survived, and he hadn't.

Gumboldkirschner, my roommate in Room 3242, won an award after three weeks of training. He had excelled, receiving few demerits, having his shoes always well shined, his belt buckle straight, his name tag above the right pocket; his poop was pat and he kept his nose clean. Gumboldkirschner, from Troy, Ohio, was an amateur wrestler and weight lifter. When he was just a freshman in the Troy high school, he had landed a spot on the junior varsity wrestling team. Lifting weights was really just a pastime, he told me.

Gumboldkirschner's first name was Harold, after his grandfather, but he had been Hank since he was two years old. He proved it by showing me a checkbook with the name Hank G. on the unused checks. Hank G. had a large build but a lean, fierce look to his face that you sometimes see in boxing posters. I think Hank did a lot of boxing and wrestling in his dreams, since he had the same fierce look about him when he'd snore at his desk, cleverly catching a cat nap without messing up his immaculate bed.

Plebes had little time for communication, but Hank G. once opened up to me after I gave him a chocolate bar. In Troy, Ohio, there was a certain route that Harold's dad used to take when driving him home on those many winter evenings after wrestling practice. The road led over a new highway bridge, and on the bridge was a plaque commemorating the death of a Troy resident in the Korean conflict. Troy had named the bridge after this courageous young officer, who was a West Point graduate. Hank G. said that he had passed over that bridge going home after wrestling practice for four long years. He said it made him think. But Hank G. had finished the chocolate bar and said no more. He turned around at his desk went back to shining his SI's, or Special Inspection shoes.

I had to ask him what the bridge made him think, and even then he didn't reply quickly. I waited, looking at his back, while he sat thinking. I saw Harold drop his shoe rag and pass a hand slowly to his face to wipe something away. He'd lowered his head momentarily, so that the tendons stood out on the back of his neck. "It's something," Hank began in a heavy voice.

He wiped his cheek. "Everybody in Troy knew who that guy was, what he did. He was a hero. Everybody in Troy goes down Holmes Road at one time or another, even if they don't live there. There's a shopping center there, too, so people from even in the north part of town pass over the bridge to get to the Interstate Cut-off. That's where the shopping center is. And I'll tell you one thing, buddy: if one man's life can mean that much—what he did for his country—then it's good enough for

Hank Gumboldkirschner, too. You can quote me on that, buddy."

The amateur wrestler then turned around in his chair to give me a doleful yet striking look of wonderment. His face was smeared all over with melted chocolate. He pawed at it with a strong, chubby hand, then licked his fingers. How foolish to think Hank G. would be wiping tears. That was the last and only time he and I ever had a serious conversation, though shortly before Beast Barracks ended, the old sentimentalist gave me the highway directions to the Holmes Road bridge should I ever be in Troy. "It's something," he said, "that you have to see."

In the high-pitched activity of New Cadet Training, the lurking bozo in me was shoved aside by a true zeal for duty and a willingness to curry favor with the powers that were. I learned my poop religiously, made a point to be early to formations, and did my best to conform to the system. It was a full-time process with scarcely a minute free to oneself, and even then relaxation was a mental and physical impossibility.

Part of a squad leader's duty was to ascertain every night that each individual squad member had "shat," showered, shaved (the three *S*'s), and powdered the feet. Garth usually came by with his check pad after taps, poking his head in the door to shout: "Three *S*'s and a *P*, men?" We'd yell back *yea* or *nay*, at times having to hop up and dash some powder on the feet so Garth could check everything off and look like the fine squad leader that he was on the reports he sent up to the Tactical Officer.

For me, adapting to the violent turnover of life-style involved a considerable repression of anxieties, and this started to show, in spite of my zeal, in a long string of *X*'s where there should have been *S*'s. On the books I was a soldier who was not fulfilling all of his duties. Tilson pleaded with me to lay off potatos and eat more salads and, on placement of the eleventh X, began considering what formal steps he should take to deal with this matter, such as submitting a request to the Tactical Officer for a drum of prune juice. But that would make *him* look bad.

The next night after taps he came in the room and asked, "Three S's and powder your feet, Mardis?"

"No, sir."

"Powder your feet?"

"Yes, sir."

"The same old S, huh?"

"Yes, sir, the first one."

"You'd better come with me."

I climbed down off the bunk, wearing my regulation gray pajamas, threw on the regulation bathrobe, and followed Garth down the long, clinical corridor, with my white optional shower thongs going *clop*. Tilson was grumpy and untalkative, his hair messy; he was dressed in a wrinkled "Navy" bathrobe, a status symbol among the upper class, being the booty of war, the traditional payment for a bet won off some Annapolis middie. We went to the Blister Rep's room.

Behind a closed door, the Fifth Co. Blister Representative was administering to the swollen feet of Company Commander O'Megan. There were yards of gauze all over the room because we'd had a long field march that day, and the Blister Rep, an upperclassman, was responsible for taping up the damages.

"This is Mardis," said Tilson dully.

"Are you Mardis?" asked O'Megan.

"Sir, I am Mardis," I said.

"Take that tone out of your voice, Mister," Tilson snapped.

Fifth Co. Commander O'Megan was a First Classman with a bright red face and prematurely thinning hair. He scrutinized me briefly and intensely, then looked the other way as iodine was applied to his wound, perhaps

21

feeling sorry he'd made us sprint the last five hundred yards of the march with him in front.

"Upperclassmen are human, you know," O'Megan said, grimacing. "I'm talking to you, Mister Mardis."

I had been watching the Blister Rep expertly wind the tape around one of O'Megan's toes. Now he stood up and tested the pain. "Not bad. . . . Relax, Mardis; fall out for a minute. Hand me that field bayonet over there, would you?" As I crossed the room to take the bayonet and scabbard from a field belt, the Company Commander gave Squad Leader Tilson a knowing wink. I returned with the honorable weapon in my outstretched hands.

"Thanks—" But no sooner had O'Megan taken it from me than he savagely ripped the bayonet from the casing and, with a barbaric commando scream, thrust it against my throat. O'Megan's face was reddening madly as he held the cold steel tight against my jugular; from behind, Tilson stopped me from recoiling. "That's the *dull* side," the commando rasped softly. "OK—let him go."

"You feel anything?" Tilson asked excitedly.

"Feel what?"

"Say *Gung Ho Fifth Co.,* Mister Mardis!"

I repeated it for the Company Commander.

"You still don't feel anything?" He looked over at a disconsolate Garth Tilson. "Like I said, it's only positively guaranteed for hiccups." O'Megan returned the bayonet to its scabbard. The Blister Rep made a few obscene jokes, and Tilson began discussing how to go about siphoning prune juice out of one of those big drums.

The following morning I would report on sick call for a laxative, but that night, as I rendered my salute to leave, the Company Commander paid me a fine military complement, and Tilson had to agree. "You may have other problems, Cadet Mardis," he told me, "but one thing's in your favor. Like the Rep says, nobody's gonna scare the shit out of you."

MEMO 2.

A case of mistaken identity. I had mistaken the Military Academy for a pleasant kind of war garden, and the Academy, in its fail-safe computer selection of nominees, had mistaken me for a junior officer. Yet once engaged —challenged—I wanted to measure up. I wanted to give them that "110 percent of twisted steel and sex appeal" they kept demanding: your everything and then some. My first 110-percent undertaking did not concern Squad Leader Tilson or even Gung Ho Fifth Co O'Megan. I sought much higher recognition.

In the frenzied early days of Beast Barracks any leftover civvie ideas of protocol were quickly ravaged into strict military properness. Good military bearing was especially important in ranks, and strict rules were imposed to insure our best possible performance. In ranks, or in any formation, we New Cadets were never allowed to look around, only straight ahead. In order to look sideways, it was necessary for a whole platoon to execute a right or left face and then look at something straightaway. To be caught "gawking" in ranks was a guaranteed humiliation, so your best bet was to "stare a hole in the back of your buddy's head," which is exactly what they told us to do.

The austere, hewn-stone Washington Hall Complex provided housing for the Beast Barracks clientele, and during the year this massive structure quartered a majority of the Corps. Its two perpendicular wings, meeting in the crux of the more ancient Mess Hall, were each fronted by a concrete apron used for thoroughfare and for forming ranks. Across the apron was the Parade Plain, some two hundred yards in breadth, and beyond that were Trophy Point, a few athletic fields, and the steep, majestic bluffs of the Hudson River.

The form-up area of the apron was where we put in the most hours staring holes into the backs of our buddies heads, or if you were in a front rank, staring holes into the trees across the Plain. If a mathematician were to calculate the total man-hours our class spent staring holes into each other's heads, the figure would approach astronomical proportion, something like the ten-year labor output of a small envelope-stuffing company.

The waste could be rationalized—at least my share of it—by assuming that all this staring nonsense was being executed for the pleasure of the "Inspector." When we new men of the Corps would finally march into the Mess Hall after a stiff twenty minutes' wait, we were as rigid and upright as a troop of wind-up grenadiers. The Inspector, visible during meals in a position near the Central Guard Room, certainly did appreciate this steely discipline. I had my own way of knowing this, since in my particular rank, I always caught a sideways glimpse of him when we broke formation to negotiate the Mess Hall steps.

For sixteen days, forty-eight meals, I did my best for the Inspector and no one else. His anonymous appreciation was sufficient—and for me far surpassed the surly, insensitive approach Tilson used: "If you guys don't look spoony out there, it's gonna be clothing formations tonight." My comparison of an underling like Garth U. Tilson to a successful, honorable soldier like the Inspector helped me rise above the surrounding pettiness. The soldier with an *inner* dignity, a true military bearing and not a paste-on model, would eventually, with determination, win out. The true leader stood separate from the lowly squabbling of lessers.

From a sideways glimpse a person can only get so much information, but information all the same. And when certain details begin to repeat themselves, day after day —such as the Inspector's red-plumed hat—a picture is formed in the mind from the residual, repeating images, after which the details can be filled in by more sophisticated glimpses. By exactly this method I determined that the Inspector was a man well above average height, that he wore a white uniform, had a red plume on his hat. His importance was emphasized not only by the white uniform—worn on special occasions—but also by the presence of the Officer in Charge and the Cadet Chain of Command beside him. The Inspector, possibly because of his stature, always seemed just a bit more rigid than the others. This indicated, so my reasoning went, his appreciation of old-fashioned discipline. And so I better adapted to a Plebe's tortures, knowing that it was an honor as well as a duty to look good and to do right for those who counted. For each, his own lucky star, or ideal; for me, the Inspector.

The seventeenth day of Beast Barracks was a Saturday, and for the first time the Cadet Boodlers, the candy store, was opened. They opened the place for two hours and did one heck of a business. This was our first opportunity for sweets, candy bars, ice cream, and the only rule was that any candy purchased had to be disposed of by 2130 hours that night. Fine with us! We hadn't had a treat for two full weeks; furthermore, most table commandants still wouldn't allow us to use any sugar or eat very much of our desserts.

A new ruling that year entitled Plebes to more food than prior incoming classes—"substantial portions"— but there was a hitch. You had to have something on your plate at all times during the meal, and if by chance you finished your portions before "Battalions Rise," then you were finished too. You'd have to recite Fourth Class Knowledge for the rest of the meal, and if you made any mistakes on the poop, most likely you'd be visiting the table commandant's room that night for some extra practice. No matter what demands your stomach made, the logical and safe thing to do was leave something on the plate.

Pacing the meal became an art. More than anything else, we New Cadets craved sweets—and the only sweetness was in the dessert—so there was a tendency to hurry through the other courses (in the correct manner) in order to have at least a taste of the dessert. Once you had finished your courses, though, and requested permission for the dessert tray, it was the road of no return. The dessert had to last you the rest of the meal, and the bites could be no smaller or larger than the regulation thumbnail size.

This was a trouble spot. If the table commandant noticed that you were chewing a bite of apple pie some fifteen to twenty times, he'd ask you if your apple pie were chewier than everyone else's. Therefore, overchewing and chewing well past swallowing were a risky method to make your dessert last. Pausing between bites was out of the question. Finishing it was deadly. And taking miniature forkfuls was detested by most upperclassmen more than finishing. In short, there was no easy solution to this complicated and tricky business of not finishing your dessert. The result was that many of us became obsessed by this frustration, often never reaching the dessert, sometimes having a bite or two, other times sweating out the seconds till "Battalions Rise" over a pie crust or crumb stacking.

These frustrations were all vented in the melee of the seventeenth day. Returning to the room with a couple of candy bars, I found most of my squad gathered there around Gumboldkirschner, who had done their buying. A delicious orgy was in store. Hank G. alone polished off two six packs of candy bars, four canned sodas, three pints of ice cream, and a large brick of saltwater taffy for his refresher. As the festivities neared an end, the boys entertained each other with a belching contest.

Any cadets who thought they were finally receiving a few privileges were painfully short-sighted. That night at supper, many of the table commandants were seen laughing shortly before the prayer. ("God, thank you for this food. May it go into the nourishment of our bodies to do Thy service. In Christ's name, we pray, amen. . . . *Take Seats!*") The table com's were jesting among themselves over some private joke which none of the Plebes knew about. The Plebes were the joke.

Virtually every New Cadet in New Cadet Barracks had stuffed his face with candy that afternoon. We had been advised how to get to the Boodlers by upperclassmen— who were rarely in the habit of giving out directions. We had been fooled into thinking they cared. They cared enough, after taking seats, to inform us that double helpings of every dish would be served and that we would eat our helpings *vigorously.* Some table commandants even made their Plebes bang their forks and demand the food. Naturally, there was plenty of dessert left to go around, but the table com's didn't miss a stitch. They saw to it that every known pudding pig and crumb stacker got a generous portion.

There was an overwhelming traffic in the latrines after supper, and some of the upperclassmen regretted their chicanery since they had to give up cigar time to organize an emergency hospital escort group. In the outdoor Sunday sermon at eight the next morning, the bright sunshine knocked out those victims who had managed to last through the night. But I was among the lucky ones. I'd eaten only two of my candy bars and hidden several more in the leg of my bunkbed, against regulations. For that matter, I still had a sweet tooth. I went to alternate chapel that afternoon and got a free coke for singing "Onward Christian Soldiers."

My abstention from the sweets on the day before had not exactly been an act of will. The truth was, I lost an appetite. Cadet Boodlers was located through the sallyport of Central Guard Room, not far from the Mess Hall steps. On my way there I had not seen a single upperclassman; many were either gone on a weekend pass or enjoying other privileges for a Saturday afternoon. So, on the way back from Boodlers, I took the liberty of gawking. What I saw sent a shock wave running through me. My arms, high in double-time position, dropped numbly to my sides. I refused to believe it!

The Inspector was standing outside Central Guard Room in his full-dress colors with not a soul around to inspect. He stood there completely alone, his brass waistplate a humble tint of brown in the shadows. My fine hero was a fire meter! His red plume was a beacon, his white uniform a fresh coat of white paint. His waistplate was no doubt an engraved phone number to call in case of emergency. I stopped in the sallyport, completely stunned.

Slowly, I recovered my senses and began to doubletime around this thing in order to give it a sideways glimpse. I refused to believe that my proud idol was a gizmo with a call box in its chest until I'd circled by again and taken in the sight crosswise with my left eye, the same eye with which I'd been glimpsing the Inspector for the better part of a month. Then I turned to circle it again, but my unconventional hairpin route on the apron did not go undetected.

"*You* there! Mister! Halt!"

I halted, dropping the tiny bag of sweets to the ground, as it was the custom to drop anything when addressed by an upperclassman. I never saw a face; he hazed me from the sides and rear. I gazed grim-faced and dead ahead, staring a hole straight into the Mess Hall steps. There wasn't a sideways glance left in my heart.

"Mister, what in hells bells do you think you're doing running circles around that fire meter there? Huh? Don't you know to square all corners? Answer me, Mister!"

"Yes, sir."

"Louder, Mister!"

"Yes, sir!" I bellowed.

"So what's the story?"

"Sir, there is no story."

"That one of your regulation answers, Mister?"

"No, sir!"

"So what's the story, Mister? Let's have it!"

"No excuse, sir."

He cocked his head to breathe in my ear. "You in *love* with that fire meter, Mister? Eh?"

The upperclassman continued his ridicule for perhaps five minutes. He braced me and threatened to confiscate the boodle, and then he snidely criticized my shoeshine, which was melting right before his eyes in a hot bolt of sunshine. Although he persisted with questions about the Inspector, I stayed silent except for the regulation Fourth Class answers. My loss was just too horrible to discuss.

I blocked the tragedy from my mind until the next day, a provocative sermon in alternate chapel fished it out. The turnout was poor for the optional service since precious few New Cadets were eager for a free coke. It was just myself and about ten fanatics, and they were probably attending to repent their gluttony—if Saturday night in the latrine hadn't been enough penance paid.

The preacher for the Sunday afternoon sessions was a young assistant chaplain from the regular army base, the kind of figure with a friendly square chin and long sideburns and who supposedly appealed to the "youth."

29

He reminded me of my Little League baseball coach. He took it quite personally that so few had turned out for the inspirational.

Over two hundred folding chairs had been set up in the upstairs ballroom of Cullum Hall, the Plebe activities center, and the ten of us who showed had each selected a different row. The youth chaplain must have thought he had a losing bingo card. He came down off the stage where the pulpit was set up, told the Private who played piano to leave, and lined up his small service in the first row of chairs.

"It hurts me that so few have turned up at a time when, uh. . . . You guys can fall out, you know—nobody's gonna bite you." The chaplain, around thirty, with sloppy black hair and stooped shoulders, frowned very significantly. "It's not that *I* really care who comes to these alternate chapels and who doesn't. You get a free coke out of the deal, and two cokes if you help take down the chairs, so now. . . . Well, we'll just discontinue the coke service. Obviously you newcomers to the Corps are by this time more concerned with your duty than with a free handout . . . and that's *good.*"

It was apparent he didn't know what to say, and with so few people to say it to, the youth chaplain was lost for words entirely. We all sat there stony-faced as he took a few deep breaths, fidgeting with his clerical collar. After a guilty pause, he smiled beseechingly at two zealots who had brought along their Bibles. "Well, looks like you two guys are the pacesetters. So you two lead the way and open up your cokes." He still couldn't get a response.

By and by, a sermon emerged about the meaning of individuality in a crowd. It is the individual, the chaplain told us, who throughout history has turned the tables. "A dot on the line—I know you boys are good in math—yes, one dot and one dot alone can be the start of a new direction, a new line, a new way of thinking. That dot is a

30

leader, believe it or not. Galileo, who changed the course of history. Socrates. Christ. The turning point—call it that if you will, boys, men. That's what you are now— men."

While we later belted out the appropriate hymns, I couldn't help wondering which way my line was headed. I considered what the youth chaplain might think if he got to Heaven and found out God was a fire meter. After the service, we stacked the chairs and the chaplain shook all our hands. I felt almost grateful to him, an identification and a respect that he had mucked his way through the ordeal, for better or worse.

The zealots all sped away to the barracks as soon as the handshakes were over, since folding so many chairs had put us behind schedule. I bolted too, but then went back, bolstering my courage to tell the chaplain the real reason for the lack of attendance. He listened intently to my explanation, which was somewhat garbled from nervousness, then laid his hand firmly on my shoulder, nodding his chin.

"You are the leper who has returned to thank his Healer. Bless you, Cadet—"

"Mardis."

The youth chaplain gave me a free coke for being honest, and though I knew I shouldn't have taken it back with me, I felt it would be sacreligious to think of doing otherwise. I didn't even bother hiding it, just set it on my desk like a trophy. Perhaps God should be my new Inspector, perhaps by way of the Above I could learn to ignore Garth U. Tilson. But Tilson didn't give me the chance. He came in later that night and busted the room for unauthorized boodle, putting us on our honor to confess.

As Tilson, hands on hips, splendid in his bathrobe, watched me pull candy bars out of the rail of my bunk bed, he shook his head, mocking.

31

"The same old bozo, huh, Mardis? You hide candy in your rack and leave a coke right out in the open. What's your excuse this time, Mardis?"

"No excuse, sir."

"No excuse is right, beanhead—and I really doubt you'll ever find one."

MEMO 3.

At West Point you mix with the best of them, the brochure reads, the Cream of the Crop. And you are there because *you too* are the Cream of the Crop, the brochure goes on, the best America has to offer. I met Larry Bob Lee in the post-nomination, army-sponsored qualifying examinations in the spring of 1969. The Army sponsors these qualifying exams to make sure you can hear, smell, see, talk, and broadjump, that you weren't born behind the Iron Curtain, and that the friendly senator or congressman who nominated you for the Point wasn't kidding about your creamlike qualities.

When the other nominees who had come to the largest Army base nearest their home (a site determined by the government) took note of Larry Bob Lee, they thought somebody *had* to be kidding. This one didn't look like a leader at all. He had wiry hair, a hawk nose, beady eyes— a mama's boy with bermuda shorts, red socks, and a thick volume of Plato under his arm. Larry Bob Lee was instantaneously dubbed "the weird one" by the others, yet Larry Bob seemed to know he was "unusual" and didn't let taunts bother him. He would laugh back at the group of nominees like a wild hyena, exposing a ratty disposition, and then go on his merry way.

The other nominees were new faces to me, types I'd never seen around St. Francis's Preparatory. The future officers, some two hundred of them in our region, arrived looking very much alike. They all smelled of sweat, wore short-sleeved shirts with enormous stains under the arms, tight slacks, and somewhere on the face had an acute blemish, like a brand-mark. On each muscular wrist was a shiny new wristwatch. They seemed like an army already.

The government was doing a thorough job of screening that year. The memories of what had happened at Berkeley, Chicago, Columbia University, the Sorbonne, the University of Mexico, and Brooklyn Community College were still too vivid to discount the possibility that the next radical target could be West Point. Each nominee, including the stand-bys, had to sign a legal document declaring that he was not and never had been a member of the Red Dragon Society, American Socialist League, Irate Orange Pickers Coalition, etc.—the same form postal employees have to fill out.

The tests took three days, checking out all aspects of the body in the laboratory, in the classroom, and on the gymnasium floor. Cadet "star men," or scholars of merit, were present to brief us on what academic pressures to expect. A film clip was shown on how West Point builds men, and we had to write an essay called, "Why am I a LEADER?" The grand finale was the psychological examination held on the third day. The psycho exam was allegedly saved until the last day so that any crackpot-weirdos would get the jitters and give themselves up.

I had the jitters myself, but I wasn't too worried about being pinned for a weirdo, not with Larry Bob Lee around. Now there was a weirdo! Still, feeling like sort of an outsider myself amid the nominees, I liked Larry Bob. At lunch on the third day I risked my personality rating by going over to the empty table where he sat in the cafeteria. I put down my tray across from him and said hello. I wanted to commend him, somehow. The psycho exam would begin in less than an hour, and here Larry Bob Lee wasn't even shaky.

"Hi!" I shouted over the clatter of the meal, which we

took together with regular enlisted men. Larry Bob didn't bother to look up; he was savagely forking at some string beans. "You almost have to have a knife to eat these mess hall string beans, don't you!" I shouted, leaning forward to sit. He didn't reply. I didn't know what else to say, so I spread out my napkin and then noticed the volume of Plato sitting alongside his tray. "Oh, *Plato*!" I reached out for it, but before my hand touched midair, Larry Bob had snatched the Plato book and dropped it in his lap. He was still hunched over his food.

I stood to take my tray elsewhere, offended by "the weird one." I remarked, "Well, nice to meet you, anyway," and started away. Larry Bob's head then popped up, snarling.

"You're no different than the rest of them, you know!" That was all he said, and I walked away.

I was wondering how Larry Bob meant that. I didn't wear a shiny wristwatch or have a perspiration problem. I had to assume that the weird one figured I was already allied with the robust crew of nominees—with Charlie and Joe Normal, and their cousin Arty. When this struck me, I felt somewhat better. Yes, I probably *did* have a lot of camaraderie about me. *Esprit de Corps. Duty, Honor, Country . . .* Yes, I absolutely did—I belonged.

The tension was apparent in the group of nominees waiting for their interview with the Army psychiatrist. The system was numerical; I had seen L. R. Lee leave the hospital foyer in an earlier batch, and I knew I'd never see him again. A few nominees who had been antagonizing him before he left said he was probably behind bars already. But no one waiting was completely confident that he himself maybe wasn't just a little weird. For instance, about five dirty jokes dropped flat when somebody whispered that the foyer might be bugged. Rumors spread like wildfire about the "meaning" of biting your nails, having a sniffle, blinking your eyes too much, seeing snakes in your dreams, etc. And in line everybody froze when the psychiatrist was heard screaming, "*Pick up that pencil!*"

The fellows in line were perspiring much more than usual. They fell into an awkward silence, nervous, terrified of all those hidden mysteries that the psychiatrist might use against them to keep them out of West Point. On mental grounds. On *moral* grounds, or grounds they didn't even know existed. That dropping pencils, or that bump on your chin, or the inability to rhyme Simple Simon could all be telltale signs of communist tendencies. And the psychiatrist was going to know all this and have you arrested for your own good. "Arrest this man! He has hairy fingers just like Fidel! Let's hope it's not too late!" Or maybe the psychiatrist knew funny things about your past that you chose to forget . . . "You're saying you weren't *aware* that old Grandma Ferguson had changed her name from Inga J. Sarjefstikov?"

"Just don't fiddle with any items on my desk and I won't lose my temper," the psychiatrist told me. "I hate meddlers, and it's been a long, hard, stinker of an afternoon." He had an electric fan pointed toward the nominee's chair; his nostrils seemed to flare a bit, then he turned the fan toward himself. *"All right?"*

"Fine with me."

"You'll have to say 'sir' if you join the army, young man. I'm an officer, if you haven't noticed. Oh, by the way, you didn't knock before you came in, so you better go back outside and knock and don't come in until I tell you to enter."

"Right."

"Say 'sir,' now. This is your last warning."

"Yes, sir."

I went back into the hall and knocked, and came back in when he told me to. The army psychiatrist said he actually hadn't told me to "enter," he had told me to "come in," which was similar but not altogether the same. "However, since there's a line out there, I'm going to dispense with some of the formalities, but for future reference, just you remember there is a difference between 'enter' and 'come in.' All right?"

The office was that of a pencil pusher; the walls were bare except for the thinly framed photograph of a two-star General, and the windows faced across to a barnlike aluminum building identical to the one we were in. The shrink was a Major; he had fuzzy hair cut very short, revealing a pinkish section of scalp, and his paunchy cheeks were near the same color. He began at once with his trick questions.

"Name?"

"Last name first, Mardis, Jaime, sir."

"Good job." Two thick stacks of pamphlets were on the desk. He took one off the lower stack, opened it up, and said, "So be it." Then he took a pencil from a formation of finely sharpened pencils, tested the point with his index finger, and asked, "What is *pi* to you?"

"It is made with a crust and inside the crust is a filling, and it is baked."

"Nothing to do with algebra, eh?"

I panicked. "But you didn't spell it—sir."

He calmly held up a moist palm, after making a mark on my pamphlet. "Please try to relax, son. There was nothing *wrong* about your answer. Now, on this subject, as it were, young man, answer me this. After *what,* repeat, after what significant indulgence . . . Let me reword this. I've said it so much today I'm going *bananas!*" His eyes flickered excitedly, like a happy hamster in its run-cage. "No? . . . ha, ha. All right, ready! After what significant indulgence and lack thereof does c-o-o-old turkey occur?"

"After wha—"

"Just answer it, now."

"Thanksgiving!"

This wasn't so bad—just another television quiz show. We went on for several minutes with routine questions about my background, ostensibly for the purpose of spot checking the forms. Next in order were some moral-type questions. "Let's imagine, Mr. Mardis, that you were walking down the street without really too much to do, and just by chance, you see this huge, dirty, roaring cement truck run flat over a tiny, wittle-bitty soft, cuddly kitten. *Smack!* What would you do?" He giggled a little bit.

I giggled back. "*Gee* . . . ha, ha. I guess I'd have to take it to the pizza shop!" I broke out laughing since I figured this was a sense-of-humor question to ascertain whether you were "army-tough." He made several quick marks in my brochure, then turned back a page and erased something and made another mark. I was getting scared again.

"Sir, I want to change that last answer. Sir, you know I was just kidding about that one—you're a psychiatrist. What I really would've done is call up the cement company and made them pay for the kitty cat's funeral. Sir, really! Maybe I would have laughed at first, but then I would have cried."

He didn't answer me. He had closed his eyes and was skimming a hand across his flat top of hair. Then the interviewer sighed and said, "You can't do that."

"Yes, sir, you can call the SPCA. You can do anything you want to because this is a democracy."

"You can't change your *answer*," he droned. "And for future reference, the Army isn't a democracy. It's the Army." The other moral questions were less controversial, such as whether a man is entitled to defend his fatherland. I remained uneasy, nonetheless, about hidden meanings in his questions, and when I mixed up the zip codes of my home and school, the mastermind closed his eyes again and rubbed at his forehead. I felt certain he was debating how to break the bad news, that I might not be right for the Point. Instead, he asked:

"Did any of the kids ever make fun of you because you look like Beaver Cleaver?"

"Sir, I don't look like him."

"Then it stands to reason none of your classmates would have made fun of you for the same, now doesn't it?"

He folded my brochure and put it on the high stack, then asked me to tell the next nominee to knock before he entered. "And don't you bother telling him about 'enter' or 'come in' or 'come in' and 'enter' because my patience is getting short and I don't want anybody's fingers in my pie . . . Which reminds me—for your future reference, *p-i* pi is one half the diameter of a circle or the radius divided by the circumference or 3.141593 rounded to six figures now get out."

In 1969 the military was acting extremely selective about its candidates for leadership, but this might have only been a front because there weren't too many leaders who wanted to join the army. Many were no doubt organizing communes in the mountains or throwing fire bombs or rioting in colleges. A left-wing fellow at St. Francis's told me he had accidentally checked the wrong "Career Choice" box on a vocational aptitudes test and was heavily pamphleted by all the academies, including the Merchant Marines. He said "the Cream of the Crop" was nothing but a bunch of hornswaggle—and I came close to punching him in the nose!

I was happy to be the best America had to offer. I had passed the Army's tests, my appointment was secure, and the West Point welcome mat was rolled my way. My congressman congratulated me long distance from Washington; Mom and Sis looked at me in reverence— my Dad thought the place would "do me wonders." And Mr. Murray, the dean at St. Francis's, was taken beyond words; every time we'd pass one another in the quadrangle, he brusquely shook his head in frank admiration.

My few confidential friends were wishing me "good luck," and at night I began practicing salutes in front of the mirror.

To add the diplomatic touch to my military contract, two upperclass cadets in uniform dropped by one day to treat me for coffee and doughnuts. They were on a mission to give official greetings to appointees in the vicinity. The cadet diplomats took me to the nearest Daddy-O Doughnut Shop, sat me down in a corner booth, and told me all there was to know about *espirt de corps.* During the conversation they reached out several times and shook my hand heartily, and made me feel important.

I was so wrapped up in my own visions, however, that I hardly heard a word they said. Out the window, on the ramp of an expressway, antennas and grillwork of passing cars were flashing in the noonday sun. I saw instead the glistening of sabers in the Khyber Pass. A diesel rig roared by—I heard the hooves of horses galloping into battle. A waitress brought the check finally, but in my wandering reflection she was a captive belly dancer of disputable virtue.

"Well, that about wraps it up," one of the cadets said. "West Point builds character, and character is the mark of a man, and so, the reasoning goes, West Point builds men."

"Yeah, it is getting late," agreed the other cadet. "Just take our word for it, you'll be the proudest son of a bitch on earth to wear this uniform."

"You better believe it," I told them.

The two diplomats were in a rental car and had to ask me directions to their next destination, a suburb some thirty miles away. "So it's simple. We just get on that ramp there, go three miles, turn to the west ten, hit the Interstate, and it's the fourth exit."

"Well, it might be the *fifth* exit," I told them modestly.

"Fourth, fifth, you can bet your lucky dollar we'll find it with these instructions, Mister. And thanks." As we stood to go, one of the cadets grabbed the check away and said, "These doughnuts are complements of the Point."

His comrade commented, "You know, this town isn't that big. Maybe Mardis here already knows his new classmate."

"Maybe I do—what's his name?"

"Some guy named Bobby Lee Lawrence."

"Sorry, I never heard of him."

It was just dumb luck that I wouldn't know until after I was a cadet that the weird one had been accepted, because if I'd had to consider Larry Bob in the landscape of my glorious illusion, I think all the glory might have drained right out. By no stretch of the imagination could I *ever* see someone fighting his way through the Khyber Pass in a pair of plaid bermuda shorts.

Midway through New Cadet Training we went to the rifle range. I'd been looking forward to this, since many pictures in the Academy brochure had shown what splendid fun cadets had on the rifle range, and so far nothing had been fun. What's more, though each New Cadet had an M-14 rifle for parading, that was the only function of the rifles until we'd been to the range and fixed our *battle sight zeros.* "If West Point got invaded tomorrow," an instructor pointed out, "and we gave you boys live ammo, you boys would still be dead 'cause you don't know your battle sight zero."

(There was an overriding need to get out to the rifle range and have our battle sight zeros fixed on our M-14's, since scarcely a week before, three hippies had been sighted aboard a platform raft in the great bend of the Hudson River, no more than two hundred and fifty

41

yards from the sacred ground of Trophy Point. If they had a *navy*, the rumor went, they could even have an air force, a balloon or something, and we wanted our BSZ's just in case.)

"Hey, Plato! Com'ere! I got some virgin peanut butter for ya to rape!"

And so I discovered Larry Bob Lee was around West Point. Two full companies of New Cadets were lunching around the rifle range mess tent; Larry Bob stood up in the sea of green combat fatigues and skillfully caught the jar an upperclassman tossed to him. He opened it with a quick spin of the lid and then shoved his whole fist inside, screaming "Rape! Rape! This peanut butter has been raped!"

Larry Lee screwed the top on and threw it back to the upperclassman. Then he sat down again, wiping his hands. A light round of applause sounded around him, but Larry Lee paid no mind; he was reading. I was so fascinated at seeing him again—and like *this*—that I quickly picked up my tray and went over for a closer peek. I might have felt condescending toward the unlikely soldier, or even hostile, but I had just learned my battle sight zero was four clicks down, seventeen clicks right, and I was experiencing a form of bliss that came quite rarely in Beast Barracks.

"*Hi!* Remember me? Say—what's your battle sight zero?"

In a repetition of our first meeting, he just wouldn't acknowledge me. I told him what my battle sight zero was, and again asked what his was. Still no response. Then I crooked over to see the title of the pocket-sized book he was reading: "*N . . . I . . . E . . .* Oh, Friedrich *Niet*zsche! Hey, what happened to Plato?" At this, Larry Bob snapped his book shut rudely and resumed eating with hard concentration.

As at our first meeting, I was offended. Larry Bob Lee

was no longer the snotty mama's boy in red socks; now he was vicious mama's man in jungle fatigues. I made arrangements to take my tray elsewhere, and when I was on my feet and moving, Larry Bob lifted up his head and snorted, "*Plato* is for kids!"

MEMO 4.

In the "last days," Squad Leader Tilson handed me a sheet that said: *Mardis—G-5.* For a second I thought I had been assigned a special vitamin, but then I realized that this was the long-awaited notice of my regular company assignment. In September, following New Cadet Training, Plebes are allocated to one or another of the Corps' thirty-odd companies (in one of five regiments), where they'll stay for four years. Yet perhaps the Big Brass actually did feel I needed a shot in the arm: Company G-5, or Golf-5 in the Army phonetic alphabet, or Golf*ball*-5, was most commonly known around the Point as Goofball-5. And they'd assigned me there permanently.

This was by no means an insult. It did mean one of two things. You were either a hero, and the best of America's best, or you were the worst of the best, a zero. Golfball-5 happened to be the Academy's "experimental" company—the melting pot—and it was ceremoniously staffed by the heros and their opposing forces, the zeros, to see just what would develop. In theory, if you add zero to anything, you come up with the same number. In theory, then, G-5 should have been the best company in the Corps. But all it took was one bungling zero to trip over his shoelaces, and G-5 would ruin the parade every time.

The heros of Golf-5 were hand-picked and carefully sprinkled around for maximum exposure, on each class level. In this way the big brass took opportunity to do their heavy-handed tinkering: each G-5 room was a test laboratory for military osmosis. The weak roomed with the strong, the dull with the bright, marathon swimmers with dog paddlers, iron-twisters were shipped in on the milk-toasters, and Mr. Meticulous laid waste to the slobs. The paperwork in the tactical department probably said different, but their high-sounding "osmosis" was never anything more than what it started out to be—a melting pot. Too often, the wrong people melted.

As a result, the goofballs had been ruling G-5 for some time, and their leadership was sufficient to drive the entire Fifth Regiment into shame. The Fifth Regimental Area was blithely referred to as the "Demilitarized Zone," or DMZ. Our ancient barracks, which were no more dilapidated than those of the Fightin' First, were also subjected to ridicule. The home of the Fightin' First Regiment was called "Old Citadel," but our barracks, equally a landmark, had been earmarked "the Slums of the Corps." We Fifth Regiment locals made as much money as everybody else (11¢ an hour), but there was no way the neighborhood could be upgraded. Golfball-5 was deteriorated beyond repair.

Traditionally, the Fifth Regiment was a nice-guy establishment, a fraternity of jocks. The reputation had come about because the gymnasium was right next door to the regiment's area, and a preponderance of athletes had once been assigned to the Fifth for easy access. This favoritism had been changed, however, by the construction of Washington Hall, which provided centralized housing for more than half the cadet companies. Athletes had long since been disseminated, but that onetime happy-go-lucky fraternity atmosphere remained on—but only in Golfball-5.

At first blush, the incoming G-5 Plebes were uncontrollably happy to be part of this tradition. Whatever the New Cadet company, our summer playground had been a hell pit, so setting foot in the fall-out territory of Golf-5 was like a God-sent miracle. Soon enough, though, the Plebes became aware of the wild schizophrenia afoot and started falling into their respective categories: hero or zero.

Hadrean Groovey, one of my first roommates, lived by the rules. He hailed from Great Barley, Minnesota, where they grow great barley. Whereas my decision to apply to West Point had come relatively late, Hadrean, on the contrary, had been hankering for a cadet career since he was knee high to a barley weevil. And while I honestly didn't know what to expect, and wanted it this way for the sake of my illusions, Hadrean didn't have any illusions at all. He had rules.

Hadrean was from a farming background, stood about five foot ten, and was a long-distance runner. He had a willowy build; a clean, placid tone to his face; flaxen hair; and the crystalline eyes of a renaissance portrait. Hadrean looked down on the only other Minnesotan among the G-5 Plebes, Frank Kirkelshaw, called him a "hick" behind his back. This occurred the same day Kirkelshaw was circulating a hometown paper his mother had sent him, which featured a picture of Kirk's brother on the front page, driving a tractor. Hadrean told me he knew Kirkelshaw's type.

The company was subdivided into three platoons, four squads per platoon, two fireteams per squad. The company and platoon commanders were First Classmen, the squad leaders were Second Classmen, and the fireteam leaders were Third Classmen. Fourth Classmen were fireteam *members,* three of us per fireteam. The fireteam leaders generally kept the fireteam members in line in daily company life, and with easy know-how, since only the year before they were Plebes themselves. Ours was Carlo Carillo, whom Hadrean criticized as Fireteam *Loser* Carillo. Carlo disobeyed every rule there was. He recognized us—let us call him by his first name—on the first night and lent us his record player on weekends. Carlo said, "Hi, soldier!" instead of "Good afternoon, Mister," and for our morning inspections he liked us to give bird whistles instead of recite poop.

Hadrean had to be a frog during a.m. inspections, since he had a whistling disability. *Burp! . . . burp!* I suppose Hadrean hated Carlo Carillo more than any living soul; nineteen years he had waited to make it from the land of lakes to the *terra firma* of West Point, now only to find out he was still a little froggie in a big pond. It wasn't long before Groovey found a cadet regulation stating that no superior could unduly force him to humiliate himself, so Carillo simply "unrecognized" Groovey and had him stand mum at attention while Mark Rutledge and I did the morning birdsongs.

The thing Hadrean said he hated the most about Carillo was that he was dirty. "So you come to West Point," Hadrean complained, "and whatta you get? You get a dirty Fireteam Leader. Have you seen his toothbrush holder? It's filthy—de*cayed.* All his belt buckles are scratched, and his darn Full Dress Coat has buttons missing! It's downright revolting, that's what it is. Even the way that bozo smiles—ugh! He's dirty all over." Coming from germ-sensitive Swedish stock, Hadrean just couldn't tolerate a nonantiseptic Mexican from El Paso, Texas.

Carillo was a cute-looking fellow who said he would have become a beatnik if the beatnik era hadn't ended before he was of proper age. To prove it, he had a set of bongo drums as his one optional desk display object. Carlo put Band-Aids over his sideburns every week so the barbers wouldn't shave them off, and every week he got demerits for having sideburns of unregulation length. He claimed the sideburns were worth all the trouble since he charmed more girls at the West Point hops, and he proved his successes by showing us a drawer half full of love letters.

Mark Rutledge, my other roommate, was an Army brat. Mark speculated that he had landed in Company G-5 because his father, a two-star general, was afraid his son wouldn't make it in any other company and had pulled strings accordingly. "You see, the way my old man is, he figured he'd put me in Goofy 5 and make me look better, or make *him* look better anyways. But the way I am, all this cakewalk shit just makes it easier for me to screw around."

Rutledge prided himself for certain accomplishments that would have made General Rutledge cringe. "You see, I've got it all figured out, and I've been around too many goddamn Army bases in my life to not know what it's all about. Now get this—I can sleep with my eyes wide open. *Yeah.* I know how to spit-shine a pair of shoes with liquid epoxy that'll make 'em last six months—no kidding! And Fourth Class Knowledge, that's a cinch. You just tape it in the bill of your hat and look up to God whenever the time calls."

Rutledge and Hadrean Groovey didn't say much to each other. Most nights, Rutledge would sit at his desk with his feet propped up, staring a hole into outer space. Occasionally, he would come to life and light a cigarette, his freckled, quizzical face in a bored pout. "What a *mess,*" he'd say to no one in particular, then take a drag off his cigarette, and go back to staring into space.

Mark had lived on at least a dozen Army bases and had attended several military prep schools; he was therefore a scarred and hardened veteran of the armed forces, and he hated what he called "the bright boys." A bright boy, by definition, was someone who made others look bad by looking good. "Ol Groovey baby—you watch out for him," Rutledge warned me. "He's a bright boy if I ever seen one."

Mark and I weren't particularly concerned about the token "hero" of the room showing us up, that is, not until the autumn Superintendant's Inspection. And by that time, there was no way we could catch up with the sparkling cleanliness of Hadrean's every item. A few days preceding the inspection, all the fledgling Fifth Regiment Plebes were summoned together by "Eyes" Seitz, the fierce Regiment Commander, to be pooped on what a Super's Inspection was all about.

"It's living hell, men!" Cadet Commander Seitz screamed at us, his famous steely eyes darting to every other face. "If the Super comes to your room personally, men, and he finds, so help me, a dead spider leg on your radiator knob, you'll find yourself on the area in half an hour! Marching off those demerits . . ." Seitz shook his head sadly. "I'll be there too, men—but that ain't gonna be in your favor, cause *I'll* be watching." He brashly tugged at his eye sockets, startling the assemblage of new Plebes.

"See those eyes, men. Take a good look—you see those eyes! Those are *hawk* eyes, Misters! My mother was a hawk and my father was an eagle and these two peepers can spot a loose thread on a button at a hundred and fifteen paces." "Eyes" Seitz took a quick look around him and hooked his finger at a Plebe in the second row. When the Plebe approached, "Eyes" jerked a thread out of one of his shirt buttons as if spinning a top. The button bounced to the floor, and Seitz laughed, "Three demerits, Mister. Out of uniform."

Even Carillo was worried about the big inspection. He shaved his sideburns a good quarter of an inch and tossed out the empty bourbon bottle he had hidden in his bottom drawer. He and Chip Hightower, the Assistant Fireteam Leader, came down to talk it over with us. They had a third roommate, who was the "hero" of their room, but he was seldom seen around the company; Hightower said you had to put the guy on his honor to make him admit he was even a member of Golfball-5.

They found most of their fireteam already motivated. I was cleaning my rifle, and Groovey, with a can of spray disinfectant, was dusting his bookshelves for "kooties." But Rutledge, as usual, had his feet propped up on his desk and was staring into the wild blue yonder.

"Hey, Rutledge," Carillo chided him, "what do you think you're doing? Don't you know the Super might be up here tomorrow?"

"I'm *prac*ticing," he answered indignantly.

"Practicing what?" Hightower drawled. "Practicing how to do nothing? You don't need no practice for that."

Rutledge said "Jesus!" and turned around. "I've told you guys already that I can sleep with my eyes open, and *you* just woke me up. How would you like it if I came in there some night and bounced you out of bed?"

Hightower, who was unathletic and soft-spoken—and at his best around Carillo—grabbed Rutledge by the shoulders and shook him. "Sober up, boy, The Super's coming. Coming tomorrow morning."

Rutledge shoved his hands away, annoyed. "Don't tell me they've fooled you two goldbricks with this Superintendant boondoggle! Well, they're not fooling me, goddammit. I'm not doing shit."

Hightower and Carillo nodded their heads.

"Direct disobedience to orders."

"Ten-four, and call Sergeant Friday. He'd be dead in the Nam."

"Doggone right," Carillo said. "You other guys, carry on. But you here—Rutledge—listen to your Fireteam Leader. I wanta talk to you as if you were my own son."

Hightower began giggling; Rutledge banged his cigarette lighter on the desk and said, "Now *cut* it out, will ya! I've had it with you guys."

Groovey was so shocked by this impertinence that he stopped dusting and looked around. Granted, Fireteam Leaders Carillo and Hightower weren't the best in the Corps, but they were still our Fireteam Leaders. "You there—Groovey—keep dusting. It looks good." Hadrean bit his lips shrewdly and went after the corners with an untwisted paper clip.

"You there—Mardis—clean that rifle some more. We got Nazis to kill."

"Nazis, schmatzis," said Rutledge. He had put his face in his hands to think. "I'll lay you five to one that no Super's gonna be up here tomorrow . . . and I'll tell you why! He's too goddamn lazy to walk up four flights of stairs, and you know it." Mark lit up a cigarette as if to signal his victory.

"Shit, you know he's right," Hightower agreed.

Carillo felt at his sideburns and frowned. "Well, anyway, bright boy—"

"I ain't no bright boy."

Carillo stole a couple of his cigarettes and put them in his pocket. "Anyway, Rutledge, doesn't it bother you that somewhere on the other side of the world there's a little Korean boy, or a little Russian boy, or a little *Chinese* boy, and that right now all these little boys are cleaning their rifles and shining their shoes and cleaning out their soap dishes just so that some day, when they finally do meet up with you, they're going to be a little bit better prepared than you are?"

"Prepared for what?" he snickered.

"For blood, stupid," Hightower told him.

"Ha, ha," Rutledge laughed. "I don't care who you're fighting for. The Army's the Army, and I know the Army. You take all those Soviets, you take the Communist Union of—you take the Chinks, the Peking boys, and you take the Moscow boys, and you put all those goddamn armies together and take a poll, see. I sincerely doubt whether you can find fifteen or twenty of them that can sleep with their eyes open the way I can. *Seriously.*"

When the room was quiet again, Rutledge winked at me and said, "Even if the Super did make it up here tomorrow and checked your rifle, he'd find something wrong, even if you goddamned battle-stripped it. You get my point—why bother at all? What they say in the *real* Army, Jaime buddy, is just let the dust fall even."

Hadrean wasn't anywhere near ready to let that happen. He was up to two o'clock in the morning with his aerosol bomb and a pencil flashlight, a search-and-destroy mission for enemy dust particles and/or "kooties" advancing upon his private desk complex. He was up again by 0430 hours and had probably spent a portion of his "rack time" sending ESP signals to the Super to come and inspect. When the cannon sounded for Reveille, Groovey was already dressed and pacing the room like a businessman waiting for a long-distance telephone call.

"You—Mardis!" He pointed at me frantically and then pointed at the sink. "I've got my Special Inspection towels out so you just watch out where you put your grubby paws."

Rutledge was yawning and slipping out of his pajamas when Groovey called on him. "Rutledge! The apparel in my half of the closet is spotless, you hear me? Spotless! And so is my half of the closet, so you better *watch it*, Mister, you watch it when you open up that closet door."

"Yeah, yeah, I gotcha, bright boy."

The inspection would commence exactly twenty-five minutes after completion of the normally scheduled Saturday morning classes. This gave us from 0730 to 1030 hours to worry about dustballs flying in through the windows, and then twenty-five minutes to hurry back and find them. I spotted Hadrean in the corridor of Thayer Hall on the way to mathematics. He looked like a man who had wandered ten miles across the desert in search of water only to see his visionary fountain shrinking in the distance. He appeared *unslaked.*

After class, there wasn't much to do in the room except stand around, and wait, and keep a watch out for dustballs—but Groovey did that. He did everything. He had mopped the floor, he had chiseled the rust out of the waste can, he had polished the doorknob and razored a speck of paint off the mirror of the medicine chest. Now, as the minutes ticked off in the countdown, Rutledge and I had to admire what a fine job he had done, bright boy or not. We both said thanks, in our own way, and in return Hadrean lent us his private cheesecloth to shine the bills of our hats.

A Superintendant's Inspection took place "in quarters," and stressed the importance of immaculate quarters over that of your immaculate person. The uniform was the everyday class uniform, with a black shirt, black tie, and gray tropical-worsted trousers. Ironically, the black class shirt looked more immaculate when it was dirty—it tapered better. Hadrean, however, defied this logic as soon as he hit the room, and changed his shirt. At countdown fifteen, he changed trousers. Then he changed his socks, tossing the smelly ones neatly in his laundry bag and rearranging the hanging bag so the U.S. ARMY stencil was clearly visible. Hadrean Groovey was not easily slaked.

At countdown twelve, Carillo came in with his rifle and said, "Stick 'em up, men!" Once he'd looked around, though, our Fireteam Leader was unbelievably impressed. "Wow! This is really something. This is *really* some*thing! I wish I had my polaroid."

"We keep *our* asses in gear, sir," Rutledge said.

"Bullwinkle. Mardis, who's responsible for this? Who?"

"Sir, it is Groovey. Groovey's responsible."

Groovey, in his fresh class shirt, clean trousers, and clean socks, was still restless. He smiled nervously, his ordinarily placid face haggard, tense, agitated. "Yes, sir. It was me."

Carlo Carillo handed his rifle to Rutledge and stood in front of Hadrean. "Put it out there, friend. I want to shake your hand. We've had our differences but—" It was hard to tell whether Carlo was serious. He kept shaking Hadrean's hand. "Just put her there, friend, just put her there"—and *shaking* it. "We've had our differences but this *room*—friend, you're a credit to this company. Just lemme shake the hand that's responsible. I tell ya. . . ."

Carillo left around countdown nine, assigning Rutledge as the "battle watch." At countdown eight, Hadrean was still staring at the hand Carlo had shaken, as if it'd been injured. At countdown seven he went over to the sink to wash his hands, but stopped. He'd hammered the taps tight after breakfast to prevent demerit-causing drips. Groovey now looked around, panicky, blushing. "Gee, something stinks. I wonder what it is." *Sniff sniff.* "Well, what do you know, I think it's me. Guess I'll have to take a quick shower."

The future leader undressed in a bolt of lightning and shot down the hall, soap dish in hand. It was going to take some powerful washing to get rid of the kooties Fireteam Loser Carillo had inflicted in his congratulatory handclasp. There was no way of determining to what extreme the vile creatures had invaded his person, but Hadrean knew what was best for him and scrubbed from twiddle to twaddle. In less than three minutes he was back with us, re-dressed and catching dustballs, his mind at peace, and his person once again immaculate.

Rutledge lazily flicked a cigarette butt out the window. "Hey, Groovey baby, did you just take a shower?"

"That's correct."

"So what's with your towels over there on the sink? You didn't use those, huh?"

"Those towels are dry towels. All towels must be dry for—"

"*I* know that," Rutledge snapped, furrowing his brow. "But those aren't dry towels; those are new towels."

Hadrean replied curtly, "They're both."

"Well, I don't like it, and neither does Mardis, right?"

"That's right," I told Groovey. "Your lousy new towels make our clean towels look dirty."

"That's *sh*ow business, *s*onny!" Groovey told us snidely. "And if you can't keep up, *give* up—*Yuk!*"

"Oh, brother."

"I second the motion," said Rutledge, yawning. He took a look at his watch and scuffed his heels out into the hall. Mark's voice echoed from the small landing of our four-room floor: "Countdown one minute . . . fifty-five seconds . . . fifty . . . Son of a!" There was a commotion of scurrying feet and loud whispers; Rutledge came storming back in the room, hissing, "Grab your rifles, boys, he's here! I seen the stars on the first floor and I think they're coming all the way up!"

For a small eternity the three of us stood side by side, bolt at attention, our rifles by our sides and our three pairs of feet each lined up in precise 45-degree angles. We could hear each other swallow. Mark Rutledge whispered, "I'm glad I didn't make that bet!" and Groovey whispered back, "Shut up!" And Rutledge said aloud, "*You* shut up." But now we froze. Footsteps were thundering up the stairwell.

"Atenn-*hutt!*" The inspecting detail entered our room. Apparently the Superintendant had decided to work his inspection backwards, beginning with the Corps' last regiment, most remote division, and the top floor thereof—us. The inspecting detail seemed to be in a hurry, either to hurry up and get started or to hurry up and get it over with—it wasn't clear. They zipped about the room testing things with the tips of their white-gloved fingers.

Overall, there was my Squad Leader Mr. Patchett; Company First Sergeant Hoggins; G-5 Company Commander Haroldson; Fifth Regimental Commander, "Eyes" Seitz; Seitz's assistant commander; two members of the Cadet Brigade staff; the G-5 Tactical Officer, Major Clifford Cutler with his assistant, a Regular Army

Sergeant; another Major whom I hadn't seen before; and of course the Academy Superintendant, who was a General.

I could hear Hadrean's heart pulsating right next to me in proud thumps as numerous voices kept saying, "This is very good. Very good." He had been slaked, but the inspecting detail wanted to be slaked, too. They chose Groovey's glistening desk complex as the one to inspect meticulously, and what they inspected was a desk so meticulous down to the last petty detail that it made them dizzy just looking in the drawers. "This man Groovey is a neatness *expert*," they said.

The Super had been hm-hawwing and making gastric noises; now he cleared his throat. "Can't you men find *any*thing? Flagrant, that is."

"You want us to dig, sir?"

"No, no, don't dig, we don't have time."

"Sir! I found a dead spider in this man Rutledge's left overshoe."

"Give 'im two," Major Cutler commanded.

"Now wait a minute," the Super scolded softly. "Is the spider dead or alive?"

It was "Eyes" Seitz's assistant who held it up. "Sir, the spider looks and acts half dead. A few minor wiggles but on the whole unreactive. Could be postmortum stimuli."

"Oh, all right, give him two," the Superintendent said, suddenly grumpy. "Are we almost ready?"

"Pencil scratch here on the rear posture support of Cadet Mardis's chair."

"Two," said Major Cutler, the G-5 Tac.

"Keep those posture supports *clean*," added the Golf-ball-5 Company Commander.

"Eyes" Seitz had yet to speak up, but as the inspecting detail huddled to make their way through the door, he boomed out: "Sirs! I got an infraction on this man Groovey!" The officers obediently turned around, curious. I could feel Hadrean tighten next to me like a giant sling shot. "I got here a disorderly soap tray," "Eyes" said. "And it belongs to Mister Groovey—see."

"Disorderly soap *dish*," someone corrected.

"Dis*reputable* soap dish," someone again corrected.

"Well, what is it?"

"What's the problem with it?"

"Look—" Seitz said. He gloatingly held up the soap between two fingers of his gloved hand, first showing it to the Super and Major Cutler, and then to Groovey. Without knowing it, Groovey whimpered out loud.

"Three demerits," gnashed Cutler. "Talking in ranks."

"And three more," laughed Seitz. "*Pubic* hair on soap."

MEMO 5.

The idea of sex does not mix very readily with the integrity of the United States Corps of Cadets. Had the Founding Fathers wanted cadets to have sex, they would not have made the uniforms so difficult to get in or out of. They would not have decreed that cadets cannot marry until graduation. And they would not have placed hidden video cameras in the bushes along Flirtation Walk. The Founding Fathers had hang-ups.

In 1969, the idea of sex was very popular in spite of the integrity of the Corps. When cadets were on leave, they were bombarded with mini-skirts, hot pants, nylon stockings, and black lace brassieres. In *Life* magazine, the cadets read about hippie love-ins; on naughty, bawdy 42nd Street they saw peep shows; in *Playboy* magazine they saw candid pictures of breasts. The cadets knew what sex was, all right.

Simply because the lascivious, immoral times rollicking somewhere outside the stone walls of West Point had popularized sex inside the walls, had titillated the Corps, the Corps itself was not due for a change. Gray-clad integrity was too powerful. The Founding Fathers had had too much foresight. And the great computer in the bottom of Thayer Hall, Fido I, issued a proclamation intended to arouse the Corps' morale: "SALTPETER HAS BEEN DOUBLED IN THE MASHED POTATOS."

Fido and the Founding Fathers overlooked one important aspect in creating this Maginot Line. (The Maginot

58

Line was an extensive construction of tank barriers built along the Alsace border, in northeastern France, after World War I to prevent any future invasion of German armor. Field Marshal Foch had suggested it. In the next war, German forces easily outflanked the impenetrable Line.) Like Foch, Fido was blindly overconfident. Cadets stopped eating their spuds.

It was not long until *Playboy* magazine had to be banned.

There is a legend at the Academy of the ambitious, untiring cadet who does unauthorized study after "lights-out," hidden under his blanket with books and flashlight. There's also a regulation at the Academy which states that you must sleep in a complete uniform—either in regulation pajamas or in nothing at all. So every night after taps, the Officer in Charge of the Day, usually a Major, and the Cadet Chain of Command, who are First Classmen, conduct several arbitrary blitzkrieg raids to make sure lights are extinguished and that cadets are wearing complete sleeping uniforms. The odds for a blitzkrieg raid on your room are about one in five hundred.

The Officer in Charge and the Cadet Chain of Command walked into a Plebe room one night after taps on the fourth floor of the MacArthur Wing of Washington Hall, flicked on the lights, and called the room to attention. Three sleepy Plebes grumbled and then, on seeing who it was, pivoted to attention. But the fourth Plebe in a top bunk did not respond as avidly.

This Plebe was snuggled under his blanket like Winnie the Pooh, engaged in the old overtime routine with a flashlight and a book. He was not with it, as they say. The Officer in Charge ripped off the blanket, thinking the bed might be stuffed—and the spectacle then presented was one of conduct unbecoming to a USMA cadet. The cadet was in a regulation birthday uniform, holding a flashlight in one hand and his manhood in the other. The book was *Playboy* magazine. The officer unmercifully had the sex criminal stand at an erect position of attention alongside his other roommates.

The crime was odious but complicated. They couldn't really get him on PDA—Public Display of Affection—which usually applied to instances of kissing or holding more than one hand of your girlfriend in public. On their honor, the three roommates were absolved of any complicity since they claimed to be unaware of his activities. (Cadets who do not report infractions are equally guilty of the infraction.) All told, enough charges were mounted against the cadet-turned-playboy to keep him marching off demerits for a long, long time, even though not one clause in Cadet Regulations specified that a cadet *could not* do what this one was doing. The punishment might well have been worse were it not for the rapid disappearance of hard evidence in the case.

Although sex was largely kept under the blanket at West Point, carnal assault was not. *Rape!* was a favorite topic of rabble-rousers such as Colonel "Tips" Porterhouse, head Tactical Officer for the Fifth Regiment. In a rare appearance, the seldom-seen-but-often-heard-from Colonel emphasized the importance of the Red Plague by saying, sincerely, in a whisky-voiced aside: "How would you like it if some slant-eyed commie raped *your* mother?" The cadets nodded their understanding.

In Beast Barracks, we attended a few propaganda skits where rape was topical (the skits were conceived by the Big Brass and executed by upperclassmen.) One version had a black-shirted Viet Cong coming upon an unsuspecting young blonde, a sort of Tarzan-Jane scenario where Tarzan comes to the rescue in the person of a machine-gun-toting Green Beret. The Beret bops the Cong and saves the girl. Another version has the blonde—sometimes played by a Cadet Hostess, other times by a cadet in a wig—taking a stroll in the park and accosted by a covey of disreputable hippies. The hippies molest her when she refuses to "get hip" with them, at which point a cadet in his dress uniform meanders by and punches out the long-haired mugger-rapists. The curtain closes with the grateful doll cooing, "Oh, my goodness!"

The skits were simple enough so as not to befuddle the new Plebes, and they were a great success, too! The captive audience not only clapped and whooped, they demanded a curtain call! Such comic relief reinforced and flattered our reason for being at the Point, institutionalized a disdain for our civilian peers, bolstered our cadet egos, and illustrated to anyone with two of everything that honor—and integrity—were keynotes to success with the opposite sex.

The problem was, in 1969, that cadets were cut off from black lace brassieres, alienated from participating in love-ins, because for all fashionable purposes, cadets were squares. You couldn't go down to New York for a weekend with your shiny shoe tips and Woody Woodpecker hair-do and expect to impress anyone. So, with the help of the Cadet Hostesses Office, the mountain came to Muhammed for a change. High school and college girls were recruited and bussed in to people the West Point hops.

The hops, especially Plebe hops, were a travesty. They took place on the second floor of Cullum Hall, where alternate chapel had been that summer. The first hop of the year, held in September, was a big shindig. The Hostesses had done a bang-up job with their recruits, scoring busloads from Wellesley, Vassar, St. Mary's the Virgin Mother. A welcoming committee had been set up, and we were all to wear our tails—our Full Dress gear.

It was a balmy Saturday night, the hop kicking off around 2200 hours. And the enterprising Plebes had learned from their upperclass brothers that the only way to get yourself a nice girl was to arrive early and snatch one up the minute they got off the bus: first come, first grab. Jerry Drury and I slapped on the cologne and were over there on the steps by 2100 hours.

Jerry Drury and I had become fast friends during the first week of regular company life, when he was collecting forms from Fourth Class rooms and noticed that I was making doodle sketches instead of shining my shoes or belt buckle or doing homework like everybody else. Jerry clapped me on the back and said I had potential.

Jerry was strongly built but flighty, and terrified of athletics on the grounds of "weak knees." Drury was a cool and canny veteran of a military prep near Chicago; he'd been around just long enough, he said, not to take the Army too seriously. Jerry had a habit of wincing as if he didn't believe what you told him, and if he did believe it, he still wished it weren't true.

We were sitting there on the steps of the dignified, antique building, located on a sheer bluff overlooking the Hudson, enjoying the slow, waning hours of the afternoon, an evening of Indian summer. Then the Officer in Charge of the Hop arrived with the Plebe Welcoming Committee, resplendent in red sashes. They told us to wait somewhere else, and went inside. One of the Plebes lingered on to say, "We don't want your kind at our hop."

"What did we do?" I asked Jerry.

"I don't know. Maybe it was because I'm smoking a cigarette." He showed me a cigarette he had hidden in a cupped palm.

Regardless of the Welcoming Committee's disapproval, a lot more of "our kind" soon showed their faces—about two hundred, at least. They had heard the lowdown about first come, first grab and had sprinted on over to get their share. Our squatter's rights didn't mean a damn now.

When the first bus pulled up, havoc broke loose. It was

truly disgusting, and the girls in the bus were probably frightened out of their wits to see two hundred robust young Americans with their tongues wagging like metronomes. Jerry and I couldn't believe it ourselves. The bus driver had to come out and push people aside just to get the door open.

Fortunately, two other buses pulled into view about then, so that some of the Plebes in back of the mob broke off to have first shot at the newcomers. The Plebes at the bus door were going crazy to match manners: "Hello, I'm Cadet Private Hillery from Company D-1! May I be your escort this evening, miss!"

"Hello, I'm Cadet Private Smith from Company C-3! May I show you around the grounds, if you please, miss!"

"Watch out you lousy son-of-a— I saw her first! I'm Cadet Elrod from—" And so on.

When the cadets in the back of the crowd saw that their chances were minimal for getting a first grab, they started to hop up and down beside the bus windows to see if there was anything inside worth waiting for, or fighting for. If not, it was on to next bus—or even to form an imaginary line for a bus that hadn't arrived yet.

Jerry and I were too amazed at the spectacle to take part; instead we climbed on the base of a small statue to get a better look at the onslaught. A few screams were heard—and some of the girls panicked and scampered back to the safety of the bus. Others refused to disembark when they saw what was happening, and with good reason, but the sex-crazed cadets wouldn't take no for an answer; some fought their way upstream past the driver to get inside where the grabbing was best.

After a while the Officer in Charge of the Hop and the Plebe Welcoming Committee emerged from Cullum Hall and began blowing police whistles. The action immediately came to standstill, and the destruction was now apparent. More than a few cadets had been trampled, one had a bloody nose, dozens had had their spit-shines ruined in the ruthless stampede. A Vassar girl was down—she'd sprained an ankle. Several more were in tears. The Officer in Charge of the Hop and the Welcoming Committee plunged through the aftermath, commanding the cadets to go inside or back to the barracks. A physician was summoned for the wounded Vassar girl. Demerit forms were issued for any Plebes who had exchanged blows. And one of the buses loaded up and went back home.

The first hop of the year certainly started like a riot, but the rest of it was anticlimactic. Once the majority of the girls had met, spoken to, perhaps danced with, shared cookies and punch with, and generally related to the Plebes as something more than stir-crazy, salivating barbarians, they were ready to go home. This only took fifteen minutes and they were bored.

When the Officer in Charge of the Hop saw that the festivities were taking the shape of an apartheid, he ceremoniously got on stage and gave his official sanction to the great fun that was in store. He also hinted an apology, saying, "Our Plebes were greatly excited to have you here." He smiled off a few catcalls. "Now, I order all of you to enjoy yourselfs!"

The cookies must have been made with saltpeter, too, because soon most of the Plebes were looking sour-faced and dismal, dispersing into their own groups, going for a work-out at the gymnasium, or downstairs for a few chocolate sundaes. There might not have been a hop at all if the bus drivers hadn't pooled together and gone down to Highland Falls for a few beers. Drury and I nevertheless attempted to hurtle the barrier that lay between ourselves and the co-eds.

"I came here tonight to try to give the military a second chance," one of the co-eds told us. "But after seeing this, I know why we're in Viet Nam."

"Why?" asked Drury. "I'd like to know myself."

"Because of your imperialistic aggressiveness, that's why!" she snapped.

"Care to talk it over on the dance floor?"

"I didn't know that pigs could dance."

There were some couples dancing, however, because some cadets had girlfriends in the vicinity who visited them every weekend. And, as I was to learn over the year, the most eager group of outsiders to show up at our socials were the girls from St. Mary's the Virgin Mother. But they weren't allowed to dance.

Admittedly, I suffered some heartbreak in the course of these hops, pretending as best I could that this was a segment from *Gone with the Wind*—the sabers and uniforms, the ballroom chandelier, the polite conversation. Soon enough, though, the Hostesses had botched it with most of the neighboring colleges and had to resort to anything they could get. By and by, my own Scarlet O'Hara was a bubble gum princess from some P.S. in the Bronx.

"Hello, I am Cadet Private Mardis of the Corps of Cadets. So charmed to have you with us tonight, Miss—"

"They call me Sammie. It's a guy's name but I've managed all right for myself. I'm here, ain't I?"

"Care for punch and cookies?"

"If there ain't anything better, sure."

I felt the same way. But Sammie quickly broke company with me to meet other cadets. Perhaps she was looking for a West Point wedding, had seen too many gang wars to make hasty value judgments on imperialist aggressors. At the end of the hop, she came over to me and asked for my address. I shrugged and wrote it on a paper napkin—any mail, even junk mail, was savored by confined cadets.

The next week I got her letter:

Dear Cadet Private Mardis, USCC,

It was an honor and a privilege to be at a West Point dance and I greatly enjoyed it the whole way. The place was OK and I had a wonderful, fine experience talking to you and Cadet Hillery from Company D-1. Cadet Houseman was also a fine gentleman like yourself. Both of you were greatly courteous and gentlemanlike towards me and believe you me, I had a fine, good time. Let me tell you a little about myself. I am a young girl of eighteen and am in my second year of high school here at P.S. 191. My interests are canoeing and yachting and water skiing, even if my swimming strokes are not the best in the whole world. Thanks again for the wonderful time,

Yours Sincerely,
             Gloria Rosa d'Aquino (Sammie)

I couldn't figure it out until a second letter arrived the next day explaining the first.

Dear Shit-Head,
Dont think I enjoyed that bullshit up there. My class counselor made me go and she made me write that letter, too. I've been in trouble lately and I had to do it. I wouldn't be in this shit school except I'm on probation. Anyway, my boyfriend would knock your face in if I told him what a hard-on you was.

                                    Up Yours!
Sammie.

PS—You look like a FOOL in that uniform!

MEMO 6.

Fido was usually the bearer of bad news, and so had a low popularity with the Corps. But I, for one, did not blame the computer personally for its dispatches. I felt friendly toward the computer and made more than one trip down to the basement of Thayer Hall to gaze with respect—from a distance, of course—at the sealed vault where he was kept. If you listened closely, in the tomblike silence of the long, cold corridor, you could hear him back there buzzing and clicking, making command decisions.

Fido's gender had probably been established by a predominance of male outlet plugs, the kind which give instead of receive. The computer had been purchased from a scientific firm somewhere for many millions of dollars, then brought to West Point and programmed to do military thinking. Not that West Point was lacking in military thinkers—it had plenty of them. Fido's purpose was to back up their authority; and this is what I liked about old Fido. The computer had to take orders just like anybody else!

Colonel Porterhouse utilized the computer to its fullest capacity. The reclusive Colonel had learned how easy it was to make a phone call, whereupon a few buttons were pushed, and seconds later have his immortal words spilling out of the computer like a hot edition of the *Daily News*. "THERE SHALL BE NO MORE BLUEBERRY MUFFINS RELEGATED FROM THE MESS HALL FOR INDIVIDUAL USAGES." On a steel-gray print-out in brisk computer lettering, Colonel "Tips" ' petty reminders had the head-line impact of a nation at war. The cadets would read the bulletin board and stop stealing muffins for good.

That fall, Fido showed the Plebes a different side to his personality by giving us some good news on a print-out, almost *too* good to be true. The print-out said what we already knew, that we were the Cream of the Crop of the year 1969 and that we were the best grouping of young men that America has to offer. But when you flipped the page, the print-out went on to state explicitly that we were the most outstanding group of young men in the *world.* Attached were twenty-five pages of factual proof.

Kids were mailing them home and buying picture frames for them. "Dear Mom: You always told me I was the best son in the world, but I thought you were just kidding. I now have factual proof. . . ." No one had put the computer on *its* honor, though. The best grouping of young men in the world had been established on "certain technical grounds" and by means of "repeated random samplings." Meaning that the researchers kept repeating the random samplings until they found a nice juicy one to compare us favorably with.

"Random" comparisons from every corner of the globe had been tabulated to set the stage for our superiority. We had better bone developments and bet-ter hair follicles than similar per capita peer groupings in Ecuador, Nigeria, or Pakistan. We had higher batting averages and larger vocabularies than in Tunisia, the Antilles, or Thailand. The print-out continued, taking on bigger game: "PREVIOUSLY UNDISCLOSED RECORDS HAVE NOW BROUGHT TO LIGHT CLINICAL EVIDENCE SUB-STANTIATING PEOPLES UNDER THE SOVIET BLOC TO HAVE DETECTABLY LOWERED INTELLIGENCE QUOTIENTS (IQ'S) RESULTANT FROM . . ." in so many words, from having to live in political captivity.

The bulk of the proof, however, pertained to the U.S.A. The researchers were clever enough to know we

Plebes were too bright and alert to be bothered with the rest of the world for long. What we really wanted to find out about were those stupid midshipmen at the Naval Academy—were we really smarter than them? "YES," was the computer print-out's answer, on page 9, Tables C, D, and L. You have more valedictorians, salutatorians, better night vision, fewer histories of somnambulism, and, collectively, the United States Corps of Cadets outweighs the middies by 1,428 pounds.

What about the rest of America? Just shut up and keep reading, was the print-out's answer. In Table R, the Harvard and Yale men were proved to be sissies and troublemakers. In Table R-2, every other domestic college awarding federally approved non-matriculated degree programs was shown to be worse off than the Harvard boys. Yep, we had everybody licked, all right. What's more, we incoming Plebes had fewer police convictions than any other college freshman class in America (O) and more combat experience than all of them put together, and those were the facts.

The researchers probably worked for a shady marketing research firm looking for a government handout. The researchers themselves were probably mustachioed Harvard drop-outs looking to get back at the alma mater. But no matter! It was all right there on steel-gray paper and in cold crisp type—we Plebes were the best grouping of young men in the whole world. Fido had told us so.

Fido said a lot of things. In fact, he might still be yapping about the best of the best if somebody hadn't thrown the switch; some computers can just go on forever.

One of Fido's multitudinous responsibilities was to keep the Corps posted on their grade-point averages. Our scores were posted every week and in every subject, computed all the way to nine decimal places. And on this subject, one cold November morning, Fido put an end to our silent "friendship." The computer opened its big yak and shoved me into nine decimal places' worth of public scandal.

To move freely in the United States Corps of Cadets, you had to be *anonymous.* To do great good or great wrong made you an object of controversy—cadet gossip. But to do absolutely nothing and do it well was an accomplishment of such grand proportions that it defied comment. Which was exactly the point.

So far that term, I had enjoyed French class. I liked it because it required little effort; I'd already covered the basics at St. Francis's and this was easy street, a rehash. The Major who instructed the class spent most of his time, and ours, conducting a group gargling chorus so the Brooklyn cadet and the Milwaukee cadet could get the hang of their gutteral French *r.* The Major didn't know, nor did anybody else, that I would be top Plebe French scholar in the Corps. But Fido knew, once he'd calculated the midterm examinations. And by the time *I* found out, it was too late to change anything; I'd been exposed to one and all as a bright boy.

The language scores were posted in a sallyport of Washington Hall, which was used by many Fifth Regiment Plebes as a safe thoroughfare to and from the academic buildings. The "language sallyport" was actually the roundabout way to go to the academic buildings, and for the same reason it was considered to be safe passage for Plebes. Hardly an upperclassman ever went that far out of his way during class hours to lay an ambush for gawking beanheads.

All the same, there was at least one ambush a month there, and as many as thirty Plebes would be slaughtered with demerits. I preferred to take no chances and returned from classes by way of a dank, obscure alley which led behind the Mess Hall docks, along a cliff, and then emerged under a quaint arch into the Slums of the Corps. In the alley you were free to gawk. You could see a squirrel struggling its way up the steep cliff, or you could see a lame-brain civilian struggling a huge drum of apple sauce onto the Mess Hall loading dock.

No ambush occurred in the language sallyport on the day the midterm averages were posted, and consequently a lot of gawking took place. When I arrived through the alley, maybe a minute and a half later than most, a crowd was gathered on the covered stone porch of Golf-5. The Slums resembled a row of quaint tenement houses; I lurched up the steps, excited to see what the frou-frou was all about.

Since this was Golfball-5, I just grabbed a Plebe by the back of his jacket. "Say, what's the commotion?"

"You wouldn't believe it! Some beanhead got a perfect. . . . Hey! It's you! Hey! Here he is! Here's *Frenchy*!" The mob turned itself on me; luckily, I was thrust behind the door as they came pouring out of the entryway shouting, "Where! Where! G-5's got a genius! Hooray!" and more of the same. Then I was discovered, my back against the wall, my books under my arm. It so happened I had a French book with me.

"Still studying, huh, Mardis? You probably study French in the shower!" An upperclassman who didn't like me had said this.

Another shoved his nose at me, a Firstie, a smile from ear to ear. "Good job, Mister, good job! That's the G-5 spirit. You won me five bucks, Mister! I knew one of our Plebes would maximize!"

Someone else yelled from the background, "So you think you're pretty smart, Mardis! You'll see!"

The mood of the crowd, at the drop of a hat, turned to derision, with a hand knocking down my books, my necktie being tugged, and then, suddenly, back to praise again. "So what if he dicks on his classmates—he's got his own ass to cover, doesn't he?"

"Let's hear it for Mardis—he may not look like much, but at least he's got brains!"

Then the Plebes present whooped in harmony,

"Hiphip, hooray, sir! Hiphip, hooray, sir! Hiphip, *horse-shit*, sir!" and the crowd laughed, at last finding a happy medium. The shouts of the Plebe minute-callers signalling lunch formation began reverberating through the barracks. The cadets, some fifteen who'd been scrutinizing me, realized they had to change coats for formation and quickly disbanded, leaving me alone to pick up my books.

I wasn't completely sure what I'd done, but Hadrean Groovey, who came pounding down the stairs to be first in ranks, laid aside any doubt. "Congrats on the 36.0 in French," he whispered, double-timing in place.

"Thanks, Hadrean. I thought maybe that was it." I stood up with my books now in order. "What'd you get?"

"A crummy 27.46. Puts me *sesenta-ocho* in overall Plebe Spanish. But you're *Numero Uno*—see you later."

I scarcely had time to dash up to my room, change coats, and make it into ranks before the bugle was blown —which was the late signal for upperclassmen. Plebes were supposed to be there three minutes sooner. Reports were rendered; then we were at ease for a few minutes while some announcements were read to the assembled Fifth Regiment.

Usually while we were at ease in ranks, the upperclass joked around, under their breath. A Third Classman, Deinling, called out, "Hey, what's the matter, Mardis? Think you can get here late now because you're an intellect. What's the matter—afraid your brains are gonna freeze in the cold?"

My Squad Leader, Mr. Patchett turned fully around at the waist, saying, "Aw, shut up, *Dein*ling. Just because the Plebes in your squad can't distinguish your name from the German spelling of *dung*heap." Powers got a stifled laugh all through the platoon. Other wisecracks went up to take sides.

"Mardis probably farts in French!"

To which someone replied, "You probably fart in your hat."

"Mardis! Hey—you still gonna do my homework for me tonight?"

And so the crossfire went until we marched across the DMZ into the Mess Hall. The DMZ was the huge sheet of concrete where the Fifth Regiment formed ranks, and it was located in front of the large section of the Slums. The Slums themselves were located well behind Washington Hall, cleanly out of sight. So when the rest of the Corps formed ranks on the aprons of the great green Parade Plain and marched proudly into the Mess Hall through the front door, we went in the back way.

G-5 was quartered in the small section of the Slums which was remote even from the DMZ and wedged quite neatly between a sheer cliff and the flying buttresses of the West Point gymnasium. With such rustic charm, the Golf-5 "Slum" had always been a sight for sore eyes—a welcome retreat for the hypertensive, overwrought Plebe returning home from a hard day of classes and hazing.

But now all that would change. My peaceful room, the calming window view of the rock garden and bubbling brook, and the happy sparrows who drank from the brook would now be invaded by hateful aliens, just like the bully squirrels who terrorized the sparrows for their acorn bits! I wished Fido had provided a special table on me explaining that I didn't know what I was doing—but no. Fido spoke, and a public figure was made. And there was my nameplate on my shirt pocket to identify me. I was no longer *anonymous.*

I was a victim of circumstance, already subjected to mob violence, persecuted for no good reason in ranks, and that day at lunch (dinner, to the Army), the table commandants interrogated me on the nature of my foul motives.

"How did you manage that, Mardis? Huh, Mister? You been goldbricking on your Fourth Class duties? Let's have it, Mister."

"Yeah, let's hear the story, Mister. How'd you do so good on that—" (The Academy lingo for a midterm examination sounded like the formula for a chemical reaction.)

"Come on, Mardis—look up here. Stop looking at your plate!"

"Yezzir!"

"Now," the table commandant, First Sergeant Bub Hoggins, asked, "what's the story with this 36.0 on your language *%!$? Huh? I wanta know, Mister! Maybe you think you're better than everybody else. Is that it?"

"No, sir."

"Then let's have it."

"No excuse, sir."

This got a laugh at the table, and I was given permission to continue eating. First Sergeant Hoggins, however, who was mistrustful of anyone whose grades were *too* good, let me know that he'd be watching me closely. "Just to make sure you're not dicking on your classmates," he explained, implying that in devoting time to individual studies, the welfare of the whole was irrevocably being ignored.

Over the next week, each and every member of Golf-5, all classes, let me know their private feelings on my success. There was no even breakdown of opinion between zeros and heros. One hero thought it was "damned good for company spirit"; others felt as Hoggins did. A zero First Classman brought by a bawdy French record, which I translated for him to the best of my ability. Deinling, who was "super-stract"—a zero on the outside but very definitely a hero on the inside—cornered me and said, "It's the phonies like you who make this company what it is! Warped!"

Hoggins and his cronies began driving around at night

to make sure my room was in p.m. inspection order, which made Groovey happy but Rutledge extremely irritable. Overnight, my desk became a virtual auction block, with Plebes and Yearlings (Third Classmen) swarming in from all over the company to get unofficial AI (Additional Instruction) on French, Spanish, Portuguese, even Map Reading. They came to snoop, gawk, joke around, observe, philosophize, criticize, and idealize. Suddenly I was a star. But I felt like a religious relic.

The well-wishers went away after it was apparent that no miracle of osmosis was going to occur, but the wrathful and ill-minded stayed. Obviously, I needed a new sanctuary, and the only suitable authorized p.m. place I knew was the seldom-used lounge of the foreign language lab on the eighth floor of Washington Hall. Every night after supper I would load up my books and vanish. I'd come back ten minutes before taps and duck under the covers before anyone had the chance to say yea or nay. And when I'd leave the company for my hideout, I double-backed, side-stepped, and took obscure staircases to assure that no one followed.

But they found me anyway. The language lab usually had no more than three or four students in it at night, upperclass cadets deeply absorbed in Russian or Mandarin who could care less about one lowly Plebe's French standing. Fine with me! Then one night, shortly before Christmas leave, I was on the earphones, listening to a few lines from an advanced dialogue and generally daydreaming of busty prostitutes on the Left Bank of Paris, when my voice-level indicator went jumping helter-skelter.

Slightly in a daze from my activity, I took off the earphones and turned my head to see what had gone wrong with the dials. Sabotage. I saw a pink, meaty hand with gnawed-up fingernails. My eyes traced up the hand along the black class shirt to see a pink, meaty face grimacing at me. It was a Plebe, a neat, husky fellow whose sensitive features did not seem to match up with his thick limbs and broad shoulders. The Plebe was sucking in his lips nervously and biting them. He looked like he'd just come in from the cold.

"I'm number *two*," he said viciously. "I thought I'd find you here."

"Pardon me?" I scratched the sides of my head where the earphones had been.

"You don't know who I am, but I know who you are, Mardis," he said, his face tensing at the eyes. "A lot of people know who you are, but I'm the one who's going to get you."

"Oh . . . my French standing. So how did you find me here?"

"I have my ways. But if you want to know, a guy from G-2 told me. You're not as smart as you think you are, Mardis."

I didn't want to hear about it, just wanted to put the reel back on and think about Mademoiselle Fifi in Paris: "*Je suis Cadet Jaime aux Etats-Unis, ma chérie Fifi. Comme j'aime les jolies jambes! Voilà!*"

The Plebe tugged my shoulder and made me look up again. An upperclassman listening to Mandarin tapes two stalls down hadn't even noticed that a wise guy was amuck in the lab. I suppose he was either asleep or maybe in Shanghai cavorting with Susie Wong. "Listen to me, Mardis!" The Plebe, number two, seemed about to cry; his thick hands were trembling, and he was grinding his teeth as he told me:

"My name's Ed Ogerby from Company C-2. That name may not mean anything to you right now, but it will pretty soon. *Because I'm going to be number one.* This is fair warning." He removed his hand from my shoulder and walked to the door of the lab. He was wearing a gray jacket, zipped it up, hurriedly tugged his gloves on his hands. He found his hat and put it squarely on his head, grimacing and squinting his eyes. As I watched, dumb-founded, I managed to put on my earphones again.

Ogerby of C-2 was insulted by my action: He mouthed some words which I couldn't hear through the phones, then he trooped over, hit a switch on my board, curtly turned up the volume (we all knew how to operate the equipment from class) and said into the microphone as I numbly listened:

"Ed Ogerby, Mardis. Company C-2. And I'm gonna be number one! Read me?" The voice-level needle had done a backflip. I gave an OK signal with one hand. Ogerby re-clicked the switches, restoring normalcy to my set, and brusquely left the lab. I thought: What did I ever do to Monsieur Fido to deserve all this?

Eventually, my life was made easier when my French marks began to show signs of deterioration. Ironically, this happened over a three-week period when I had to devote all my spare time to passing a computer sciences course.

MEMO 7.

Major Clifford Cutler was not a tall man; he couldn't have been more than five feet eight with his hat off. Nor was he well-proportioned; he had big feet, spindly legs, long simian arms, and a bullish chest. But none of this mattered because Major Clifford Cutler had "The Look." The young G-5 Tactical Officer had a way of jackknifing his shoulders and thrusting forward his chin to give his snide, razor-clean face all the prominence of an upraised hatchet. He knew how to smile with his bottom teeth, how to knot the muscles in his cheeks. He knew how to make his eyes glower like black diamonds under the low, gold-leaf bill of his officer's hat. The Clifford Cutler "Look" would have made an excellent cover feature for *Gestapo Illustrated*.

In 1968, Major Cutler arrived at West Point fresh from the Nam; he had himself graduated from the Point in the early 60's and had proceeded directly to the war. So the story went, the courage of the ambitious young officer over there had brought him a succession of uncannily rapid battlefield promotions. Three times in a row, his immediate superiors were killed off in action and this gave Clifford instant rank. It was called "field promotion." Apparently *he* wasn't unnerved by these coincidences, but the Lieutenant Colonel who remained just above him in the pecking order was, understandably, a little nervous. So young Cutler was sent back to the States with a few medals and pats on the back and told to relax awhile.

The position of a West Point Tactical Officer (the officer in charge of a cadet company) was essentially an "honorary" duty, a two-year rest station. But Cliff Cutler was far too restless to goldbrick it for two years. He'd been assigned Golfball-5 as his cadet company, a company which had been in last place in the Corps for seventeen consecutive years. Major Cutler had said he could make it *first*. When he'd said that, however, G-5 had only been last for sixteen years. Now he only had a year left to turn the company called Goofball-5 into *Glory-Hog* 5.

Cutler usually addressed us in the musty basement of our division of the Slums, standing on top of a locker bench. "They say that war is all hell, boys, but it's all *glo*ry!" he'd say, misquoting MacArthur. "And this is war! War! You hate all those other som'bitching companies, you hate their guts. 'Cause it's gonna take some powerful hate to get us to the top this year, men, a lot of hate. Hate your enemy—but respect your enemy. After all, they're cadets just like you, but for right now, they are the enemy."

Mark Rutledge, who had told me the story about Cutler, had a low professional opinion of the Major. Cutler wore all his medals, citations, and badges on the left pocket of his smart olive-green dress jacket, while most officers only displayed distinguishing medals. Rutledge said this was a sure sign of a bright boy: "I'm telling you, *no*body in their right mind wears their Good Conduct medals, except maybe on a drinking spree. And even then, you don't pull 'em out unless the barkeep says he ain't gonna serve you. But that Cutler, he wears that tinhorn stuff like he was proud of it."

Rutledge proved to be quite correct. The Major explained it to us one night. "I'm proud of every single thing the United States Army has ever done for me, and

I'm not ashamed to show exactly how proud I *yam*. Just look here on my field—and you'll see a Silver Star and a Purple Heart. You don't get those from sitting behind a typewriter, men. But look closer, and you'll see my Good Conduct badges and even an old rifle badge. Small potatos, some would say, but not to *this* Major. I'm proud of every single one of them babies and I'm not ashamed to show it!"

The gung-ho factor of G-5 applauded this gutty remark, but Major Cutler signaled for quiet. "When you boys get over there—where the real action is—there ain't gonna be any applause. So you better get used to it." Cutler looked at the faces of his men from the locker bench, then cracked a smile which more closely resembled a sneer. "I *yalways* say that only actors need applause, anyways. Not soldiers. A soldier gets his applause from a job well done, and he gets it *here!*" Cutler bounced a fist off his solar plexus. "Deep inside his gut."

In his first year as the G-5 Tac, the iron-fisted Major had tried to terrorize the company into improvement. He'd taken the First Classmen, who ran the company, and literally pinned them up against the wall to make his demands. When his rash demands could not be met, Cutler punished the Firsties. Yet, *no one,* hero or zero, liked to be held responsible for the G-5 mess—this was something that had been going on for years. And in what was probably G-5's finest hour, the zeros and heros had combined forces to fight the demon officer.

The foremost victim in the ensuing battle between the Tac and the Firsties had been a Plebe named Wook Keeng. Keeng was a fainter, and he had fainted in four out of seven Full Dress Parades, causing the company to default in the most vital area of Corps-wide competition. Cutler could not keep Wook out of the parades because, in repeated checkups, the doctors found him in perfect health. In other words, Wook—and defeat—couldn't be stopped.

The Firsties affectionately called their scapegoat "The Secret Weapon," for it was they who harassed the Plebe into his many tailspins on the field of honor. With the parade losses, the First Classmen had gone on to defeat Major Cutler, and to place the seventeenth zero in the book of G-5 records. Now they were gone, but Cadet Wook Keeng was not. Thanks to Carlo Carillo, my Fireteam Leader, Wook had managed to endure and *overcome* the many hardships of his Plebe year.

Wook Keeng was of trim physique, an expert gymnast, and quick of mind—an ace mathematician. He was from Oakland, California, and used a lot of slang in his speech, and for his friends, Wook always had a warm greeting and a keen oriental smile. Third Classman Keeng lived in our barracks unit, and each week, like clockwork, he brought Carlo Carillo a check for ten dollars. I asked Carillo, discreetly, what the money was for, and then I found out how Wook Keeng came to owe Carlo the sum of $2,000—and was happy to be in debt.

During the 1968 battle with the Tac, the Firsties' first counteroffensive had been to poll the Plebes for their stud factors and send the Plebe with the worst stud factor down to the PX as Rubber Representative. Wook Keeng was sent down to the PX to buy the prophylactics. The upperclassmen didn't tell him that Rubber Representation had long been banned in the Corps and that any nincompoop gullible enough to walk into the Post Exchange and ask the shop girl for four dozen "rubbers" would be reported to the MP and would soon be marching the area.

Wook was soon marching the area. The counter girls were acting unusually skittish that autumn because an overzealous cadet had tried to see the name tag of a particularly attractive shop girl and had grabbed her breast instead. Naturally, Wook would never have done

81

such a thing, but the shop girls were wary and not taking any chances. They weren't wearing any name tags either, but when Wook asked for the "rubbers" with that inscrutable smile of his, that was all it took. They called the MP and the MP called Major Cutler. Major Cutler put Wook on the area, marching off demerits. Then he changed his mind and put ten upperclassmen in his place.

After the Rubber Rep episode, one of the Firstie's girlfriends happened to get pregnant, and the Firsties decided to blame it on Wook for his failure in the line of duty. *Wook* was to blame for the pregnancy, even if his stud factor was zero! They taunted him night and day: "Hey, beanhead—so you're the guy who wants to turn the orderly room into a nursery, huh!" "Hey, Wookie! Where's my cigar!"

In part, Wook had feathered his own nest. When the poll was taken to appoint a Rubber Rep, the Fourth Classmen had been instructed to compute their stud factors by dividing their age in years by the total number of times they'd "gone all the way" with a member of the opposite sex. There was a tie for last place, Wook's denominator not being the only zero. But Wook was too smart for his own good in calculus. He told them his stud factor was *infinity*, and won the cake.

"Hey, Mister Infinity! Who's gonna be pregnant next?" During the second Full Dress Parade of the season, this remark caused an ailing and tormented Wook Keeng to faint dead away. A parade passed without incident, and then, in an unusually warm Halloween weekend parade, the same jibe caused Cadet Keeng to faint again. Major Cutler took Wook and gave him a good talking to. Cutler learned of the harassments and, sympathetic, punished the First Classmen implicated. But by now, the indignant Firsties knew how to lose a parade: "Hey there, Mister Infinity!" and down went Wook again.

Cutler put Wook in the hospital. Of course, his company had already lost, or worse, defaulted from the autumn parade season. The hospital found nothing wrong with the Plebe; yet in the resumption of the parade season the following March, the cadet fainted once again in the Grads' Day Parade. He was placed in the hospital again; they found him normal again.

Plebes were known to faint when the hazing got *too* tough. . . . But this was Golfball-5! And Wook Keeng was the Secret Weapon. He felt pretty bad about it, too. He felt bad about himself, so bad, in fact, that he decided to call it quits. Wook was an organized fellow, and this was a weakness which he could neither organize nor accept. He was worse than a loser. He was a defaulter.

In early April of 1969, Keeng put his papers through for resignation. Major Cutler was of course thrilled, but the Regimental Tac, Colonel "Tips" Porterhouse, saw the matter in a different light. Once the resignation reached his level, he called in Wook and told him to bear with it, that if you fall down, get up, and if you fall down again, get up again. The Colonel said that forty years ago, in the *Old* Corps, it was unusual for a Plebe not to faint. You had to get your sea legs, the Colonel told Wook. "And even more important," the Colonel said, "you've got to find yourself a girlfriend."

Wook went to Carlo "Hot Sauce" Carillo, the Plebe with the best stud factor in the company. In high school, Wook had been the president of a Junior Achievement bulk paper company, and had saved money. In an act of great determination and some desperation, Wook had sent home for his bank book, gone to see Carillo, thrown the bank book on Carlo's desk and said, "Carlo, if ya find me a girlie, there's two G's in it for you."

Carlo wrote over forty letters in search of a girlfriend for his client. When at last he found one, and she actually went to the hop with Wook, and *danced*, Carlo was so amazed by the situation that he refused Wook's money. The girl was a sophmore at Barnard College, a liberal arts student majoring in Far Eastern Studies. Carlo refused the money, but Wook insisted: "I'm no welsher, Carlo. Every week I'm still making time with this tomato, you're getting my John Henry for a sawbuck."

Two weeks after his first date with the Barnard co-ed, Wook strutted into his Squad Leader's room and made an official report. His stud factor had descended from infinity to plus eighteen. The girlfriend rented a car for a visit, and before long the stud factor was a respectable 3.6. Wook didn't faint in one spring parade after Grads' Day. He was no longer Mister Infinity. Wook could now stand in ranks with pride, and without fear of a relapse. The Firsties could jeer, but to no avail—Wook was now 3.6 and declining. But so was G-5. They went on to lose the spring season anyway.

As a Third Classman, Keeng wasn't immune from peer criticism. Our crabby First Sergeant, Bub Hoggins, for one, had it in for him and would call out in ranks, "*Hon*orable Mister Infinity," and such. Wook would crack back, "Cheese it, chum, or you'll be having knuckle sandwiches for lunch!" But it wasn't necessary for Wook to defend himself in our first Full Dress Parade because this year Cutler wasn't taking any chances. He had put Keeng down for a regimental grading assistant, a pencil carrier.

G-5 won that Full Dress Parade, its first in six years. Our score wasn't tops in the Corps, but we won the regimental honors, and, after all, Major Cutler never did say we'd be first in the Corps; he just said "first." The following two parades were rained out, so G-5 remained first for an astounding four and a half weeks. In addition, on the slippery, marshlike athletic fields, the company intramural teams began to win steadily, since it was easier to cheat.

The rain ceased, and a Full Dress Parade was promptly

scheduled for the coming Saturday. We were about a week into October. On Friday morning, Wook dropped by Carlo Carillo's room. We'd just had a Fireteam Inspection—mostly birdcalls—and I'd stayed behind to listen to Chip Hightower's radio. As usual, Wook had an optimistic smile and greetings for all, yet there was a troubled look to his bright eyes.

"Hiya, Hightower. Hey, Carlo! Relax there, Mister Mardis. I'm OK." Wook sat down backwards on a chair. Carlo asked him how the old stud factor was. "It's A-1, Carlo. And don't you worry, I'll have the old ten-spot for ya tomorrow, per usual."

"Thanks, 'cause I need it."

Hightower began toying with the radio dial and remarked, "Why, Wook baby, I bet your old stud factor's better than Marlon Brando's by now."

"A clean .87!" Wook smiled proudly.

"Geesers!" Carlo whistled. "You must have made up for lost time on summer leave."

"And how!" rejoined Wook. Then his tone changed. "Say, uh, guys, what's the scuttlebutt? Like the Tac has you guys out there in the rain every day drilling for these lousy parade AI's, and where am I? Cooling it in my room cause I'm a bigshot grader. You think I'm a P.C.?"

"What's that?"

"You know, a privileged character."

"Naw, naw," Carlo assured him. "Nobody thinks nothing."

"Maybe the Tac thinks I'm a bozo."

"Cutler thinks everybody's a bozo," Carlo said.

Hightower turned off the radio. "You ought to feel lucky you *are* a grader, Wook boy. I wish *I* was a P.C., I tell you."

Wook flipped back his hat and grinned. "You know, I must be a D.A. A dumb ass. Who else would complain about being a P.C.?" He gave Carlo a punch in the arm and left.

A company meeting was held in the basement after supper that night to get our blood flowing for tomorrow's parade victory. Cutler looked like he'd just come out of a press conference with the Angel of Death. He was radiant but solemn. Our victory, their defeat. The assembled men of G-5 were silent as the Major quietly shook his head in approval, his bottom teeth glinting. "I say it's the best army in the world that feeds its officers steak three times a week. Sure hits the spot, don't it?"

Major Cutler cracked his knuckles and signaled for the Company Commander to bring forth the gold regimental banner. The banner had been ours since the original parade victory, and after the first rain-out, Cutler told us we'd had it "going on a month." As of the past weekend, which made four weeks and two days, it was "going on two months." Clifford Cutler stood on a bench holding the banner like a spear. He glinted respectfully at the limp, weather-beaten yellow pennant.

The Tac loosened his tie a notch, then adjusted his hat. He curled up his lip as he looked at the banner. "Gentlemen, I'd suspect that if you wanted to buy a banner like this, it wouldn't cost you more than fifteen bucks. This flimsy piece of cloth here ain't worth more than fifty cents, and this old pole here, why . . . I wouldn't give ya five bucks for it. But gentlemen . . ." The Tac spoke defiantly, his eyes narrow and hard. "This banner can't be bought. This here banner has to be *won*."

Cutler handed the flag to a cadet and, stepping from the bench, said, "We have a special guest here with us who thinks we can *win* that parade tomorrow—and I'll be damned to hell if he's wrong." The Major made his way over to another locker bench; we watched in suspense. Cutler reached up and brought down the handle of a hanging, recoil-type screen. The company was momentarily stunned.

He unreeled an old, faded world map which had been painted over in bright colors to resemble a vicious horned pig with long bloody tusks. The words GLORY HOG were inscribed in giant letters across the bottom of the beast. One of the pig's eyes was Alaska, one of the fangs was the Cape of Good Hope. This was certainly no art treasure, but Golfball 5 got the point, all right. "This, gentlemen, is the *Glor*—" Cutler's voice was already drowned in the uproar.

The men were screaming wildly and chanting and singing, and a few zeros in the hubbub made clever noises. But the Major was too overcome by the glory of this imminent victory to ask for order—he sailed his hat across the lockers and boomed over the shouts of his men, "*Need I say more!!*" and the cheering surged on for five hoarse, heartfelt minutes.

Our friendly cadet Company Commander, Hopalong Haroldson, a track star, then took the bench and waved his arms for quiet. "Sorry fellows, but I've got some routine company announcements." He looked at Major Cutler, smiling guiltily. "Now, you all know to be out there by ten twenty-five for a last go at that turning movement. Now . . . Wook . . . Where are you, Wook?"

Wook held up his hand. "I was just tying the shoelaces on my loafers, chief!"

Haroldson laughed nervously. "Just make sure they're tied by tomorrow, Wook, because you're marching in the parade. I got a last-minute memo from Colonel Porterhouse, and it looks like he's changed most of the Fifth Regiment's grading assistants. You, anyway. A guy from B-5 is taking your place."

"OK—you're the boss!" replied Wook.

Major Cutler appeared to have aged ten years in ten seconds. His eyes were suddenly glazed, sunken; his steely jaw, usually so bold, was contorted. Haroldson concluded the announcements and asked, "Any further comments, Major Cutler?"

Cutler pulled down his hat, grinding his teeth. He stood by the Glory Hog, which offered no moral assistance. The Colonel had made a review of parade proceedings and had wised up to Cutler's ploy. Major Cutler said, "You men just carry on . . ." and the rest he mumbled.

"Sir?"

He cleared his throat and said louder, "You men just carry on like the hell bastards you are. All hundred twenty-*two* of you!" At that, the old map on which the Glory Hog was painted accidentally triggered itself and went *swwook—ping!* back up into its casing. But it had sounded like *Wook—Keeng!*

The morning of the parade, I was letter carrier. I had my uniform specially laid out so that after class I could dress quickly; then in my spare minutes I sped from room to room in the division handing out letters. When I entered Cadet Keeng's room, he was in the process of placing his "tar bucket," or Full Dress Hat, squarely on his head. He held the detachable plume in his teeth. "Thanks," he said when I gave him the letter from Barnard College. "My old lady," he said. "Here—knock the living daylights out of it."

He had handed me a thick dictionary with which to pound his Full Dress Hat squarely on his head. All cadets had a grave fear of having their tar buckets fall off on the field of honor, and Wook was no exception. The common safeguard was to pound the implacable hat down onto your scalp with a book. If Wook had ever reported to the hospital in his Full Dress Uniform, there's a strong possibility that the doctors could have made an instant diagnosis.

"Harder!" Wook said. "It still doesn't fit right."

"But doesn't it hurt you this tight?" I asked him.

"You bet your life it hurts," he answered.

"You're sure you want it to hurt?"

"You're darn tootin' I want it to hurt. Come on, once more. . . . *Ouch*! All right." He stuck the plume in and looked at himself in the mirror, satisfied. I'd hammered the tar bucket all the way down to his eyebrows. He thanked me taking the time and was opening the letter when I left.

At 10:25, all one hundred twenty-two of us were on the DMZ and squabbling over who was taller in our tar buckets, since ordinary height arrangements were changed by the altering fits of our dress hats. When at last we were lined up, it was far too late to practice the turning movement as planned. Cadet Commander Haroldson shrugged his shoulders shamefully, then faced Major Cutler to render his saber salute.

The Major was standing opposite the company formation on one of the stoops of the long section of the Slums. Other Fifth Regiment Tactical Officers, all in sparkling dress green uniforms, were present at intervals along the length of the barracks in front of their cadet companies. Some chatted, but Cutler was like stone. His assistant, a Regular Army Sergeant, was also motionless. When Haroldson saluted with his sword, Major Cutler finally made a move. He looked the other way.

The bugle was blown, reports were rendered, and "Tips" Porterhouse, wearing sunglasses and smoking a cigar, walked hurriedly "front and center" to salute Cadet Regimental Commander Seitz. More bugles were then blown, our Glory Hog banner was unfurled, and in the crisp sunlight of the autumn morning, the parade was on. Platoon after platoon, company after gray-clad company, bayonets glittering atop their rifles, marched through the sallyports of Washington Hall toward the Plain.

Ten minutes later, the entire Corps was standing in the middle of the Plain listening to a boring address. Some senator who thought the military budget shouldn't be cut. Talking during Parade Rest was exclusively an upperclass privilege, even in G-5, so the Plebes listened. I listened to a curious argument in the rank behind me, between Carillo and Wook Keeng. For a while they were speaking in whispers, but now Carlo Carillo was mad.

"I *need* that ten bucks, I'm telling you, Keeng baby. Today's the regular day and I need that money. Like I'm broke. I got a *date*. Hey, come on—say something already! You think I like begging? Not that you owe it to me, but a deal's a deal, damn it all."

"*Shad*dup, Buster."

"Listen, you lousy punk! Don't tell me to shut up! After all I've done for you and this bullshit. You fool with me, Keeng, and I'll call up that little dollface and tell her what the real action is. I'm just asking you for my legal due, wise guy. I got a date. I *need* it. You think I'd be reminding you like this if I didn't?"

"*Shaddup.*"

Other voices joined in. "You tell him, Wook." And, "What's this, you panhandling the parade or something, Carillo?" And, "Don't get Wookie riled up—you know what can happen!" And, "Hey, aren't you two bozos interested in the defense budget at all?"

"I'm interested in my own budget," Carlo grumbled. He lowered his voice again. "All right, Wook, one last chance. You handing over that ten spot or not? Yes or no?"

"Go fly a kite."

Carlo started sputtering curses. Then he said Wook probably still had a stud factor of negative infinity. He said nobody had ever put Wook on his honor about the stud factor but maybe now was the time. The senator on the podium had just remarked, "Yes, for the next part of my speech I would like to discourse somewhat on the disarmament program." There could be a dozen "next parts," and the sun was gaining altitude, and the zeros of G-5 were getting itchy. The fun of having Mister Infinity back in a parade was simply too hard to resist.

The soul of Golfball-5 had been born again.

"Yeah, Mister Infinity," someone snickered, "you been lying about your stud factor maybe?"

"Hey, Infinity! Tell us more about this girlfriend of yours. You say she's only six years old?"

"If she's only six, at least she can't get pregnant!"

"Hey, Infinity baby! I got a girlfriend for you—his name's Bob."

Wook did not answer.

"Wookie old pal, what's zero minus infinity?"

"Shut up you guys," a voice said. "We got a parade to win."

"Oh *yeah?*—Look!"

"I got dibbs on him if he falls forward."

"I got dibbs if he falls backwards."

Wook fell sideways and it was a free-for-all to see who could grab him first. There was so much greed to see who'd be the lucky fellows to carry the casualty off the field that the rear three ranks of Company G-5 appeared to have been struck by a large bowling ball. As it turned out, four cadets were "needed" to carry him off, and a fifth cadet to carry the rifles of the pall-bearers. As for Wook's rifle, it had somehow landed on top of my shoes. I stared downward for a long instant, then grabbed the weapon and hastily caught up with Wook's procession.

"Beat it, Mardis. We don't need you."

"Go back to the parade."

"But I have his *rifle.* It fell on my *feet.*"

"Not so loud," one of the bearers told me. "We're being watched." True, the senator had stopped speaking, but he slowly resumed his tirade as Wook's caravan moved slowly, slowly across the wide green Parade Plain. Wook himself was slowly coming to and muttering, "Where am I?"

"You're in heaven, Mister Infinity. That's where you are."

"Now beat it, Mardis. We're taking Wook to the hospital. This has gotta look good."

"But what about his rifle?"

"He won't be needing it in the hospital, stupid. Take it to his room."

The rifle bearer agreed that nobody would need their rifles at the hospital; he handed me one of his and we started for the barracks. "Last year I got out of three separate parades thanks to Cadet Wook fainting all the time," said the cadet, a zero First Classman. "And here I am again."

As I restored Wook's rifle to its rack, I happened to notice two piles of methodically ripped up papers on his desk. One pile was obviously a check; I found a piece that said "Carlo Caril—" and other shreds that added up to "Ten dollars and no cents." Since I hadn't much else to do for the next hour, I sat down and pieced together the other pile, like a picture puzzle.

The picture was not a pretty one. This stack was the shredded remains of the letter I'd delivered—and the tragic remnants of Wook's studly love affair. His Barnard girlfriend had written that she had changed her major to Latin American Politics and was now dating her professor, Señor Lopez. She had dropped Wook, as he himself might say, like a redhot potato.

And so, a young woman at Barnard College arbitrarily changes her major, and a United States Army Major is defeated. The cadet company known as Goofball-5 zeros in for the eighteenth year in a row. But the cadet sometimes called Mister Infinity would never again faint on the Parade Plain of West Point. Wook had made it to the hospital in his Full Dress gear, and the doctors could diagnose the problem, once they'd pulled it off his head: Hat, 6$7/8$ inches. Head, 7 and $3/4$!

MEMO 8.

My first explosion occurred shortly before Thanksgiving, on a weekday morning. By popular standards, I had it good as a cadet; I was in an easy company, had been recognized by a majority of the upperclassmen, had fared well in academics, and had made a relative name for myself as a halfback in intramural soccer. In two muddy games, I'd kicked upperclassmen when they were down.

But underneath, trouble was brewing. I had been reading a book on Buddhism, another on palmistry, and subscribing to the *Village Voice.* I had written poems, too, which probably created more tension than relief. I felt an increasing estrangement from my classmates; since Plebe life had leveled off, my classmates were more free to be themselves—which somehow frightened me. Most of them tended to behave like beligerent chimpanzees who knew how to do pull-ups and operate slide rules.

I felt pressured that I didn't have enough time to myself, that even in my escapes, like French, I was still processing the Academy's information input rather than understanding it—or understanding myself. Rather stupidly, I undertook a "hollow-sleep" program to create more hours in the day. This program, which I'd stumbled across in an obscure medical encyclopedia in the library, stated that the central four hours of an average eight-hour sleep were basically a carryover period between the more important first and last two hours. The hollow-sleep program suggested that the world could get more done if sleepers would wake up and employ the central four hours toward some activity rather than sleeping the whole night through.

The program sounded fine with me. The professor who had originated it reported that he had experimented with himself and found his normal waking activities to be unimpaired by "hollowing out" his usual rest. His only dissatisfaction was an uncommon grogginess during the additional four hours, and that sometimes, when he did succeed in rousing himself to a full state of consciousness—by drinking coffee or tea—he then had difficulty getting back to sleep for the vital second leg.

The professor, who had been born in 1893, said that after six weeks' experimentation he went back to his customary sleeping habits of eight solid hours. He suggested, however, that a younger person might adapt better to the revolutionary sleeping formula and thus cultivate an extraordinary time-saving device which would certainly be an asset to him for many years to follow. Reading this, I was convinced that the hollow-sleep program was a godsend and that Cadet Private Mardis was that "younger person" who would justify the professor's research. I wanted to collaborate, but on looking up his name in the index, I saw "1893-1953." It looked like the plan was in my hands alone.

As anticipated, on the first two nights of the plan I experienced extreme grogginess and low efficiency during the hollowed-out four hours of my sleeping span. On the third night my efficiency accelerated sharply, but I was unable to return to sleep. I'd been employing the newfound time toward mathematics, using my formerly allocated mathematics time for daydreaming, dawdling, doo-daddling, and general personal activities. On the fourth night of the hollow-sleep program, the professor would have been proud, because I rose sharply, executed four hours of exacting mathematics, and returned to sleep concisely for the vital second leg.

But when I woke up at the Reveille cannon, I was seeing and hearing double. According to popular standards I should have been happy, should have greeted the morning with a cheerful visage. All my shoes were shined, my brass was shined, my desk was spotless, I knew my poop backwards and forwards, and I'd done enough mathematics homework to tide me over three weeks. Thanks to the hollow-sleep program, I'd gotten *so* many extra things accomplished! I may have looked good on paper, but I felt rotten. And seeing and hearing everything in duplicate didn't help my frame of mind.

I made it to ranks for breakfast only through Fireteam Leader Carillo's friendly persuasion—he came back after me when I didn't show. There I sat at my desk, neatly dressed in my short overcoat, my regulation gray scarf tucked to the regulation left side, and in a deep depression. I was giggling but on the verge of tears. My two roommates had been too sleepy to notice my odd behavior; they'd scampered on down to formation at the five-minute bell. I had seen four of them leave. Now two Fireteam Leaders led me down the stairs, saying, "Granted we're we're all all out of our mind mind to be in this crummy-ummy place, place but you've gotta play the game game."

Outside, a fierce wind was blowing off the river, adding to the desolation of the cold stone architecture. In the dawn darkness, the men of the Corps seemed to be a massive huddle of silent gray figures as they stood in formation, waiting for the bugler to signal the march to the Mess Hall. My Squad Leader snapped at me for being late, then rendered his report to the Platoon Leader. The time was approximately 6:13 A.M., and it occurred to me that at the same month, day, and hour some fifteen years

95

ago, most of the men now shivering in this cold formation had been safely in their individual homes all across America eating warm oatmeal and watching Captain Kangaroo. The thought of it made me giggle heartily.

After breakfast, my senses cleared up remarkably and I was better able to cope with my feelings. I returned hastily to my room with a few pilfered blueberry muffins and tried to absorb myself in the biography of Buddha. I identified with his perilous quest, appreciated his poignant failure to adapt to his social role. I wondered what the Buddha would have done if he found himself in a cadet situation? Would further suffering amend his alienation? Would the Buddha have wished for a greater Academy good and have taken measures sufficient to effect a change? Or maybe the Buddha would never have become a cadet. . . . These were questions beyond my scope—ridiculous questions—but I kept asking them.

"Hey, Mardis, snap out of it and sweep the floor," Rutledge told me. *Would the Buddha sweep the floor for his roommate?* Would the Buddha even have a roommate? I looked around at Rutledge, a lanky freckle-faced fellow, the droll Army brat. He said, "Or is sweeping the floor too much to ask?"

I stood up, took the broom, and began sweeping the floor methodically. Groovey packed up his books and left for wrestling; he seldom spoke to me now, but he didn't speak to Rutledge either. I think he was waiting for the soap-dish saboteur to confess.

Rutledge took one of the leftover muffins, gobbled it down, and told me, "Christ, I don't want to go to boxing this morning. You know, I don't know why the hell they don't do away with that subject. I mean think about it, you know?" He talked to me while I swept. "Like, the future wars sure as hell aren't going to be hand-to-hand combat, and even if they were, you're not going to slug it out, right? Plus, for example, let's say you get into a fight in some bar in Philly. You really think anybody's gonna use this shit they teach us over there in the gym? Not a chance. Why, shit, you think people are gonna square off against each other and blow a whistle? Hell no, they're gonna be kickin' and bustin' bottles and that kind of stuff. So my point is, why the hell do Plebes have to have boxing class? It's just a haze, as far as I'm concerned."

"Right." I stooped down to pick up some dustballs.

"You been creeping around at night, Mardis?"

"Sort of."

"What'sa matter, can't sleep? Seriously, pal—your girlfriend giving you problems?"

"No."

"What's this here?" He began thumbing through the Buddha book. "Buddha, huh? Yeah, I heard of him. The A-rabs and all that. Yep . . . yep . . . looks interesting, all right. You go in for this kind of shit?"

"It's interesting."

"Yep . . . sure is . . . Hey, check this out!" He'd opened the volume to a glossy photo of an ancient temple painting of a snake pit with several bare-breasted virgins standing around. "Not bad, huh? I'll bet the old Buddha was a hard-on, all right. OK—see ya at class." Rutledge flipped on his cap and strode out of the room.

The last thing in the world I wanted to do this morning was box. I'd almost forgotten about class and had to force myself to arrive at the gymnasium in time. So far, I'd maneuvered quite well in boxing, but we had yet to engage in bloodshed. It was coming, we all knew, and the slim, cocky young Aryan who was our boxing instructor assured us that "it would be no picnic."

"Today's the day you've been waiting for, men!" The time was 7:35 and Major Reiner, the boxing coach, was leaping with energy. We men of the boxing class stood before him in the South Boxing Room, our mouthpieces in our mouth, no shirts, no medallions or jewelry, just gym shorts and our high-topped sneakers. "Today is the day you men can finally prove yourselves to each other—Are you *ready?!*"

We shouted back at him that we were. "Go get your head pieces!" boomed the assistant coach, Major Madison. Madison was heavier built and not as agile as Major Reiner; the two of them worked the class with a brains & brawn routine. Reiner would use "Moose" Madison as a dummy in demonstrating certain punches, then ask a member of class to inflict the same damage on the Moose. When the Plebe boxer invariably made a fool of himself against the Moose, Reiner would tell a story that illustrated the proper techniques for the punch. Their antics added a certain frivolity to class that served to keep us in "fightin' " spirits—laughing away our fears.

Today Major Reiner had a game for us to play. After a fifteen-minute warm-up on the punching bags, he instructed us to join elbows and form a large circle—like "Ring Around the Rosie." Major Reiner stood inside. His blue eyes were bright and his bottom lip glistened with saliva. "This, men, is your first conditioning drill. What we want is plenty of noise and plenty of action—get your guts pumping."

He chose a cadet to stand in the center, and had the cadet choose his own opponent. The boxers had to keep punching until Major Reiner decided the bout was over. After that, the defeated would join the circle again, and the winner would choose a new opponent. The rest of us were to scream at the top of our lungs throughout. Anyone not screaming loud enough would know because Moose Madison would be skirting the outside of the circle. If you felt him punch you in the kidneys, or kick you in the pants, that was his signal that you should scream louder. Reiner stayed inside to referee.

The bout and the noise began. Blood was quick to flow, the whistle was blown, and the defeated rejoined the circle. A couple of boxers got a kick in the ass. "Nobody told you to stop screaming, did they?" Reiner shouted. The noise went up again, and the lone boxer circled around to select another opponent. We were all in the same weight range so there were no pathetic size discrepancies, but the boxer managed to find an opponent a great deal smaller than he was. Reiner didn't like it.

His whistle blew, the circle fell silent, and three students got quick kidney punches from Moose Madison. "Keep shouting!" the Moose told us. "That whistle don't concern you!" The noise went back up again as Reiner placed the small cadet back in the circle and himself chose the largest cadet there to fight the cowardly boxer. Blood came quick again, but this time there was no whistle. Reiner shoved the larger boxer, who then continued his assault and beat the weakened cadet down to his knees in a matter of seconds. Blood was all over the mat. Rainer sounded his whistle and told all of us to be quiet.

"This is what happens when you guys try to get chicken shit with me. All right, get up," he told the fallen boxer. The fellow stood up, his chest smeared with blood, his leather headgear halfway off. The larger boxer stood with his head lowered, guilty. Reiner had the defeated rejoin the circle and ordered us to start the noise again. I heard the cadet next to me make a gut sound—he'd been punched by Moose Madison. I shouted louder than ever. Reiner was strutting inside the ring, pointing at different cadets, jeering at them, revving us up. Then he chose a sufficiently large cadet to contest the new victor.

They squared off with each other for some fifteen seconds, uncertain, until Reiner pushed one from behind and started the blows flowing. It was a long bout, lasting nearly three minutes, but there was no blood. Reiner, irritated, made us go quiet again for more instruction:

"You see these two big lugs? They may be big, but they've got hearts of chicken shit, men!" The pair of them stood there breathing heavily, perspiration gleaming off their chests and stomachs, saliva trickling out of their mouthpieces. "Who's got enough balls here to come in and knock the shit out of one of these guys? Huh? They're already winded—it shouldn't be *that* much trouble. OK, since nobody wants to step out, I'll make the decision." He told the newcomer to the ring to rejoin the circle, and had the class scared-cat, Sheen, step in to box the large cadet, Puska, who'd just boxed two bouts. The whistle blew, the noise started, and so did the blood.

Sheen darted around the circle, trying to be scarce, but each time he'd try for refuge in a swaying corner of the human arena, either Reiner or Madison would thrust him back in the direction of Puska. The coaches were ridiculing Puska, too, calling him a big sissy, so that Puska got a dull glint in his eye and went after Sheen with the intent of doing damage. It only took one blow and Sheen fell to the ground, pleading for mercy. But Reiner made him stand up again, and as soon as he was up, Puska pulverized him. We screamed louder and louder as Puska did his work, but there was a lull when Sheen began shrieking that he'd lost a tooth. I got a hard kick in the pants: "Nobody told you to stop, Mister!"

Reiner had Sheen removed and sent Puska back to the circle for a rest. As we raged, Reiner wheeled inside like a caged animal, pointing at us and wheedling us, slapping our headgears. "Who's next!" he kept saying. "Who's got the guts?" His voice was indicipherable in the uproar, but you could read his lips as he danced about the ring. After he was satisfied with the orchestration, he chose a cadet—there were some forty of us making the circle—and the new cadet chose the fellow standing next to him, for simplicity's sake.

The class lasted another sixty minutes, each student having occasion for at least two bouts, or more if he were victorious in one of them. I lost my first bout without incident and without a bloody nose; then toward the end of class I was chosen again and won with a left to the body followed by a right uppercut. I then chose a new opponent and tried the same winning combination, which didn't work. After I delivered the left to the body, my opponent came up with his own right uppercut and bowled me backwards. I heard whistles and sirens, managed to roll to the side of the ring, and finally stood up only to be shoved back toward the other boxer. We exchanged blows briefly; then Reiner tossed me out and had the new victor choose someone else.

As soon as I was part of the ring again, I felt a kick in the ass: "I've been warning you, Mister!" I started screaming more feverishly, my ears ringing numbly from the blows to my head, my face stinging and temples pounding with a headache. The action in the ring was now a blur, and my arms interlocked with the sweating, chanting bodies next to me seemed to make me an unthinking dog in a pack, howling and grappling at some strange object we had all declared our enemy. During the initial bouts and first signs of blood I had been thinking about what the Buddha would have done in this situation—but now, with my nose feeling flattened in my face and the pulse pounding in my head, I found a surge of violence pouring through my body, an eagerness to get back in the ring and make up for what had been done to me.

But the whistles blew and blew, and class was dismissed after the Majors gave us brief critiques. A few minutes later I was sobering up under a shower. I stayed there a long time, then dressed slowly and started for the Cadet Hostess Office, where I usually dropped off for coffee before 10:30 mathematics class. My heart was still racing and my head was still humming from the class. I was certainly wide awake, if that's why athletics were held early in the morning. Sound of body and sound of mind. Now I was seeing the world in triplicate.

Somehow I ended up in the basement of the Golf-5 barracks, nestled in a corner near the soft drinks machine with a can of root beer. Cadets seemed to rely on certain foods as security objects—and when things got very tough for me, I'd have myself a root beer. I kept hearing Moose Madison's voice: "*I'm warning you, Mister!*" I was thinking how scared Sheen looked as he ran around the ring trying to escape, then how Puska had looked as he worked Sheen over. I thought of the Buddha remonstrating with his material father. Then I dwelled on sine and cosine equations—sentimentally, because by this time mathematics class was already in session.

If only the professor were still alive! I told myself. He could advise me what to do. I sipped on my root beer for more inspiration and glanced down at my shoe shine. I was wearing my Special Inspection shoes, my SI's, and on one of the shiny black tips I saw a terrible long white scratch—the destruction of weeks and weeks of careful, painstaking attention. I didn't even know how the scratch got there, which made it worse: I was a victim of my own negligence. I began to sob about then, because a scratch that deep on your SI's was really more than a cadet could bear.

Toward lunchtime, I was discovered by two First Classmen. Apparently someone had reported sighting me in my depraved condition. I vaguely recall that they wouldn't let me take along my root beer as they carted me up the stairs to the orderly room, saying, "This ain't Disneyland, Mister! When are you going to get that through your head?"

Crackers! is a term not to be found in the United States Corps of Cadets Regulation manual. You could find "disreputable behavior" or "conduct unbecoming to a cadet" or "failure to properly perform duties."

Just as there was no clearcut violation for the cadet captured *in flagrante derelicto* with his *Playboy*, there was also no allowance in Regs for cracked cadets. Such events were baffling.

"Mardis, do you want to see the youth chaplain?"

"No, sir."

"Do you care to call your mother?"

"No, sir."

Different voices were questioning me in the orderly room, some hostile, some compassionate. "Did you lose your French standing, Mardis?"

"No, sir."

"You can't just skip classes and get away with it, you know, Mister. But we've got to have a damn good reason before we send this thing up to the Tac."

"Try again, Mister. And make it spoony this time."

I looked up at the concerned faces, myself miserable, dejected, tired, ashamed. I tried remembering a few lines from the Military Code of Conduct. *I am an American fighting man.* I will never surrender of my own free will. If I am captured I will continue to resist by all means available. I will accept neither parole nor special favors from the enemy. However, if you let me go back down to the basement and get my root beer . . .

Such thoughts depressed me further, because I knew I probably would bend under a prison camp torture, give away allied secrets, lose the war, disgrace my country.

"Come on beanhead—let's have the poop."

It was Hoggins, the First Sergeant, leering at me with his sunken, beady eyes, his gnarled face, his bad breath. The orderly room door had been closed and a transistor radio whined with the news in the background. A number of upperclassmen had foregone lunch formation to quiz me, making themselves feel that much more important. Hoggins said, "Whatsa matter, Mister? Don't get your rocks off in chapel, so you started preaching Buddha now. Think a chink swami's gonna help you out there on the area? You've had it, Mister!"

Hopalong Haroldson, the Company Commander,

intervened. He was a popular, easygoing sort, often with an encouraging smile and a kind word for the Plebes. He endorsed "positive leadership." He told Hoggins to lay off.

"You're too easy on these bozos," Hoggins told him.

"Listen, Mardis," Haroldson reasoned with me. "We appreciate your honesty, and your intelligence, in trying to tell us why you didn't go to mathematics, but don't you know you'll probably be slugged for this? You know what that means? A six and six—six months confined to quarters and six months on the area. Now, if you want to attach an explanation to the violation form, that's fine, that's your prerogative. But *believe* me, it'll be a lot better for you in front of the board if you can just give us a simple explanation right now and cut the harble-garble. You're on your honor, you know."

I took it from the top. But each time I began to describe one of my reasons, a dispute would erupt and Company Commander Haroldson would step aside for a brief conference. No, that wouldn't look good on the violation form—Buddha, no; a scratch on his SI's, no; not enough sleep, no; displeasure with boxing class, no. A partial concussion might do, but that would require a medical examination, and if an examination didn't turn up anything, then they'd be back where they started.

After much dispute they finally settled for "mental unpreparedness not pertaining to classwork per se." I think they liked the way it sounded. Haroldson gave me the rest of the day off on the condition that I go on emergency sick call, to put him in the clear. The paperwork for this would also legitimize my unfit condition. I was told to prepare a Delinquency Report explaining how the unpreparedness did not pertain to classwork.

I was also ordered to discontinue the hollow-sleep program. In my room, I hid all the Buddha books and, in frustration, put a big scratch on my other SI so they'd be even. I felt sorry for myself and pretty angry at that scatterbrained professor. But then *I* felt pretty scatterbrained. Taps was at 2300 hours and Reveille was at 0600. The professor's sleep plan had specified an eighthour nocturnal, and a West Point cadet only had seven.

MEMO 9.

In Beast Barracks, we New Cadets had been forced to write the story of our lives. Garth U. Tilson had brought back my autobiography to me in Room 3242. It had a rejection slip on it. "*No,* Mardis. No, no, no." He shook his head disgustedly. "*No* way. No way I'm gonna let this silly gooseshit come out of my squad." Garth saw the terror in Gumboldkirschner and my other roommates. "*You* guys were all right. But this silly piece of gooseshit"—he waved it in my face—"don't do the job."

Our squad conditions had become so mechanized at that point in Beast that when Squad Leader come in room we no stand up. *Efficiency!* Tilson told us, and he allowed us to get away with a sitting position of attention while he was in the room. This way we could get back to what we were doing faster when he left. But when he was in the room and we at our desks, our hands flat out, chins tucked in, backs rigid and straight, we looked like Egyptian sphinxes. Beneath all that efficiency, perhaps Tilson thought he was a Pharoah.

Garth Tilson had slapped the autobiography on my desk and told me to write another one—more *military*, he said. The autobiography was to deal with significant events leading from your birth up to your entry into New Cadet Training. Gumboldkirschner, I remember, snickered smugly. Hank G. had no doubt written about the Troy highway bridge on his, a sure-fire tearjerker for engineering officers. The Big Brass would probably read it and have it published in *Army Engineers Newsletter*—perhaps they'd even build a bridge where Hank could hang his own plaque!

Admittedly, my first autobiography was not too military, hen-scratched and confusing, with lots of arrows and crossouts. But the new one seemed too military to me, too efficient. It was in the logical fashion, also in neat capital letters with good margins and page numbers. But what was missing was, in Academy lingo, "the human side of things." What this thing needed was maybe . . . a nice poem. I hadn't written poems as a civilian, but I was writing a few now, and I wanted the "Big Brass up there" to know about it because I was writing *Army* poems! Human and efficient at the same time.

> Army blue
> Army gray
> Jesus Christ
> What a day

I inserted the poem near the end of the autobiography. I felt confident that it was at least as good as the verse in *Bugle Notes*, the inch-thick volume of chants and trivia which Plebes had to memorize verbatim—"The Commandant's Cat," "On Brave Old Army Team," "How Many Lights in Cullum Hall?" and so on. But I should have known Garth U. Tilson didn't like poetry. He came storming in again, slightly frantic.

"Have you still got the first one, Mardis? Apparently you're not capable of making sense. . . . But if that's the way you want it. Gimme the other one."

"I tore it up, sir."

"They'll send this back, I tell you."

They didn't send it back; instead, they sent me to Goofball-5.

I'd mentioned preparatory school and how weak we mortals be, how the funnels led from kindergarten to a college diploma and a polyester suit and the only real drama an automobile flat twice a year; I talked about my Mom & Sis and how my father made me mow the grass and like Errol Flynn and Buck Rogers a lot better than him; I also discussed popular trends, stated that I was not a hippie vagabond since I knew that old revolutionaries slept on park benches. I told them that Christ might have had long hair but His inner being was better represented by the orderly celebration of specified ideals and behavior patterns—i.e., morals—but when you really came down to it life was more like a lizard making its way on a chain-link fence. I put the poem in at this point and concluded the personal history with an affirmation of faith in America and in the United States Corps of Cadets.

Garth Tilson took the autobiography away from me in August 1969, and Major Clifford Cutler handed it back on December 2, 1969. I sat in conference with the Tactical Officer in his small, neat office on the eighth floor of Washington Hall in the Department of Tactics. In the aftermath of the hollow-sleep fiasco, I had been living with bitter anxieties of a doomed man, waiting for the verdict to come down. Some of the men of G-5 laughed at me; others offered their condolences or a trivial favor. In the Corps, you didn't skip class and get away with it.

"Cadet Mardis," the Tac said grimly. "Do you know what a six and six is?"

"Yes, sir," I gulped.

"That's what the punishment is for this offense."

I closed my eyes to hold back the tears; then I opened them again, curious why Major Cutler had handed me the autobiography. He pointed to it.

"Mardis, you exhibit nice, neat hand-lettering on that paper."

"Thank you, sir."

"That wasn't a compliment, Mister. That was a statement of fact."

"Thank you."

Cutler scowled and cracked his knuckles; then he tightened his tie and, glazing his eyes, leaned forward. "But the rest of it is *gar*bage. Don't think I'm not being honest. That kind of crap you put down there turns my stomach. He tapped a button of his jacket, still leering. "It makes me *puke.* However, it so happens everybody ain't as sensitive as me. I guess you know you won the FFA award." I expressed my ignorance in this matter, and Cutler made a noise like he was spitting. He took back the autobiography, commenting, "The same kind of crap, I guess, too." The Major leaned back in his chair and crossed his arms.

"Because you won the FFA—and it don't mean a shit to me, buddy—some powers that be here in the Tactical Department have seen to it that you're getting off light. *Real* light. And don't think I like it, either, Mister, because I know your type—I've seen them before. And I don't like what I see. But it seems I don't *run* this show." Cutler was becoming angrier as he spoke; he began tapping a pencil on the desk, and his face was tight and restless. He reached over to the window sill for a small plaque and set it in front of me with sarcastic politeness. "Now take your trophy and get out of here before I lose my temper. I don't like you and there's no use pretending."

I got out of there, though Cutler had to call me back because I'd forgotten to salute. Once I was in the outside corridor, however, and could safely look at the plaque, the mystery was solved. I had made Honorable Mention in the Freedom Foundation of America essay competition, and for so doing the powers that be—"Tips" Porterhouse, most likely—had given me a reduced sentence. The essay topic had been "My Hopes for Freedom."

Who am I? An American!
What am I? An American!
What is this? America!

C/PVT J. MARDIS

The Army poem that I had written into the essay was stenciled in gold on the plaque, above the Freedom Foundation logo. The plaque seemed impressive indeed, but on unsealing the attached envelope I saw that I was one of 750 Honorable Mentions in the Armed Services. It was a form letter. There were 400 fourth places, 300 third places, 200 second places, 100 runners-up, and a winner. I was pretty far down on the ladder, but Colonel Porterhouse didn't know that. He'd only seen the plaque.

I'd completely forgotten about the contest. Early in the fall Carillo went on weekend leave and told me I could use his record player if I shined his combat boots. I shined the boots on top of one of Colonel Porterhouse's that-time-of-the-month computer dispatches. Among his many suggestions on how to improve morale while improving yourself—the optional section of the memorandum—I noticed, as I shined, a piece on the Freedom Foundation essay-writing contest. Rules were included. After the left boot was done I wrote an essay, and mailed it in the same night.

I suppose the Colonel was deeply touched that anyone cared enough to read the optional section of his dispatches. I suppose he had gone through my file and seen that I had a fine grasp of "the human side of things." Whatever the case, and to everyone's surprise, including my own, I received the highly unusual punishment of *no* punishment at all. That night word came down, and a mob carried the news to my doorstep.

It was a miracle, and the upperclassmen, especially the zeros, were jealous beyond their wildest dreams. They wanted an *immediate* explanation of what "mental unpreparedness" was—and how to use it to your own advantage. They wanted to know how I'd worded my attached report and what I had said to Cutler. A few cynics put in that I'd gotten off because my father was secretly a General or a powerful politician. As with the French score, the crowd simply refused to listen to my side of it, and when I proudly held up the FFA plaque, the group became unhappy.

"Quit dodging, Mardis, and spill it!"

"P.C.'s die a young death, Mister! Now you just tell us what page of Regs this unpreparedness shit is on!"

But no one would believe me; they were positive I knew some special loophole in Cadet Regulations. Later, even Rutledge tried to pry the secret out of me, and when I showed him the *Who am I? An American!* he said, "Oh, a *bright* boy."

I was overjoyed to get back to regular life. A week as the doomed man had shredded my faith in the West Point Way further and further along the seams. Now, the official pardon patched it up quite neatly. And being forgiven, I quickly discarded all the "silly gooseshit" which had gone into my secret nonconformity. Buddha's perilous quest, I thought, was nothing but warmed-over bologna. Poetry was bad, too, I figured, but I did write one last Army poem as a sort of tribute.

> Stone Walls
> Ancient Halls
> Cannon Balls
> Duty Calls

Christmas leave was soon due, and the increasingly jubilant mood of the cadets made for a buoyant company life. My conspicuousness as a "privileged character" all but vanished in the helter-skelter weeks preceding Christmas leave. Each cadet was too wrapped up in his own plans and dreams for the long-awaited holiday, too busy buying gifts at the PX and arranging for military junkets, too engrossed in cranking out a last-minute term paper to persecute or pursue one humble Plebe who had broken the rules but had learned his lesson.

Rooming assignments now changed with the rotation of "detail," or the upperclass chain of command. Evidently I'd been deciphered as having a short supply of outstanding leadership ability, since one of my new roommates was Boyd Royelle, self-appointed kingpin of company Plebes. My other shortage was apparently in motivation for all things normal: the other roommate, Ralph M. Aberby, was the hardest trying Plebe of them all. At least once a day he'd say, "If at first you don't succeed . . ."

My two roommates were too excited about Christmas when we first moved in together to pay me much mind. They scarcely noticed that I was a much better cadet than ever before, almost a hero. My bed was made tight, I dusted my bookshelves, I was early for formations, etc. I spent little time in un-cadet-like activities. They didn't notice, but the absence of any criticism—from the hardest tryer and best leader—was reward in itself.

They accepted my almost nightly departure for the language laboratory—even encouraged it.

"Go do your thing!" Boyd Royelle would say.

"If I could speak this spic, I'd be up there myself," Aberby said.

The new room was located one unit over from the old place. The atmosphere here was more sociable due to the odd circumstance of having three Plebe rooms on one floor. Our room was quick to become the gathering grounds, the bull-shitting parlor. Such congregating was now allowable since, at the change of detail, visiting privileges were put in effect for Fourth Classmen.

G-5 was fortunate to have the most unusual Plebe in the Corps, a man whose assignment to hero classification or ? would have been a difficult task for even the computer. This Plebe was a genuine war hero, a decorated Vietnam veteran of two tours, yet by nobody's standards was he the classic "stract" cadet; in many instances he didn't give a damn. His name was Williams—Willie—and he was from somewhere between Virginia and West Virginia originally, and he lived right next door in one of the Plebe rooms.

Willie was often on hand for the bull-shitting sessions, and old Willie had more stories to tell than the rest of us put together. His eyes were a cool blue and his manner was that of a homespun philosopher. He was built broad and rugged, sturdy. He told us in his strangely gentle voice that he once took on twenty men in a brawl, but now, with his karate training, he could take on "upwards of forty." Willie was twenty-five years old, and how he had been admitted to the Corps at that age, no one knew. He said, "A General owed me a favor."

In Beast Barracks we had all heard of Willie as the man who told his table commandant to "go take a flying leap." For unknown reasons, Willie never received any demerits, and he did as he wanted to do. He attended all classes and formations, but at his own pace. When the other Plebes would be bracing, Willie would stand around whistling, and the worst haze I ever saw him endure was, "Aw, come on Willie, play the game." To which Willie replied, "Gimme a break, Sarge." Even Cutler was afraid of Willie.

Willie never returned to the Corps after Christmas leave. He was destined for parts uncharted, never to be seen or heard from again. Great speculation then grew up over what Willie's purposes actually had been as a member of the Corps. The "official" reason for his separation was that he was failing in several subjects, which made sense, because Willie didn't enjoy studying. So why didn't they tutor him? He was obviously great officer material.

The only explanation that left no stone unturned was

what Willie himself had told a roommate one night, while the former was polishing off a little jug of sour-mash whiskey: Williams was more than a cadet—he was a spy for the CIA. He had come to spy on Company G-5 and the Corps at large for suspected un-American acts pertaining particularly to drug abuse, pot smoking. The roommate said Willie had even done some spying on a few questionable officers!

Being acquainted with Willie's front porch expertise in spinning a yard, the Plebes on our floor discounted any notions about the CIA's interest in Company G-5. And the idea that West Point officers were having pot parties at the Officers' Club was, of course, preposterous. Willie had flunked math, they said, and just didn't want to admit it. I might have gone along with this version myself had Willie not acted rather curiously one night.

On the first weekend of our new room assignments, I was wasting half an hour at my desk, trying to develop a mood to go over to the hop. Royelle and Aberby had both left earlier to meet their respective dates. Royelle's fiancée had come to visit the Point, and Ralph Aberby had found himself a willing victim in the dating files of the Cadet Hostess Office.

Consequently, the room smelled like a cologne and deodorant factory, so I'd lit up a few sticks of incense left over from my not-so-distant nonconformist days. I sure felt lucky those Buddhist follies were done with. I'd had to bravely pull myself up by the bootstraps from that lonely day in the basement; now, with an assist from the FFA, I was back in top working order. I was apple pie à la mode. I was Cadet Private, USCC, USMA, US of A at your service, miss. I was filing my nails when Willie walked in.

"*Abba-kadabba-bobba-hobba-gooboo!*" he said in his southern drawl.

"Oh, hi, Willie. I figured you'd be at the hop dancing up a storm."

114

"I don't think my girl back home would like that, Jaime boy."

I felt self-conscious because I'd never had a private conversation with Willie, had been a mere listener during the bullshit sessions. But I liked him and respected him. He was the real McCoy, not a schoolboy soldier like some cadets. Willie pulled up a chair next to mine, real friendly-like, and pulled a pack of cigarettes out of his sock.

"Sorry they ain't the real thing," he said, offering one over. I didn't catch his meaning, so he went on. "Sure wish I was out in Frisco havin' me a hippie wing-ding."

"You and me both, Willie," I replied politely.

"Smells right good in here."

"Doesn't it? The guys stunk it up with deoderant, so I thought I'd—"

Willie gave a downhome war whoop, scarcely blinking an eye. It scared me out of my wits, but I thought maybe this was his way of being friendly. "It's Saturday night all right!" I told him cheerfully.

He twisted his face into an evil look. "*Sure* do wish I had the real thing on a night like tonight."

"What real thing?"

"Aw now, come on. You know what I'm talkin' 'bout."

I didn't want to sound stupid, so I shrugged my shoulders. Willie flicked his cigarette ashes on the floor and muttered, "*Shiiit.*" He then leaned back in the chair and put his feet on Aberby's desk to stretch. Willie told me that he and I were birds of a feather, that he and me was P.C.'s and could get away with tricks because we knew the "secret to life." He began a fifteen-minute yarn concerning an adventure of his which had resulted in Willie learning the secret of life. He said that as a young boy, he got lost hunting squirrel in the backwoods near Lookout Mountain, that he wandered into a tribe of Katchakee Injuns, that the Injuns took him in as a brother, and he'd spent the better part of three months with the tribe learning how to make canoes, how to snare quail, how to

115

skin a deer, how to make love to a squaw, and how to smoke the peace pipe with his Injun brothers.

He gave me a knowing wink and brought his feet down off the desk. "It was through the peace pipe I learned the secret of life."

The story had some interesting parts. "Tell me, Willie, isn't it a birch tree that you strip to make the fabric for a canoe?"

"Hell no, boy. You're lucky if you can skin a toothpick off a birch tree. Sycamore's what you want."

"How did you get back to civilization?"

"Phooey," Willie said from the corner of his mouth. He reached down and took a tin of snuff from his other sock, opened it, sniffed it, made a face, and tossed it in the waste basket. "Screw civilization," Willie said. "Just gimme another taste of that peace pipe. Now you can trust me, buddy—where's the loco weed?"

"Loco weed? You'd probably have to go to New York to get loco weed. But Jesus, you're sticking your neck out to do that around here."

"Amen and say it again," Willie laughed. "But I'm gettin' ornery and I need me some of that stuff so awful bad. Why, I hear it makes you smart as the dickens." He tried to look tearful. "And my math grades is *so* bad. Why, one little cigarette and I'd be a star-man."

When I warned Willie against it, he snapped back: "Now cut the hogwash, city boy!" (He'd tell you he was another Daniel Boone, if you asked him.) "I have my own way of knowing that the reason you pulled that hanky-panky not more'n a week ago is owin' to you remunera-tin' on the *secret uh life*—and I have the same trouble myself. Now whether a man gets his consolation in the Holy Book or the Teachin' of the East is his own best behalf. But I know, as your brother of the mercy, what you're up to now . . . Now, don't try and fool old Willie. He knows. He knows all the secrets, just like you. Now, come on—"

116

Willie wrapped his fingers around my wrist and applied pressure until I cried out; then he eased up, gradual-like, and let go. "I'm desperate," he said solemnly.

"Willie, you oughta go on sick call," I said with some sarcasm.

"I thought you were my friend, Jaime my man."

"Yeah, but . . . I don't know. Talk to your Squad Leader, or the chaplain or something. That's what they told me to do. That's what you do when you get nervous in the service."

"Don't tell me about the service." He sullenly headed for the door, wiggling one leg to adjust the feel of his cigarette pack in the top of his sock. I was puzzled, also angry, that Willie should think I was smoking marijuana on the sly. He stepped into the hallway, then promptly returned and stood full at attention, framed by the open door. His lips were wide in a smile as he threw me a crisp salute.

"Good work, Mardis, and keep tight on this. It's *classified!*" At that he spun around in his form-fitting dress gray uniform, and clomped away. I saw him later at the hop with a pair of opera glasses, peering down from a balcony over the battle-scarred dance floor of Cullum Hall. Whether he was looking for the real thing or for some honey-pie just a little bit cuter than the one back home is a subject as controversial as his real motives for being at the Academy. My only regret in dealing with the cadet secret agent was my own oversight. I forgot to ask Willie what the secret of life was. But—what the heck—it was probably classified.

MEMO 10.

History of the Army was the Plebes' most dependable snoozing class, and the Majors assigned to instruct us were more like accommodating hosts. They passed most of the class time with bedtime stories—their reminiscences of the way it used to be in the "Old Corps." But prior to examinations the professors "pooped" us thoroughly on what questions to expect, a measure which took us—and them—off the hook with good test scores. There was some evidence that our lighthearted professors competed with one another before exam days to see whose class would come out smarter.

Even if your poop failed you, a minimal amount of military horse snort could bail you out:

Q: The Colonial Army was vastly assisted by the arrival of General LAFAYETTE and his ——troops. (a) American (b) Prussian (c) French

More than two-thirds of a class could guess this one right, which was the kind of percentage the instructors were aiming for. If the competition was tough, however, a professor could give students partial credit for *any* answer—in this case, because Lafayette had eventually commanded American troops and because the Colonials were in part aided by Prussian troops.

At midsemester the Military Science curriculum shifted from History of the Army to a more practical

118

course, Map Reading. Sadly, in the realm of reading maps, no partial credit could be given for free-flowing horse snort. The numerics of cartography demanded one and only one answer: the correct answer.

Q: The depth of the crater in Area B (hint—measured by the concentric rings) is:
(a) 15 feet (b) 15 litres (c) 15 yards

In such a problem it would be a tossup between feet and yards, so only half the class would get it right, which was not the kind of percentage the Majors wanted. The Majors were, alas, confronted with the problem of making us learn, and to make us learn, they had to first wake us up.

The instructors didn't try to heap on meanings to make Map Reading seem more exciting than it was; they admitted to be as bored with the course as we were. The Major in charge of our section said, "You think it's a haze for you—just try teaching it some time." He complained that the Big Brass were wasting thousands of man-hours by scheduling the course right after lunch, when cadets and officers alike could care less about concave slopes and horseshoe ridges.

Major Kipper, a spry, slender young man who seemed to hop when he walked, gave us his case. "This summer you'll get the same information that we cover in nine weeks, only you'll get it—and learn it—in three days. Why? Because you're awake. So you tell me why they don't put athletics after lunch. Bear with me, men; I realize it's tough to keep your eyes open, especially when I turn the lights off for this projector. But it's the regurgitation theory, which I'm sure you're familiar with, and these answers have got to be pat."

The Major felt sorry for us, frequently apologizing for his obligation to keep us awake. The toll in ranks was frightening—even the most alert cadets were consistently falling off during a projection session, their heads on their books, drool running from the corners of their mouths. With the lights on, the shades up, and the windows open, we'd still be nodding, nodding, bobbing, melting. . . . One fellow melted so fast he cracked his forehead smack on his desk and had to go to the hospital.

Major Kipper could no longer afford to be compassionate after the cadet injured himself. He had been using the delicate touch and would command, in an even voice, "Jones, wake up Gilbertson—just a nudge will do." If Jones were half conscious and didn't hear, Major Kipper would patiently have the next cadet wake up Jones; then he would tell a bewildered Jones to wake up Gilbertson.

The entire class failed the first week's exam, at which the Major's comment was, "I told you so." The cadet had beaned himself while we were going over our mistakes, and it was then that the Major's kindness dried up and he began wielding a long wooden pointer to make his points.

Our desks were aligned in a quadrangle with the instructor's desk and projector at one end. Major Kipper began lecturing us from a center spot in the quadrangle, pointer in hand, and would poke us in the arm for a comment or whenever he felt like it. During the projector sessions, when the casualties were the worst, he spot checked us in the dark with a pencil flashlight. If any student showed signs of melting, Major Kipper would bang down the long pointer on their desk, making a noise like a thunderclap at midnight. "Sorry, Mister, but you've got to learn this."

By contrast, English class (I was in the Advanced Section), which followed Military Science, was stimulating. The cadets were stimulated because they knew this was the last class of the day. The English professors were stimulated because they were English professors. They pounded the landscape of our quickened minds with shell after shell of literary nomenclature, a relentless barrage of didactics, then over the top with a banzai charge of diagramed sentences.

The English professors loved to diagram sentences. In a way, it was like Map Reading. "Now, gentlemen, identify if you can which of said authors would compose a declarative sentence such as illustrated in Group I. Please notice the predicate adjective placement." The English professors were after the facts of life, not the fantasies. "On page 168 of the assignment, second paragraph, a statement is made by the hero to a shopkeeper. Without looking at your books, what was that shopkeeper's name, and what was the nature of the hero's statement?"

I hated the English professors, in spite of my better intentions. I would arrive in English class seeking intellectual reassurance that neither the youth chaplain nor a letter from my mother could provide, and here these men of letters would peevishly rant about Poe's reliance upon onomatopoeia. "Without onomatopoeia, the dullard called Edgar Allan Poe would have lived and died a penny-ante pulp-grinder. Without onomatopoeia, Poe would have flopped!" One cadet made the mistake of asking when Poe and Onomatopoeia were married.

The professors for the Advanced English class took themselves very seriously. Not only were they soldiers of the world and scholars of the universe, they knew how to *enunciate*. They faked British accents at times, to give them more authority. I could picture them crying into their pillows at night because they were born in Pierre, South Dakota, instead of Great Britain. Their sentimental readings of Poe's poems were so eloquent and *enun*ciated that a professor once actually got his tongue caught between a gap in his front teeth. He learned onomatopoeia the hard way, I guess.

Classes were not conducted by the iron fist, or even the velvet glove, but by the limp wrist—which was their status symbol. The English professors had knuckled their way up through the ranks into the Advanced Courses category, and with that settled, they were free to sit back comfortably beside their imaginary fireplaces and discourse on their private brand of esthetics to the captive audience. Of the three professors who taught our sections, one was intensely quiet, one was outspoken, and the other was tactless. The latter made a wisecrack about the Vietnam war one afternoon in a lecture, and the next week he disappeared altogether from the Advanced English Department. The remaining professors explained that he had "gone back to the University."

The two regulars saw no link between leftist thinking and liberal arts training. We were required to read for the sole purpose of gleaning tidbits that supported the Advanced English Department's pet theory: "Man is basically an aggressive and predatory creature." One professor was soft-spoken but unyielding about this belief, while the other, Major Wilks, crammed it down our throats at every opportunity. On this touchy issue of "Advanced English" classification, the Big Brass just wanted to make sure they had their asses—and our advanced minds—covered. They'd commissioned Wilks and his sidekick to brainwash us about the primal nature of man.

Whatever the nature of man might be, the Army didn't take any chances on potential *wrong* interpretations of the material they assigned us to read. One of our primary goals, as stated by Wilks, was to "make sure we could hold our own in any circles." That is, so we could render a compact interpretation of *Moby Dick* in terms of aggression—the Army way—and not some muddle-minded "the whale is a symbol of lost purity," which a civilian might try to sneak over on you as the crux of Ahab's personality problem.

"The deeper truth is the truer truth," Wilks would rave, "and the deeper truth never varies. I mean, look at the facts. Look at what the author puts on paper for us to see. The white whale is itself aggressive! And they'll do it every time. A less-experienced civilian will fall for the cheap shots, go for the easy victory, and he falls down into what amounts to nothing more than the author's booby trap. But the military man will drive down deep for those truths. Let's examine the experience of Mr. Melville as represented in the persona of his protagonist. We know him to be a man of action, an adventurer, one—as it states in so many words in Chapters VII and VIII—who refuses to be taken in by subterfuge. The author, as amply represented in the persona of his protagonist, drives for the deeper truths. He is—and I might quote a plethora of excerpts—*is* a man of some bearing and integrity. . . ."

In prep school I'd been taught that man was basically an aggressive and *self-destructive* creature. But maybe Wilks was right. In fact, Wilks had to be right, because if you contradicted him in an essay, it was automatic self-destruction, and no one ever did contradict him in an essay. Because it was self-destruction. So why bother? All you had to do for a high mark was hook up the official interpretation to the poem, short story, or novel, and spew out the basic aggressive and predatory traits of the characters in question. Your score would be that much better if you could recall the first and last names of characters, the page numbers of key events, and if somewhere you mentioned the author's full name, including middle name, his time on earth, the year the book was published, and the number of pages in our edition of the book.

For a pastime in class, I would imagine Wilks holding his own in an intellectual conversation. Major Wilks would be somewhere like Paris, participating in a high diplomatic function. The Attaché to the French Consolate, tipsy on cognac, would demand of Major Wilks an American interpretation of Stendahl's *Charterhouse of Parma.*

Wilks would tap his pipe in an ashtray, take a sip of spiked ginger ale, screw the pipe around in the side of his mouth, sigh gracefully, furrow his brow, produce a butane pipe lighter from a pocket of his dress whites, light the pipe, puff on it, suck his lips briefly, set aside the ginger ale and cross his arms.

"*Well?*" the French Attaché would wince, his patience taxed.

Major Wilks would say, "Yes, I am familiar with the text."

"*Well!*" the Attaché would snort again. "Do you opine that Fabrizio has a socialist mind? By American measures, of course!"

"Of course," Major Wilks would rejoin, scratching the tip of his beaked nose with an index finger, a subtle act of sarcasm.

"You have read the book, I assume!"

"Yes, I am familiar with the text," Wilks would take his pipe into one hand and appear to look far, far away. "My last reading of the aforesaid text was in April 1957. My reading of the 437-page unedited volume, published by Liveright and Sons, was indeed a pleasure. I regret that Mr. Stendahl lived no later than 1842, as he was an excellent and prolific writer. Now, in response to your query, and coining a phrase, Yes, I opine Fabrizio, who represents the persona of the author in his protagonism, to be of the nature of what is so conveniently tagged by our modern times as 'a socialist.' But politics aside, Mister Attaché, if you dig down deep for the truer truths—if you do not deceive yourself with what amounts to be Mr. Stendahl's linguistical booby traps—you will discover ample evidence that Fabrizio supercedes the petty tag of 'socialist.' No, to coin a phrase, Fabrizio—and bear in mind that he is representing the persona of the author— is too complicated a man to fall for the cheap shots. The author takes him much deeper. Fabrizio is, as the author overtly hints on page 200 of the Liveright text, *is* a predatory and aggressive beast *down deep,* where it really accounts. And if you choose to call those two traits the basis of capitalism and free enterprise, such is your prerogative, Mister Attaché, but you would be contradicting your own premise, and I trust, as an officer of the French Army, that you would not do so, *irregardless* of what Mr. Stendahl states on page 200 in clear, black-and-white print. For if you did, you would next be obliged to peer into your own *Heart of Darkness,* as it were, and that, dear sir, is an ugly task, even for a man of combat experience."

The Attaché to the French Consulate would toss his cognac in Major Wilks's face, a weak gesture of defeat, and stalk away with his pride assaulted. Major Wilks would react by dabbing his nose with a cocktail napkin, a slow smile emerging on his tired lips, his brow relaxing into smooth furrows. He had held his own, covered his ass, "as it were," on all four sides, and could now savor the sweet taste of highbrow legitimacy as represented in the persona of spiked ginger ale.

When the tactless professor was "sent back to the University," the three Advanced Sections were combined into two. We had occasional joint sessions and lectures, in which Wilks always upstaged his soft-spoken colleague by out-talking him. It was possible that Wilks was envious of the quiet professor's British accent and felt he had to compensate.

In one joint session, Wilks went on for forty-five minutes about the run-on sentence. The Major told the cadets that run-on sentences were "repugnant and anathema to the true spirit of diction." He declared that "a goodly portion of sorely learned scholars" were guilty of run-on sentences, among them military men. He mentioned no names, but advised that he would take harsh measures against any run-ons he encountered. Good military diction was quick and to the point, the best kind of communication there is, he said, for it was the military who made the final decisions pertaining to life and death. Any officer who spoke or wrote in run-on sentences was placing his troops in jeopardy.

Wilks himself spoke in five- and ten-minute sentences, separated, joined, linked, and divided by a platoon of imaginary commas and semicolons and "inasmuches" which placed him incontestably in the big leagues of intellectual comprehension. But it sounded like a run-on sentence.

Wilks never graded a paper of mine until the classes were combined and I was assigned to his section, and when he did grade my paper, the Major was appalled. "R.O.S. factors herein make essay TOTALLY illiterate" was the message on the title page. "R.W." Re-write. What he got back was a predatory version of a Faulkner story as told by Dick, Jane, and Spot. He liked it.

Faulkner was a popular writer in the Academy's English Department, because Faulkner had once been an honorary guest at the Point as a lecturer and "friend" of the Corps. There were pictures all over the library of the aging Faulkner in his bowler hat shaking hands with officers and cadets. Faulkner had left one of his bowler hats behind as a gift, which was now in a glass case on the second floor of the library. Another glass case contained an open letter to the Corps of Cadets telling them what a pleasure his stay had been. There was a dark stain at the bottom of this letter which I suspected was from a spilled glass of bourbon.

During my week as the doomed man, Major Wilks gave us a short story to read by Edgar Allan Poe. He had his own motives; he wanted to tell the newcomers to the class his lengthy version of why Poe was a failure as a cadet and as a man, but a success as a poet. The morbidity of Poe's story made me feel wonderful. The Regimental

Board would probably cut my heart out too, but it would keep on beating. I pondered this during class.

After class, Major Wilks corralled me and asked me what my problem was. I took the Fifth—no excuse. "I didn't see your fist one time today," he told me, meaning that I hadn't volunteered any answers to his "queries." We stuck out our fists instead of holding up our hands.

"You evidence qualities of learnedness," he said. "I see sorely little excuse that you should not participate in class discussions."

"Yes, sir."

"Do not think I am deceived by Cadet Rick's fist sticking in front of your desk. If he persists thusly, you must knock that fist away. That is what a man must do."

I'd thought I could get away with not sticking out my fist because Cadet Rick, who sat on my left in the quadrangular desk arrangement, had begun sticking out *both* fists. We were seated according to grade-rank in class, which meant that Rick had an English average a few meager decimal places worse than mine. Being on Rick's right made me his immediate competitor for sorely learnedness, and he went crazy trying to prove he was smarter than I, that I really belonged on *his* left.

Each day after class Rick would ask Major Wilks for his daily oral grade, then he'd hurriedly calculate his new cumulative average on a slide rule and chase me down the hall to say he only needed three hundredth of a tenth to overtake me. Or to overtake my last posted average. It drove Rick wild that I didn't calculate my new average every day to know exactly where I stood in the competition.

Rick had been on my left for three grade postings, so to hasten his rise to power he'd developed his savage technique. When Major Wilks addressed the class with a learned question, Rick, his black eyes gleaming, would squirm in his seat to be called on. I wasn't sticking out too many fists, so Rick got the bright idea to stick out both his fists, one in front of my desk, and one in front of his desk. He would wiggle his fists and whimper eagerly for the master to acknowledge him.

I hadn't minded Mr. Rick representing me in the potato count, but after Major Wilks mentioned it I began throwing up more fists. Then I won honorable mention in the FFA essay contest, notice of which was posted on the English Department bulletin board. Rick became more savage than ever. I'd try to put out my fist and Rick would knock it away. So I tried putting it toward the fellow on my right and he'd knock it away, figuring me for another Rick. After a few classes of bruised knuckles, I decided Major Wilks' questions weren't worth answering anyway.

Major Wilks felt his questions were worth answering. For that matter, he was *stimulated* by all the hand-to-hand combat which took place over his learned queries. He felt wanted. But he felt hurt that I wasn't among his gang of brass-knuckled scholars. He cornered me after class and made me stand at attention.

"My good man," he said, clicking his cheeks, "your sore lack of participation in class says to me two things. Firstly, that you are mute, which I know is not the case. And secondly, that you refuse to exhibit the two essential commodities that distinguish man as a superior beast, i.e. predation and aggression. Your writing has improved, son, but I see you rapidly declining in what might be called an inverse ratio of progress to the aforesaid. I'm trying to tell you you better shape up your butt or I'll have it busted out of the Academy. I happen to love this place like my mother and it sorely grieves me to see a Freedom Foundation winner like you setting a bad example as a young shitface. You read me?"

"Yes, sir," I answered.

He was quite upset. "What have you got to say for yourself?"

128

"No excuse, sir."

This irked Major Wilks; he lowered his chin, his characteristic move before embarking on a blistering oratory, and began, "Then this is the thing that—" whereupon he stopped and blew up his mouth like a chipmunk. I think his tongue had enunciated itself into that little gap between his teeth. But he went on. "Speak, Mister, speak. I want to hear the facts, the facts behind that no excuse."

"Yes, sir. Sir, the facts are as follows. Not too long ago I got in trouble at the company because I didn't know the system the way I do now since I won the Freedom Foundation of America award because back then, maybe three weeks ago, I wasn't sleeping enough and reading things on Buddha, palmistry, such as that—the life line, you know, sir—and all these things kept adding up, adding up until finally one day at boxing, or after boxing, I lost my head, not entirely of course, and believe it or not, I never got punished, luck you'd have to say, which made me think, really think of how much the Academy meant to me, and even vice versa, but I realize this isn't the whole reason I don't stick out my fist anymore but that doesn't mean it's not a *deep* factor, being that these deep factors are often—how shall I put it?—causal to the more superficial booby traps of the learning process, and that, sir, in a nutshell, is about half of it."

"Mister Mardis," the Major said in a wise tone, "do you know what this is?"

I was slightly impressed with my speech—stimulated. "No, sir! Tell me, sir!"

"It's the *worst* run-on sentence I've ever heard."

MEMO 11.

Long ago, in the "Old Corps," the lower classes didn't have a Christmas leave, and Santa had to make a special trip from the North Pole to West Point to drop off all his toy guns and wind-up soldiers. The stir-crazy cadets would make cruel fun of his disreputable uniform—*red,* with frilly sleeves, baggy at the knees. Santa's beard needed policing for dried egg nog, his sleigh boots needed a good spit-shine. Santa stopped coming to the Point, and eventually the Big Brass gave all classes Christmas leave . . .

From July 1 to December 1, the Fourth Class had to know the countdown days until Christmas leave, and after December 1, the countdown hours. In G-5 it was a standard joke that no three Plebes would give you the same number of days until Christmas; and when we got to the hourly countdown, our figures differed well into the hundreds. The Plebes in other companies were less fortunate; they had to know the exact countdown hours or be punished, and sometimes the *power of the hour,* which was something I never completely understood.

In a way I was like Willie, never too interested in the hops because my girl back home wouldn't like it. She had written me sporadically during the year, and after reading the first letter, I should have suspected that Dolores didn't fully apprehend what a cadet was, what it meant to be a cadet. Maybe I didn't either, but she certainly didn't. She asked in her letter if the cadets in Beast Barracks were going to the Woodstock Music Festival.

Most cadets had a picture of "the girlfriend" as the one regulation optional display object on their desk. Boyd Royelle, my new roommate, reputedly had the best-looking girl of all the company Plebes. I had to believe this myself when, one Saturday, Major Cutler made a room inspection and hungrily grabbed up her picture. "This is *some* girl you got, Mr. Royelle," he said. "Take my advice and hang on to her." Boyd Royelle swelled up with pride and replied, "I *intend* to, sir!"—not a regulation answer, but this was an exception. Embossed at the bottom of her glossy photo was "2nd Prom Queen**Jackdale Junior College**1967."

I had nothing quite so prestigious to display, and Ralph M. Aberby had even worse—an empty frame. When questioned about this, Ralph boldly stated that he was still waiting for his girl to send him her picture. But he was darn sure going to be ready when it got here. Ralph was much too protective of his newly aquired lovely to paste up the mug shot he'd just pinched from the files of the Cadet Hostess Office dating service, afraid that someone would recognize her. "*Hey, that's number 23!* I've seen her card! Likes to cha-cha and play checkers!"

My picture of Dolores was a snapshot which I'd chopped up and silhouetted in broken pieces against another snapshot of a West Point parade. I wanted to be unusual, and the usual response was, "Why'd you ruin the photograph?" and I'd think, Which one? hahaha. . . . It was my intention, however, having turned over a new leaf, to secure a classic 8 x 10 glossy print as soon as I saw Dolores during Christmas.

After a shrewd refusal to be Emergency Holiday Rubber Rep, and a mandatory last-day haircut, I was homeward bound. My Mom, Sis, and Dad were there at the airport to meet me, but I was too preoccupied with panting after Dolores to sincerely welcome their hearty congratulations. I told them I had an urgent, confidential mission to accomplish regarding a civilian young lady.

They said, "You're even beginning to sound like a cadet!" We were still in the airport terminal. I perceived many passersby openly gawking, pointing, looking back at the young man in his cadet gray uniform. That's right, lady, I ain't the sky cap! A black Air Force Second Lieutenant walked by and I felt we should exchange a salute—even a little scuttlebutt—but we didn't. In fact, he gave me a snide look.

"You look like such a man in your uniform!" my Mom said to me.

"I wish I were a cadet!" my little sister screamed.

"The Point has done you wonders, son," said Dad. "I can tell."

I confided that I wouldn't be myself until my urgent mission had been carried out. They understood, handed me the car keys, said they'd take a limousine into town with my bags—they never got to ride in limousines anyway. I understood. And in minutes I was speeding down the nighttime expressway past the U-24 cutoff and past Daddy-O's Donut Shop, for the first time ever driving a car as a cadet, headed at breakneck pace to a scribbly address on the back of a crumpled envelope I held tightly in my teeth.

My destination was the point of origin of the last personal correspondance Dolores had forwarded to me. In other words, I was driving to the return address on Dolores's last vague love letter. It was also her last letter. In my heated excitement I surmised that if she weren't there, just about anyone would do in aiding me to accomplish my mission. The last letter had said she was living with "beautiful people." Fine with me! The more the merrier! And if any of them were guys, well . . . I'd just deliver the old left to the body and a right uppercut

132

to make more room for myself. And if anybody got sassy, I'd quote Buddha at them, show them I didn't need to go to Woodstock to be hip!

Dolores had dropped out of high school since I'd last seen her, but I didn't care; that just gave us something more in common. I'd dropped out of society myself. Now I screeched up before an old, tattered house, some three stories high, with a massive tree in front that gave it the appearance of a scene from a mystery drama, *or* a romance story. The neighborhood I knew, having once delivered pizzas here as a summertime job—and it was none too reputable. Why Dolores had dropped out of high school and come to live in a place like this was beyond me.

As I walked up the buckled sidewalk, I gazed at the upper floors of the house, noticing a few lights being flicked on and off, figures dithering behind pulled shades. I went up the squeaky wooden steps—no porch light to speak of—and knocked firmly on the door. I was wearing gloves and took one off to hold in my hand, as was protocol for most officers when paying visits. I had to rap several times more before anyone responded.

Finally, "*Yeah?*"

"Is Dolores here?"

"Whadda you want?" It was a man's voice, dull, unfriendly.

I told him again I wanted Dolores, and he asked if I had any identification. "Why do I need identification?"

"You mean you're not the heat?" The door opened and a very-long-haired fellow of perhaps thirty peered out at me suspiciously. When he was satisfied that I was not a policeman, he opened the door all the way. He had a shaggy beard, sagging eyes, was wearing only a pair of trousers. "She's watchin' TV. Who are you?"

"I'm an old friend of hers—Jaime Mardis."

He looked at my hat, then down at my trousers, which had black stripes running up the sides, then parted his

133

lips in a frown. "Man, you're a walking paranoia trip."

"Pardon me?"

"I said I don't know what your trip is, but, man, you're *heavy.*"

"Just tell Dolores I'd like to see her."

A small group had come down the stairs; one of them said, "Where'd you put that stash?" It was dimly lighted inside and difficult for me to make out who was who. Then Dolores came forward, telling the others in a clear tone that it was all right. She stepped out on the porch, shutting the door behind her.

"Why, Jaime, what a surprise."

We shook hands. She was pretty, if somewhat haggard, her hair long and dark, her eyes deep and sensual, her face smooth, calm. I swallowed hard as I realized her tousled hair and bell bottom jeans implied, indisputably, that she had become a hippie. I wept silent tears, knowing full well that hippies and cadets were rarely compatible.

I tried to make conversation. "What's on TV?"

"Oh, some stupid movie. I wasn't really watching it, anyway." Her air was lilting, charming, sensitive. I was crestfallen after my exalted expections. But my thermometer hit the top when she took my hand softly. "You look *just* . . . fine in your uniform, Jaime. It really turns a woman on!"

"It does?"

"Sure it does. Didn't you know that?" Dolores gave me a lovely smile, which seemed to linger on indefinitely in the shadows of the porch. It struck me that my whole cadet career so far had been worthwhile, just to hear that one compliment. Then she tried to make conversation with *me.*

"When do you leave for Vietnam, Jaime?"

"No, no, that's all in the future. I'm just a cadet now."

"But don't cadets go to Vietnam?" She seemed in an

awful hurry to get me over there. Yet my duty was to explain.

"Well, when they graduate, I suppose some do." I went on about how some graduates had been killed, and whenever they were a special announcement was made in the Mess Hall in their honor. "But you can get run over by a milk truck, for that matter," I concluded.

She suggested we go somewhere, that I probably wouldn't be comfortable inside because they weren't my type of people. I took her word for it, then we went in so she could get her bag. The long-haired fellow and a couple of his comrades were lounging on two studio couches in the living room. They looked at me disapprovingly, then looked at each other the same way, remarking, "Some bust, all right."

My enthusiasms were restored when Dolores and I went joy riding in the car. She seemed very interested in my tales of cadet life, and I was very interested in telling her. Soon we were spinning along a secluded drive in DuBois Park, which wound around to the picnic area. Dolores had been listening so intently to my woes and glories that she was now startled to find us alone, parked on the dark picnic grounds.

"Why, Jaime, I'll bet I know what you have on your mind!" She tried to be cross. "Can cadets do this sort of thing on leave?"

"Don't worry, I'm not going to get in any trouble."

"But, can I?" She was serious—I'd babbled so much about the infinite restrictions and punishments that she too felt threatened. I laughed uproariously, then set out to paw away six months of loneliness and repression. The windows had just begun to fog when a searchlight dashed across the windshield. Dolores tensed and panicked. "I'm *holding!*" she whispered.

"Holding what?" I snapped back. "Now let go—I'll solve this." I rolled down my window and saw what appeared to be a highway patrolman with a four-foot flashlight.

He was looking at the license plates of my mother's station wagon. I opened the door to climb out and Dolores again warned me that "she was holding," but I had no time for lovers' talk. As soon as my head was in plain view, I got the light right in the eyes. The officer told me to hold it right there. Then he whispered some code into a walkie-talkie that was on his belt.

He approached, cautiously. "OK, let's see your driver's—" His light beamed up and down my body. "Why, you're one of them—you're a cadet, boy. That's what you are, isn't it?"

"A *West Point* Cadet."

"Well, why didn't ya say so." He shut off the light and mumbled another code into the walkie-talkie, then shut it off and breathed a sigh of relief. "Where's that at, anyway? Up in Colorado or something?"

"It's in West Point, New York."

"Yeah, I thought it was there somewhere." The patrolman had a tan uniform, a wide-brimmed hat with a badge on the front, and wore a bomber jacket unzipped. On the same belt as his transistor was a night stick and a big gun. Above the belt was a happy, pleasant paunch— but his face had a nasty sneer. "We've been having trouble in these parts," he told me. "That's why they called *us* in." He was explaining why he, a highway patrolman, was doing park duty.

I told him this was my mother's car and he said that's what he figured. "You got somebody inside there?" I told him it was my girlfriend, and after taking a tentative closer look he said she wasn't bad. I said thanks.

"You know this park ain't no safe place to be bringing your girlfriend these days—not even for a soldier. It's changed since you been gone."

"I'm here for Christmas leave."

"I figured as much."

"I guess I'll have to go someplace else."

"Well," he drawled, "seeing how you're on Christmas leave, and seeing how you and your young lady friend are getting along and whatnot— You know, the best I ever done for myself was two stripes, but I respect you West Point fellas. So, I figure, maybe I'll just smoke this dollar-and-fifteen-cent cigar I got here"—he tapped his shirt pocket—"and radio on down the road to the other boys to make sure you don't get disturbed here. I figure it's the least the community can do. I'll just drive on back to the park road and have my cigar and be your official chaperone."

"Why—"

He raised his hand, took a step back. "Merry Christmas, boy. Wish there was more like you."

Dolores had overheard, and when I was back in the seat, and the officer gone, she wrapped her arms around me and gave me a big wet kiss. She said she'd never seen anything like it. "What a *man!*" she cooed. All flattery aside, I was impressed with myself. In my heart I had known that no park guard or deputy sheriff would dare insult or jeopardize the integrity of a West Point Cadet, not in 1969 when there was so much else to keep them busy. They were *proud* to see a red-blooded boy like me having some good, red-blooded fun for a change. That officer and I had an inner understanding that only those in the profession of arms could fathom—we were brothers of the sword.

With my masculine attributes so firmly established, Dolores could do little but whimper as I carried out my mission of delight. She kept drowsily repeating "and I'm holding" until I got so tired of it I decided to throw in some lovers' talk of my own. "Make love, not war!" I whispered huskily in her ear.

After a while, Dolores said, her breath bated, erratic: "Jaime?"

"Yes, what is it?"

The whisper of her voice was hesitant, timid, almost-guilty.

"I want to get married."

"You *do*?"

A West Point wedding flashed through my mind— gleaming sabers, bride bouquets, classmates cheering.

"But do you think it's right?" Dolores asked.

"Well—" My heart was pounding in uncertainty. The vision of an 8 x 10 glossy print now came upon me, with an inscription: "Mrs. Second Lieutenant Mardis-to-be." I told her an engagement would be nice, but rings were awfully expensive.

She sighed happily. "Well, I'm glad to hear you say that. Anyway, his name is Greg Dice, and he's a real nice guy, really he is. Oh, I know some people don't under- stand him, and I doubt you'd even like him, but, well . . . I *knew* I could ask you for an *honest* opinion."

I felt as faint as Wook Keeng in a Full Dress Parade. Such brutal frankness, and in such a delicate, tender moment as this, granted that no station wagon could ever take the place of Holiday Inn. "How do you know I'm being honest?" I asked throatily.

"Because cadets can't lie, silly! You just told me so!" She sat up and clapped her hands merrily. "Let's go have a hamburger! I want to call Greg right now from the pay phone!"

This was one botched-up mission to joke about back at the company, I told myself, duly shattered. Dolores detected my hurt feelings, though, and apologized. She thanked me again for being honest. I thanked her for being honest, told her honesty was the best policy, and went on for some while about our fine, commendable document, the Cadet Honor Code. As it turned out, Greg Dice was at the hamburger stand having himself a hamburger. Dolores went to him eagerly.

The rejection made me feel unbearably lucky to be a cadet. *Proud*, all the way down to the regulation square cut of my toenails. Yes, I philosophized, these civvies weren't too spoony—funnyI had never noticed it before.

The rest of my leave was spent waiting to go back to the Corps, where a man could be a man, and a boy could too. TV did not interest me as it once had, nor was I inclined to look up old friends or professors from St. Francis's. I could see myself driving an armored command vehicle over to Shopping City and blasting away at the windows, but that was ridiculous. What I really wanted was to get back to the Corps and forget about the outside world.

Once my parents had their curiosities satisfied—and my father cancelled his usual business trips—it was back to the same dull doldrums I had experienced as a teenager. Or so I looked back at my home life from my newly cultivated standpoint of maturity. I didn't mention my blunders at the Academy; instead, I built myself up and played the part of homecoming hero."Wow!" said my little sister, age eight. "You sound just like Captain America!"

MEMO 12.

Ralph M. Aberby was plump, blond-haired, ill-complected, aggressive, and had the greedy, jittery eyes of a dog with a sweet tooth. Ralph had done seventy-five push-ups in his underwear every night during the month of December to be sure he'd look like a strong man for Christmas leave. Ralph's voice was shrill and often broke, so that when he snarled, *"There's one fart from high school I'd like to meet up with!"* his vicious threat sounded like a choirboy's imitation of Humphrey Bogart.

On the depressing Sunday afternoon of return from Christmas leave, I found Ralph M. Aberby in his underwear, flexing his muscles and squeezing problem areas on his face as he gazed with sweet memory at the spanking new 8 x 10 glossy print his "gal" had given him. I knew that someday he'd make her a fine husband, because the minute I walked in the room Ralph showed me the picture and spat out, "If I ever catch you, I mean if I *ever* catch you gawkin' at her the wrong way, I'll flatten your face, Mister. You understand me?"

With a girl in his pocket suitable for marriage, Ralph felt as good as, if not better than, Boyd Royelle. Ralph had a way of joking about these things to let us know he was serious; he told Royelle he was as good as him or better, and so was his girl. Royelle replied that she certainly looked like a fine woman, and Aberby was lucky to have her. "You're damn right I am!" Aberby snarled. "You're lucky to be in the same darned room as her picture, too!" Royelle had laughed good-naturedly, understanding these foibles of men with the precise depth of a natural-born leader.

Boyd Royelle was six foot three, had a sensitive, husky voice, made good grades, played varsity basketball and was a soloist in the Cadet Choir. He had blue eyes, freckles, and red hair, was slightly arched in the back, and he fully accepted his role as a natural-born leader. His gravity and resignation in carrying out responsibilities implied that he was not happy as a jaybird to undertake these responsibilities, but when there was a job to be done, and a man to do the job, the man damn sure did that job—*his best*! Boyd Royelle was dripping with leadership qualities, and Aberby, the hardest tryer, idolized him.

Ralph Aberby was also a basketball man, but no matter how hard he practiced, he couldn't make the varsity like Royelle. Ralph also sang in the Cadet Choir, but no matter how loud he yodeled, he would never be a soloist like Royelle. Ralph tried his darndest in "stract" subjects like math and engineering, but his marks were always lower than Boyd's. One time, Aberby feverishly attempted to organize a volunteer Plebe basement detail, but Boyd Royelle had organized one the week before.

On becoming Boyd's roommate, Ralph stopped competing and started imitating. He tried to walk like him, talk like him, behave like him, and almost, it seemed, to *be* him. If Boyd decided to brush his teeth, Ralph stood over him at the sink waiting to brush his own teeth. If Boyd shined his shoes after breakfast, Ralph shined his own shoes, using Boyd's polish. If Boyd did calculus after supper, Ralph did calculus too, and would borrow Boyd's slide rule because it "looked more accurate." He accidentally borrowed Boyd's hat, accidentally borrowed his deodorant. One time he even got their underwear mixed up.

Boyd didn't like me more than Aberby but be did pay

141

more attention to me, mostly with morale-boosting sermons. In the new room I had begun to try again—to make up for the class-skipping incident—and Boyd found this commendable. In his words, the measure of a man was when he could *profit* by his mistakes. Of course it had struck him that this was his osmosis mission in having me as a roommate: to encourage me in the ways of the goodly. And he did; he complimented me on everything and anything, on how I swept the floor, on my shoe shine, my math grade, my hair part. As it stood his encouragement was welcome, but it began to drive Aberby mad with jealousy.

One night in December, Boyd had said that I had a "good, clean hair part," and Ralph, hurt to the point of tears that his hair part had not been mentioned, spent over an hour developing his at the sink. When he was finished, he turned around and announced that his hair part was better than both of ours put together.

Royelle said, "Do you think it's really wise to spend an hour of study time parting your hair, Ralph?"

Ralph seethed "You're just afraid to admit it's better, that's all, Royelle! It's better than Mardis's, a blind man could see that!"

On the afternoon of return from Christmas leave, I told Royelle and the gang in a bullshit session about my episode with Dolores. The story got a big laugh. Later, however, in the quiet minutes of dusk, Royelle counseled me with the solemn sincerity of a priest. He said my laughter did not conceal the pain of "holding the losing end of the stick," and that I must always remember that any sacrifice will bear forth some good, that I could think of losing my girl as just another challenge that a man—of commitment—must face. Blah, blah, blah. Then Royelle went to take a shower.

Aberby was eying me contemptuously. "You're no better than *me* or anybody else, Mardis," he sneered. "You might fool everybody else, but you can't fool me with your lies. And I saw you looking at my girl—you just keep your beady eyes off her, so help me!"

"What would I do with your girl?"

"Cause you don't have one, that's why! You don't know the first thing about women. I know more than you do!"

Supper that night in the colossal, banner-strewn Mess Hall was boisterous yet mournful, an echo of the freedom of Christmas leave but a grim prelude to the dreary months of winter that lay ahead. Plebe duties had been read out in ranks, so after supper I went to the Central Guard Room. I was Minute Caller for my platoon, and this duty required copying the weekly menus and any special formation times from the Guard Room bulletin board.

When I returned to the room, another bullshit session was taking place, but I wasn't interested. I took down my book of Cadet Regs to refresh my memory on the uniform flags, which were flown at dawn to let the Minute Callers know which uniform to call. Sometimes the Minute Callers got the flags mixed up, and one platoon would be wearing long overcoats while another platoon would be wearing short overcoats. Minute Callers paid for that.

As I studied the uniform flags, Aberby bragged about his girlfriend. He made it sound as if she was a grand princess, and he had been granted the privilege of meeting her because he was such a fine fellow and she'd "heard about him." The gang was falling for it, and I'm not sure whether LaDonna knew the real, hard facts of Ralph's romance. But I knew because I hung out at the Cadet Hostess Office every morning and I had seen Aberby there *often*. And I had seen Aberby's girl *often*. Jerry Drury and I used to choose hands from the dating files and play poker with them. Aberby's girl had been in several losing hands.

I had no cause to expose him; however, I began to feel less noble as Aberby continued to embroider the knightly aspects of his courtship: "Has she got any girlfriends, Ralph?" "Sure, lots of 'em," he answered, "but they're all in love with me. You should have seen me at that party I was telling you about. Hells bells, they were hot for me all right."

I turned to Ralph. "Now *how* did you meet her again?"

Aberby was condescending. "Like I said, I was walking around Cullum Hall one Saturday in my dress gray, and bang, up she comes and plants a big wet one on me. *I* took it from there."

He was talking more to the group. They needed girlfriends, and Ralph's success spoke a lot louder than my failure. One of the Plebes muttered, "Ah, Mardis, you just wish it was you, don't you?" LaDonna gave me a glance of sympathy. Aberby was stalking the room as the temporary spokesman; he pointed at me and rasped, "This bozo here would be lucky to get a rat in the gutter to go to the hop with him!"

"The gutter?" I said. "I guess you all know that Ralph here got his girl out of the dating files at the Hostess Office, and that's even worse than the gutter. Right Ralph?"

No one had to bother asking Ralph if he'd actually resorted to the taboo files—he looked as if he'd had an attack of rabies. He was growling at me, and twitching, and frothing at the mouth. The group couldn't stop laughing; they fell on the floor, holding their sides, and then stood up and fell down again, hysterical that Ralph had them believing he was a Don Juan in disguise. One of them took the picture to look for touch-ups, and Ralph snatched it back, screaming in his shrill voice.

Boyd Royelle had laughed briefly, but now he wore a serious expression. He quieted the room by asking whether an honor violation had been committed.

"Hell, no!" Aberby said, frightened. "I just left out a part, that was all. That was how we met, I'm on my

144

honor." He leered at me. "The Cadet Hostess arranged the time and place, that's all."

The men agreed that the love story wasn't an Academy matter, at the very worst a quibble. But Royelle said sternly, "Well Ralph, just let this be a *lesson.*"

The room was cleared, and Aberby was silent for an hour, biting his nails. Then he tried to pick an argument with me. But I just agreed with him. Yes, he was a better man. Yes, at least he had a girlfriend. He was stronger, and I was a zero and he wasn't. I told Ralph he was right and went to lie in my bunk—against regulations, since it was still too early.

Royelle said, "Jaime, you know it's still a little early for that sort of thing. I know it doesn't happen often, but there *could* be an inspection, you know."

"So what?" I said. "This is G-5, not F-1."

"That's not the right attitude," grunted Royelle.

Aberby squawked that I was a zero at heart, and I told him he was right. He couldn't bear not being able to argue with me, now that he wanted to; to compensate, he started grunting and heaving over his push-ups on the floor next to our bunk, where I had the top. After every ten or fifteen he'd stand up and take deep breaths and say something like, "I'm glad I'm not lazy like some people in this room," and "Gee, you stink."

The next morning I was to be on duty as Minute Caller, and I wanted to have sufficient rest to be up and action-ready. The next morning was also the official beginng of the *Gloom Period,* which would endure, for all practical purposes, until Easter Sunday. In Gloom Period, the sky would turn officially gray, the building faces would take on an ordained melancholy, the grounds would be officially sparse with barren trees and dirty snow piles. But it was a morale boost, a comfort in the city-state of West Point, to know that the Gloom Period was decreed and anticipated and not just a stint of dreary weather that occurred on its own. Regrettably, the Gloom Period gave the men of the Corps, and the officers, an "official" excuse for quickened tempers and foul dispositions. "You think *this* is bad, Mister," we'd been told. "Wait'll the Gloom Period gets here!"

As Minute Caller, it would be my duty to rouse to life a platoon of dead men who had not been required to spring up at the break of day for more than two weeks. To carry out this mission, all I had to do was wake up early, check the uniform flag, dress in the proper uniform, review the breakfast menu, and start screaming at 0605 hours. But something went wrong. On the first day of Gloom Period, 1970, as the Fifth Regiment of the United States Corps of Cadets marched across the DMZ into breakfast, the Third Platoon of Company G-5 was missing in inaction.

Shouts of terror startled me from my sleep. I saw the time, ran down the stairs in my pajamas, and vainly, nobly, tried to call the minutes in reverse, an uncommon procedure. "Sir, Reveille Breakfast Formation was ten minutes ago!" I didn't know what the uniform was and I couldn't remember the menu, so I shouted out that we were wearing "coats" and having "eggs." "I repeat, Reveille Breakfast Formation was ten minutes ago, sir!"

The sleepy ranks on the DMZ had been too groggy and uncaring to notice that the spot where Third Platoon usually stood was not occupied by a grayish clump but by a deep black void. Only when the bugles had sounded and reports were rendered did the Second Platoon Leader realize that something was wrong. Not only was a whole platoon missing—so was the company Chain of Command, which was quartered in my barracks unit. The Second Platoon Leader had deserted the Reveille formation to play Paul Revere.

The New Company Commander, Cadet Captain Charles L. "Chuck" Coogan, was late. His new staff was late. My new Squad Leader was late. As I called out the

146

minutes in reverse—"ten minutes ago! eleven minutes ago!"—cadets came floundering out of their rooms in various stages of undress, confused and babbling. They cursed the Minute Caller, they jabbered excitedly, they bolted back and forth between rooms to make sure they weren't alone in this predicament.

In the confusion, both Hoggins and Coogan tried to take command, from different floors. Hoggins, for the sake of expediency, told his platoon to throw on their coats over their pajamas and get to the Mess Hall post haste. Coogan stopped the half-robed cadets as they bounded down the stairs and told them to go back and clothe fully—he wasn't having his company late *and* out of uniform. But Coogan was too distracted to notice that some cadets had sneaked by wearing slippers, trousers, pajama tops, and raincoats, that others were wearing tennis shoes and no socks, or civilian shirts instead of class shirts. The company zeros, in spite of the waking terror, were making the most of it.

The atmosphere at the G-5 breakfast tables was like an aftermath of a surprise dawn bombing—bewilderment, vengeance, pieced-together uniforms. Coogan, in defiance of his own orders, had dressed in a zipper jacket and a dirty T-shirt, loosely resembling the Academy's bronze statue of Douglas MacArthur. Over their coffee, more than a few zero upperclassmen were happy with the situation, joking and comparing pajama tops. But Coogan wouldn't be content until the responsible party had been paid In full for this mess—namely me, the Admiral Yamamoto of the enemy attack fleet.

After breakfast I was captured and escorted to the Company Commander's room—he was still dressed in his battlefield outfit—and there I received a merciless browbeating. He and Hoggins and a few others stood me up against the wall in a stiff brace and hazed me for forty-five minutes, until they were hoarse. I learned that I was unfit to be a cadet, I was a disgrace to the Corps, I was rotten to the core, and that I had further disgraced my duty by making a mockery thereof: i.e., calling the minutes in reverse. They told me I was apathetic and incompetent, they told me I wasn't even fit to be a hippie, they told me Plebes had it too easy, and they asked me what do you think would happen if this were Vietnam, and before I could answer they answered for me:

"We'd all be dead now, Mister."

"All because of you, ya dirty dildo!"

To further inquiries, I answered, "No excuse."

I was punished with three months confinement to quarters and extra guard tours instead of punishment tours, on account of inclement weather. Even Buddha couldn't help me out of this one. My attached report was concise and easy to understand. "No excuse."

Ralph Aberby was abnormally cheerful that night in the room, but any of his spirited ridicule was lost on me. I was too distraught; I'd wanted to start the year off right and here I was, a doomed man again. At Taps I wound my clock, the clock that had failed to go off, and for the first time that day it occurred to me that I was not to blame for what had happened. I'd set the alarm for 5:45, but it now read 6:00. If I needed to call on any god, it was Shiva the Destroyer, because this looked like dirty work. I asked Aberby if he'd touched it the night before.

"Hell, no, I didn't, you screwhead," he told me.

I thought for a minute, then said, "You're Letter Carrier this week, aren't you?"

"That's right," he mumbled. He was working on a calculus problem, the same one Boyd Royelle was working on. He'd told Boyd a few minutes earlier that he would beat him to the answer.

"Did you get up at five to deliver the papers?"

"Better than you," he said. "You bozo."

"So how did you wake up? You don't have a clock."

"I don't need a clock."

Royelle looked over from his desk. "Are you trying to

say Ralph used your clock and didn't reset it? Because if you are, Mardis, I can say that I didn't hear any alarm go off at any time this morning."

"You're on the other side of the room, too," I said.

Aberby had been tense; now he loosened up, began scratching himself, and said, "You're just a sore loser, Mardis."

"Goddammit, you used that clock—put it under your pillow or something—and then you reset it for six and didn't pull the pin back out. Didn't you, Ralph?"

An argument exploded and Royelle took Aberby's side. I said Aberby had quibbled about his girlfriend, hadn't he? But they ganged up on me and said I was trying to stick the guilt on somebody else because I couldn't accept the fact I'd made a big mistake. Finally I stopped shouting. My suppositions about whether the pin had been pushed in or pulled out, or whether anyone had heard the alarm at five, or whether Aberby had it under his pillow were only making me look more ridiculous. I threw the clock out the window.

"Now you've wasted the clock, you dildo," Ralph laughed. "I knew you were a real sickie."

"What's the point?" asked Royelle.

"Nothing," I said, "except that if Aberby doesn't need a clock to wake up at five, we'll just make sure he doesn't have access to one. I'll wake up with the cannon for Reveille."

"Goddammit, somebody's gotta call those minutes, Mardis," Royelle said. "And I don't think it's too damned wise of you to risk making half the company late again for some silly trifle. I'll call 'em myself."

"Jesus, you really are a hero, aren't you, Royelle?"

He didn't like it. "I don't think hero is the word, Mardis. But I *can* say that somebody's got to call those minutes on time, and if you can't, I will."

Aberby was beside himself with joy, so excited that his teeth were grinding, his eyes glittering. "Oh, Mardis, you're really a loser, man, really a loser. I spotted you a long time ago. Shit, and I have to be in the same toilet with you. Some luck."

Royelle opened a drawer of his desk and pulled out a tiny travel alarm, wound it up and looked at it. "This thing ain't much, but it'll make sure somebody wakes up in this room tomorrow morning by six." He flipped it shut and placed it by his calculus book, then picked up a pencil to resume working on an equation. He'd had his say.

"Still gonna beat ya, Boydie buddy," Aberby said, picking up his pencil and putting it in his mouth like a cigarette. "You know," he said, "Mardis is right about something. I shouldn't trust my biological time clock as much as I do—why, I might even oversleep myself." He made a face at me and turned to Royelle, but the natural-born leader was bent over, concentrating on his calculations.

Aberby left the room and came back with a borrowed clock. "You touch this, Mardis, so help me," he said, "and I'll flatten your ugly face."

And so Ralph Aberby won back his honor, or whatever it was he wanted, at my expense, and all before the watchful eye of his matinee idol, Boyd Royelle. I should have demanded he go before a Cadet Honor Officer, but calling the minutes was *my* responsibility and I was guilty for not doing it. This was it. The cadet code of manhood said that no cadet should ever "dick on his buddy" in the line of duty, that you should never cast the blame on another. To dick on your buddy was a moral crime much worse than any infraction in the book—and I looked bad enough as it was. This code had come about naturally, I suppose, from the great brotherhood felt among the members of the Long Gray Line.

MEMO 13.

Not even a Siberian radarman could match the loneliness of a Plebe on guard duty. *Clop, clop,* back and forth, *clop, clop,* about-face. After a month of Saturday night guard-tours, I was ready to defect to Siberia. There, at least, an occasional enemy submarine or missile-bearing blimp—or blip—might pass by on the screen. But here, in the various empty divisions of the Corps where I was stationed, the worse threat we ever got was a half-drunken janitor banging his mop against a radiator in the basement.

Even so, the mission of the Plebe guard was to stop and question all persons advancing on our post. "Halt, who goes there!" Should the party be disinclined to provide proper verbal identification, the guard was equipped with a bulletless rifle to defend his post. If a nuclear attack should occur, we had our dress bayonets hanging ready.

All barracks were guarded every Saturday night (in case of attack when the Corps was out hopping) by Plebes either assigned for the duty or doing special punishments. You seldom guarded your own regiment. In G-5 we once had a guard from the First Regiment who had commanded Carlo "Hot Sauce" Carillo to identify himself as he left for the hop.

"Halt, who goes there!" cried the guard.

"Screw you, Jack, I'm in a hurry."

151

"Halt, I say!" The Plebe lowered his rifle to a ready position and refused to let Carillo go by.

Carillo wasn't in the mood to play soldiers and told him, "Now shove over, you nincompoop!"

The Plebe had neatly fixed his bayonet and shouted for assistance, failing to remember what company this was. Three men of Golfball appeared and tackled the guard, stole his rifle, and tied his hands with his cross-belts. The guard broke down and started crying.

With the exception of the guard fixing his bayonet, the relationship between Golf-5 and its Saturday night watchmen was informal: they were usually invited in a room for ginger ale and to chat. But a guard in any other barracks was forced to be the miserable, methodical slob that his "standing orders" called for, especially in the First Regiment. The Fightin' First upperclassmen who stayed home on Saturday night certainly weren't fun-lovers, and when they found a DMZ Plebe in their area— a Golf-bozo, no less—their fangs quickly filled with venom.

To heighten my punishment, Fido had seen to it that all my tours were pulled in the First Regiment, where it was assured that the duty would indeed be a duty and not a cakewalk. A division could be completely empty during my tour, and still the Cadet-in-Charge-of-Quarters would stage a lightning inspection every quarter hour to make sure I was *clop-clopping* and that I remembered a guard's four standing orders. ("I will guard everything within the limits of my post and quit my post only when properly relieved, etc.) The only consolation I could muster was that I had a deeper understanding of the psychology of a windup toy.

Somehow, they even managed to deprive me of this trifling pleasure. An ugly head would stick out of a room and say, "You're a soldier, Mister, not a robot! Just remember that and act like one!"

My most frightening experience was when I got caught marching with my eyes closed. I'd been measuring my *clops* on the second floor between stairwell and outside window, pretending that I'd been blinded by an enemy signal flare yet still unwilling to give up my post. We were supposed to alternate floors every fifteen minutes, and when I'd spent an inordinate amount of time guarding the second floor, an upperclassman on the third floor had sneaked down the stairwell in his bath thongs to reconnoiter my dawdling.

By my decreased vision I shall increase olfactory and auditory sensibilities, I was thinking as I *clopped* back and forth at my post. Should the enemy attempt to approach, I shall detect the sound of their movement and/or sniff out their alien odors. I will smell the curry sauce on their breath at a hundred paces, I shall ascertain that they say "Hare Krishna" instead of "God bless you" when they sneeze. If nothing is said when the enemy sneezes, I will still know it is the enemy. Curry powder will make anyone sneeze. I will radio this information back to the command post, then blast away with my carbine.

I had begun to notice that every fourth *clop* had a peculiar resonance, as though every fourth *clop* was really a *clop* and a half. It was twelve *clops* from stairwell to window, and twelve *clops* back, a total of twenty-four *clops*, which, divided by four, made an additional sub-quotient of six half-*clops*, or a total of three extra *clops* per complete trip. Very interesting. I pondered this, then decided to pause after each fourth *clop*, at the sound of the half-*clop*, and bend down to examine the floor for loose tiles, squeaky boards, or other podiatric hazards. My eyes had been closed for so long I couldn't remember what the floor was made of.

I was at the stairwell, on the verge of blindly examining the third trouble spot—the first two inspections of four and eight *clops* having turned up no palpable impediments, just a little dirt maybe—when I detected an alien odor. Half stooped, I raised my head and sniffed, as a mole does on coming up for air. My highly sensitized olfactories picked out Old Spice After Shave Lotion and a lesser trace of the knockwurst and sauerkraut we'd had for supper.

"Peekaboo, beanhead. For Chrissake, what are you doing?"

My rifle was already shouldered, so all I had to do to come to attention was stand up to full height. I did so, alertly, but I was still in a sort of trance.

"Can't you open your eyes, Mister?"

I blinked them a few times. An upperclassman in a wool bathrobe was standing right in front of me, a slide rule in his hand.

"Did you lose a contact lens, Mister?"

"No, sir!" Hearing my own voice returned me to my senses—and my sense of duty. "*Halt*!" I shouted as loud as I could. "Who goes there!"

"You mean *me*?" the fellow asked. He was standing a foot away. "Man, you're a real case. Are you from next door, F-1?"

"Identify yourself!" I told him. Anyone passing in the hallway had to be identified. He succumbed to the ritual and I gave him permission to proceed. He proceeded by asking me what my problem was.

"Sir, I have no problem!"

"But why are you stooping, and why were your eyes closed? Are you a shot-put man?"

"No, sir."

"Then that wasn't an exercise? I've seen shot-put men count off their steps before with their eyes closed. Some of them even heave with their eyes closed. I guess you're in a tough company," he said sentimentally. "I had hell when I was a Plebe. I know how it is. What company are you in, Mister? Come on, relax. Can't you see I'm about to recognize you?"

"Yes, sir. Thank you, sir." I set my rifle against the wall and started tugging off the white glove on my right hand. Our handshake would seal the "recognition." I commented that I'd had a rough week over in the Fifth Regiment.

"Say no more, friend. You're in B-5, aren't you? I know your C.O.—he's a bitch if there ever was one."

"Yeah, I've heard about B-5. But I'm in G-5, thank God."

"Put your gloves back on, Mister! Get that rifle on your shoulder! *Post haste!* Get it!" The friendly upperclassman was red with rage. "I'll be damned if any self-respecting man in the Fightin' First would recognize a G-5 Plebe! Up against that wall, Mister, 'cause we've got things to talk about! You call G-5 a company? Bullshit. You scum of the Slums, you second-hand douchebag—you've got the nerve to come in the First Regiment and do this goofball shit! You just wait right here while I get my quill pad!"

He lurched up the stairs to the third floor, taking two at a time, his bath thongs going *clop-op* on each step. If nothing else, I'd solved the mystery of the extra *clops.* The fellow had diligently imitated my pace to conceal his progress down the stairs, but each measured step he had taken to my four had ended with an identifying *op.* The friendly upperclassman came back with a buddy and also summoned the C.C.Q.; together they hazed me and made me recite Plebe knowledge for an hour: Standing Orders, The Commandant's Cat, The Mission of the Academy, and so on. As if that wasn't enough, the friendly upperclassman hazed me with his slide rule, asking me cube roots, square roots, and the power of the hour until Monday Reveille Breakfast Formation. "It doesn't surprise me that some douchebag G-5 Plebe can't figure the power of the hour!" he sputtered. "But for your information"—he consulted his slide rule—"It's 1,024."

Two weeks later I had a rare opportunity to repay the friendly upperclassman for his hospitality. At optional brunch on Sunday, I loaded up my hat with pieces of fruit snitched from empty tables in the Mess Hall. I did this every Sunday now, hastily escaping with my cornucopia through a seldom-used door at the base of the "poop deck," a huge stone tower which formed the axis of the Mess Hall's five wings. This door opened onto a basement exit, but there was also a stairway leading up the tower to the language departments. I would dash up the six flights with my booty and then take an elevator down from the language floor to a back door opening near the Mess Hall loading docks. From there I could make it safely back to the Slums via the alley, without fear of being spotted. I enjoyed the escapade as much as I did the fruit.

That Sunday I was feeling as gloomy as one could feel short of being suicidal. The optional "informal" brunch was hardly adequate compensation; I ate sparingly, mechanically. Afterwards, as I stole fruit, piling my hat full, I didn't get the usual thrill. No one bothered to question me, no one attempted to follow my flight up the stairs, as had sometimes happened. I was so dejected that I stopped on the fourth flight up and had an apple, gazing back down at the occasional upperclassmen departing by way of the tunnel, which was exclusively for their use. A group soon emerged, laughing like hyenas. I could see them down below, five of them. They had come stumbling and pushing out of the Mess Hall and had stopped to laugh their heads off at some joke.

I dropped my apple core on them, and when it hit, their laughter stopped instantly and they all looked up.

"Who's up there!" one of them roared.

Then another cried, "We see you, Mister! You just stay right where you are!"

That voice! A chill went over me—it was the friendly upperclassman from the Fightin' First. After two hours of hazing, it was a voice I could not easily forget. I knew that even if they saw me, they couldn't recognize me, because I could see them plainly and their faces all looked blandly the same. I dropped a banana on them.

"You stay right there, Mister! We're coming up!"

The stairway inside the tower had an extremely wide central space. I could bombard them accurately if they tried to come up, then make my escape when the fruit was exhausted. I counted four oranges, three apples, and one banana. Down below, their voices were echoing in a tactics conference. I dropped the banana to let them know I was waiting.

"You've had it, Mister! I order you to come down here right now! Are you there, Mister? Show yourself!"

Apparently the slide-rule king had taken command. In reply, I gave them a Tarzan yell. That was the final straw; they were now rushing up the stairs to overtake my position. As they reached the second landing, all in a huddle, I began my fusillade. Judging from their shouts, I must have beaned at least two of them with my apples. But they kept coming, and I had to abandon my position—and my oranges—in order to save myself.

"Stop, Mister!"

"Come back here, beanhead!"

"We know who you are! Halt!"

My would-be captors were wasting their orders on me as I fled—I knew they didn't know who I was. I'd put my coat flaps up over my eyes to make sure of that. To identify me, they'd have to catch up with me, and I knew this terrain like the back of my hand. Avoiding the elevators with their slow doors, and the men's room where they'd look first, I cleverly ducked into an unmarked door that led to an ancient fire exit. I climbed up the musty stairs onto the roof of New Washington Hall, some ten floors above the level of the Plain, and stayed there for an hour, relaxing in a beam of sunshine.

When my nerves had calmed, and the sunshine went away, it was the Gloom Period all over again. From the roof I could see the distant bend in the Hudson River, specked with bobbing masses of ice. The gray, angry river reminded me of a story Chip Hightower once told me about his father, who'd been captured in World War II by the Nazis but had managed to escape. His father had made it as far as the Rhine River, where all he needed to do to be safely back in Allied hands was swim across. He'd staged the escape in midwinter; there, at the Rhine, he had waded knee-deep into the icy water, at which point both his legs cramped against his wishes. He fell in headlong and had to awkwardly crawl back out like the worst kind of amphibian.

This was not an escape to go down in GI annals. Hightower senior had painfully trudged back to the prison camp in his wet clothes, caught pneumonia, gotten frostbite; at the camp his rations were cut in half, and he was placed in solitary confinement. The misadventure seemed relevant when I found I was locked out on the roof, my face and hands feeling the first bite of numbness from the February wind. My only recourse was to scale precariously down a heating unit three floors to the engineering department, where I shocked an officer who was fully engrossed at a drafting table. The descent wasn't so dangerous as it was dramatic—wide landings bordered the windows of each floor—but the officer who let me in the window was beside himself and not at all impressed with my gymnastics.

"What is the meaning of this, Mister?"

"Sir, I was locked on the roof."

"It's not the responsibility of the Engineering Department to rescue dumb asses in distress."

"No, sir—but, sir, I had no choice. I was trapped."

"Like I said, I don't come here on Sunday to be disturbed by people knocking at the window. Fill out this demerit slip for me, Mister." The officer, a young Major, resumed work as I filled out the form. I asked him what violation I should put down.

"Oh . . . *I don't know*—think up something, just so it's

worth about three." I needed to write a violation which wouldn't arouse too much suspicion when I handed it in at the company. I wrote, "Improper Entry to Engineering Department." The Major signed without reading it over, on my confirmation that I would receive a token three demerits for the infraction. Three demerits weren't so bad, really, but in my situation it meant another guard duty on Saturday night.

MEMO 14.

The Corps of Cadets were as unimpeachably pious a group of young men as existed in the civilized world. Though they might err and say, "You goddamned mother-flipper," or inadvertently exclaim, "Jesus Flipping Christ!," such verbal slippage could hardly be considered blasphemous; this was merely the chaff of which the building blocks of character are formed. The true, deeply pious character of the Corps was exhibited every week when the cadets showed up on time for Sunday morning Chapel—long-faced, serious, and rigorously prepared for spiritual betterment.

Although the Academy believed each man should answer fully and on an individual basis to his god, there were nevertheless certain laws pertaining to worship to which all were subject. The first law said you had to be in Full Dress Uniform and in Chapel Formation every Sunday no matter what. Another law said you had to shut your eyes during all prayers and open them after all prayers. You had to sing all songs requested, loudly. And no matter how strongly you might feel the spiritual pull during the sermon, no eye-shutting was permitted—you had to save it till the next prayer. (Catholic and Jewish cadets received greater blessings because they got more "rack time" in their less brilliantly lighted services.) We Plebes learned most of our religious law in small intimate sessions just after regular Chapel, when we were braced and hazed by our guardian angels, the upperclassmen.

Sunday Chapel at the Corps was an official function to unite West Point with the public domain. Our visitors were either dignitaries or specially invited civilians, and it was for their benefit that we had to appear alert in services: "If those civvies can stay awake, so can you guys!" The Big Brass were quite naturally worried (in 1969) about undesirable outsiders barging in on the showcase ceremony, so any guests which cadets wished to bring along were screened, and at times turned back at the Chapel doors for having a "disreputable civilian appearance." Once, two officers jettisoned a beautiful young woman because *her* hair was too long.

Simply stated, on Sundays the Big Brass wanted the Corps of Cadets at its Sunday best, to show them off as the best body of young men America has to offer—good, wholesome, clean-cut, *nice* boys who obeyed God and wanted America free. The Chapel was one which God might have built Himself, a towering hilltop Gothic structure with enormous stained-glass windows and a pipe organ that was reputed to be the largest in the Western Hemisphere. Over one door, a series of irate biblical figures were carved in stone: a plaque explained that these little guys were after the Holy Grail. In this setting, with the Cadet Choir chorusing the virtues, a few three-star Generals taking in the show in the front pew, the pipe organ blasting away, sunlight filtering through the stained glass, the cadet faithful awake and *interested*, one's pulse quickened and one's soul was tendered upward in a grand, heavenly salute. God returned that salute.

The chaplains and officers who spoke at our Sunday services were very hard-nosed about their religious beliefs because they'd all had a truckload of religious experience in war, which was, coincidentally, their favorite subject. It was in *war!* that men needed religion most, we were told. The officers said that soldiers hated war more than anybody else because they had to fight it—but

God helps them—and the chaplains told us that chaplains hated war more than anybody else because it was they who had to tell the bombed-out and battered-up soldiers exactly how God was helping them. This made lots of sense. But the way the chaplains and the officers fondly discussed their wartime experiences made one wonder whether they hated war as much as they claimed to. After all, both the officers and the chaplains were skilled laborers, and how could they talk nasty like that about their skills? With any other job, they would have lost their union cards.

Our chaplains alternated: we had Airborne chaplains who had paratrooped in the Normandy invasion, we had Navy chaplains who had been trapped on the bottom of the ocean in a submarine, we had a Lieutenant Colonel chaplain who'd been in four Hollywood movies and gave 10 percent of his residuals to the church. On some Sundays a chaplain would give a short sermon and then hand over the podium to a guest speaker, some famous-in-certain-circles soldier who had a Christian experience to share. When an officer spoke, a non-chaplain officer, it was generally in the form of "testimony," and these speakers invariably began their remarks with, "I really don't know what to say—" which invariably got them a laugh, for the wrong reason.

Staff Sergeant Guthrie R. Roko was the first enlisted man ever to speak in the West Point Chapel. He had won the 1969 Sergeant of the Year contest, and according to the program, his prizes included the opportunity to shake hands with the President, a free trip to Tahiti, a thousand dollars in cash, and the honor of being the first enlisted man ever to speak in the West Point Chapel. Roko began his remarks with, "I ain't really sure what to say . . ."

Staff Sergeant Roko was about forty-five years old, with a crew cut, tiny eyes, and the twinkling expression of a practical joker. He was on the short side but had huge hands which he was apparently proud of because he kept cracking his knuckles into the microphone. Roko wore a big, gleaming wristwatch; he leaned back and looked at it, stated the time, and said that he'd talk for exactly five minutes and that was it. "If I'm five seconds over five minutes, I'm giving you permission out there to can my a . . . act." He lit up a cigarette, telling us,"They might call me God's gift to Sergeants, but believe me, folks, I'm just a *regular* guy!"

A chaplain appeared and took away the cigarette, and Roko apologized. "There, ya see? I can't get away with nothing. OK." He looked at his watch. "Four minutes and fifteen seconds. Guess I'll have to cut the part about my second wife, heh, heh. *OK.* I grew up in the slums of Pittsburgh, and by the time I was ten I was running with a street gang. By the time I was fifteen I had a police record as long as your arm. I didn't get in the Army by choice. It was either the Army or two years in jail. And believe me, I didn't want either. But from the standpoint of the here and now, I can tell you straight that the United States Army was the best thing that ever happened to me."

Roko gave a quick overview of his career, up to the point where some joker down in Fort Hood, Texas had dropped his name in the hat for the contest. "But once I start something, I finish it," he said. "And look where I am now. West Point." He had that starry-eyed gaze contest winners often have. "And next week I'll be in Tahiti, all because I finish what I start, even though at first it may seem pretty stupid." Sergeant Roko flexed his shoulders, looking back to give an "A-OK" wink to the Cadet Choir behind him. "I don't claim to be smart," the Sarge went on. "You might even say I'm stupid. But in all my stupidness, let me tell you a little story which is the point of my speech here today at West Point. I can't figure it out, but maybe *you* can." *You* was spoken so directly into the microphone that the feedback whistled for ten valuable seconds.

"OK—be that way, ya crock of . . . ya broken clock, heh, heh." The story was about World War II. Roko had been part of the first wave in Italy, had been captured by the Wops (*cough-cough*), the Italian forces, was held prisoner just long enough so he's never had a taste for spaghetti since. He was then liberated behind enemy lines by the shellings, to find himself along with a few other American stragglers, including a chaplain, hiding out in a deserted town waiting for the Allied advance units to break through.

"Me and my buddies was catching forty when the chaplain went off to find some water. This son of a—(*cough-cough*) these cigarettes—this one fellah who was supposed to be keeping guard didn't do such a hot job and sure enough a fascist patrol comes through town and finds us just like sittin' ducks, the . . . I could have strangled that guy. Anyway, we didn't know it, but the chaplain had taken a pistol with him, God bless 'im, and when—"

When the chaplain spied his captured comrades, he had concealed himself in a tactical spot and opened fire on the fascist patrol when the group marched by. Where the chaplain had learned to fire a pistol, Roko didn't know, but one fascist was down and the other two were easy to handle. "Now you tell me why that chaplain took that pistol with him to look for water—I still don't know. But here's the message, if you haven't already figured it out for yourself, and always remember this. A man of God is also a man, and don't ever let anybody tell you different. When he's got nothing better to do, he does God's work. But when he's got a *man's* work to do," Roko said, pausing for effect, "you can bet your lucky dollar he's gonna be in there with the best of 'em."

He concluded humbly, "Thank you, gentlemen, and I think my five minutes are up." A spasm jolted the assemblage as everyone wearing a watch double-checked the Sarge's promptness—and after that, a hearty round of applause went up, initiated by a General who started clapping in the first pew. Staff Sergeant Roko grinned happily, radiantly, clasping his hands high over his head like a champ. This week, West Point . . . next week, Tahiti.

Hadrean Groovey was not only germ-fearing, he was also God-fearing. One Saturday afternoon in Gloom Period, Hadrean paid me a charity visit to show he felt sorry for me and to tell me that worse sins had been committed than making your platoon late for breakfast. Hadrean was all pepped up on the subject because he'd just received an appointment to be an alternate Sunday School teacher. Two Sundays a month he'd get out of Chapel to spread the good word among eight-to-ten-year-olds, the children of enlisted men serving time on the base.

I was sitting alone in my room, brooding about guard duty that night, when Hadrean made his appearance: armed with a thick Bible and wearing a Sharpshooter's medal on his dress gray jacket. Nobody wore a rifle badge unless it was for Expert, but Groovey had undoubtedly worn his Sharpshooter badge home on Christmas to make a big impression and hadn't gotten around to taking it off yet.

Hadrean had picked me out as a pagan and a sinner—he hadn't forgotten my hop-mongering, Buddhism, and overindulgences in sleep—and now he'd decided to come by and save my soul. It was a noble gesture, but had a practical side too. He could get in a little additional practice before he had to face all those eight-year-olds.

After he'd told me what dishes had been served at his family's yuletide table, how the Great Barley High School track team was getting on, and how his sister bought her

165

first brassiere, he got to the point. "Mardis, are you a latent hemophiliac?"

"A wha—?"

"I'll say it again." Hadrean's eyes became keen and critical. "I said, I fear that you might be a latent hemophiliac, Mardis, and I want to help you. I spoke to my high school track coach back home and I was telling him about some of the bozo shit that goes on around here. I mean like back in the other room, how you and Rutledge and Carillo were always—I mean *always* talking about girls. And I mean *licentiousness* about their female parts and mammon glands. Anyway, my coach says that when guys go out of their way to prove how wowie-zowie they are, it can be a sign of latent hemophilia."

"I think I get the message, Groovey boy, but you're a little mixed up, aren't you?"

"Please be patient! You know what I mean. You don't like girls."

I sighed. "Have you heard the one about when you start accusing others of something, it's only because you're afraid of the same thing yourself?"

Hadrean repeated this to himself and frowned. "I wish you'd listen to me, Mardis. I'm trying to help you. As I was saying, the track coach of my old high school said this *could* be a problem, and the minister of my old church agreed with my coach when I spoke to him. The lust for mammon can often lead man astray. Right off I thought of you and that stupid sin magazine, the one with the harlots."

"Oh, yeah. I remember that one." I was irritated with Groovey, but also interested to see how far he was going to pursue his evangelistic mission. "Anyway, Hadrean, that was never my magazine, it belonged to Rutledge. But 'mammon' doesn't mean what you think it does— and neither does 'hemophilia.' So what about Rutledge? Have you already talked to him? And what about Carillo; don't leave him out."

"I thought of you first. I'm not saying it's true." He gritted his teeth and looked down at his Bible. "I just wanted to . . . Hey, you're not mad, are you?"

"Why, of course not. It was really *thoughtful* of you to come by and warn me of the problem."

"So you're not hemo?"

"No. Why, are you?"

Groovey's face went sour. He then whined, "You haven't changed, Mardis. Still a wise guy. And here I came by to try to help you. You're beyond help. You can't even listen to reason."

I apologized for making a joke out of something that was a serious matter. I swallowed hard. "What else did your track coach say, Hadrean?"

"He's not just a track coach, he's an English professor, too. He studied psychology in college."

"What else did he say?"

"Aw, he said what I told you—that when people start yakking about sex all day long and looking at pictures of girls and stuff more than usual, it could be a sign that, uh . . . I forget his exact words. But hemoism, it leads to hemoism."

"*Here?*"

"I'm not accusing anybody of anything. But when I spoke to my old minister and told him what my track coach said, he said that was exactly right. Now I remember. Too much sex talk is just an act to hide latent queerness." He breathed deeply, apparently wishing to drop the subject. "Anyway, I thought you should know."

"Thanks." We were silent, then I said, "Isn't what's his name—Puska—isn't Puska your new roommate?"

"Yeah, why?"

"Have you seen his wrestling magazines? He's got a lot of them."

Hadrean minced his lips. "I haven't read them."

"Well, it's pretty weird! Puska brought 'em up here one night when we were having a bullshit session. I tell you,

167

it's more evil than looking at *Playboy*. Puska showed us some of the pictures and then took off his shirt and tried to imitate. It was pretty weird, Hadrean. He hasn't done that in your room?"

"He's gone all the time. He has wrestling now."

"Well?"

"Well *what!*" Hadrean looked at me mistrustfully. "You don't think Puska is a latent hemo, do you?"

"You said it, not me, Hadrean. But don't worry, I'm not going to tell Puska you suspect him of anything."

Hadrean gritted his teeth again, pondering. Puska was a big lunk, swarthy, spoke in a bass monotone, and memorized batting averages in his spare time. When he wasn't memorizing batting averages, he sat dully at his desk with the latest wrestling magazines, like *Ring Masters* and *Wrestling Roundup*, and picked at fat callouses on his palms which he got from lifting weights.

Puska's favorite saying was, "Go stick a dick in your ear." He huffed this about fifty times a day for any number of reasons; somehow Puska equated his basic human rights with the right to tell someone, "Go—in your ear." If Puska ever got captured by the enemy in a war, the chances were that the first thing he'd tell them even before name, rank, and serial number would be his colorful expression.

PUSKA: Go—in your ear!

COMMANDANT: What does the American swine say?

INTERPRETER: Sir, he says, "Go—in your ear."

COMMANDANT: That's awful.

But that's the kind of stuff Puska was made of, and Hadrean Groovey knew it.

Groovey quit nibbling his cheeks now to ask me why I thought Puska might be a hemophiliac. "I *don't* think he is, Hadrean. The only point I was trying to make was that muscle magazines aren't much different from girlie magazines. They're both evil, through and through. Too much gawking at anything can take you right to tempestuous lust."

"Do you really believe that?"

"So help me God, Hadrean. . . . This is no longer funny, either." I got up from my desk and took some fresh white shoulder belts from a drawer to attach to my cartridge box. For guard duty we had to dress pretty fancy—sort of like George Washington—and I didn't want to get any demerits for soiled belts. I held up two and unfurled them like streamers to see if they were the same length.

Hadrean watched me with pleading eyes, his fair, boyish face strained with wisdom. He had come to feel sorry for me but really hadn't done such a good job of it.

"Is guard duty rough?"

"It's a job," I said.

"I guess you don't get to go to the hops now."

"I'll get over it. They aren't so great anyhow."

"Maybe you can get permission to go with me to my Sunday school class! . . . or maybe that wouldn't be so good. I mean—" I pretended nonchalance as I deftly tucked the white straps into the brass buckles of my cartridge box. "I've been going to the gymnasium," he said. "I'm trying for the Corps Squad cross country team. . . . Listen, how long ago was it that Puska came up here with that muscle magazine? He's normal, anyway. Besides, he's strong, he's not like you—I don't mean—I mean. . . . Awww, what the heck, Puska ain't no hemo! You're just trying to play games with me, Mardis. You're just mad because I came up here and talked about stuff you don't even know about." Hadrean was whining again, talking in short, choppy spurts.

"What'd you say?" I asked. "I wasn't listening—I was pulling this belt tight."

Groovey got to his feet, put his hat on, tucked his Bible under his arm. "I said I don't think you're sincere, Mardis. But at least I've learned one lesson today. I know now not to cast pearls before swine. You and Carillo—especially him, the dirty little spic—he isn't even an American. You'll all harvest what you reap, I guess you know that. Rot in hell for all I care."

"Hey, wait!" I threw my catridge box on the bed. "Don't leave feeling like that. I know you came up here to do me a favor, and I appreciate it, but gee, it's upsetting to learn these new things like you say—latent weirdos and all that."

"Just so long as you heard me," he answered firmly. "I'll leave the rest up to you."

"Oh, I'm keeping my eyes open from now on, all right." I laughed and shook my head in dismay. "Your track coach sounds like a pretty smart fellow, you know that? Where'd he go to school?"

"It was a good school. I forget the name offhand."

"I guess he thought you were in pretty good shape."

"I wasn't in that good of shape," Hadrean said modestly. "Too much turkey and sweet potatos. But sure, he said I'd improved."

"Had a special workout, huh?"

"Yeah, we jogged around the football stadium. In the snow, too. Slipped a couple of times."

"Well, thanks again for dropping by. But I better get my gear ready for guard duty. . . . Oh, Hadrean—your coach reminds me of a soccer coach I had once, a real nice guy, always punching ya in the arm and goosing ya, and running around with a jock strap on like a space mask."

Hadrean was all softened up, had a smile as wide as the Missouri River. He rapped his Bible with his knuckles, beaming, "That's my coach all over again!"

"Yeah." I looked downcast. "But you know what, the poor guy got fired."

"*Awwww,* no. Why?"

"They found out he was a hemophiliac."

I was lying, of course, but Hadrean was too pulverized by the fable to question my sincerity. His face went sour again; he walked away in a kind of silence, mouthing words but not saying anything. I thought Groovey needed a little tragedy in his blood to calm him down, to stop him from trying to divide the company even further. Zeros and heros were bad enough, but hemos?

MEMO 15.

My confinement to quarters, my guard duties, and my reduced status in the company were all deepening shades of gray in my private gloom period. The motif was apathy. Only by saying, "I don't care," was I able to make the leap of faith necessary to sustain a life force. Apathy was the different drummer I marched to. Apathy was that encouraging voice that whispered in my ear, "Why bother?" If the Big Brass had put me under a microscope to check for osmosis, they would have seen a solitary amoeba stumbling through its bleakhouse routine for only one purpose—to find and absorb the life-sustaining globules of apathy. It was Cadet Private J. Protoplasm.

I had discovered a great thrill in looking at my feet when I walked. No one noticed. In the cold, harsh wind, it was difficult to make out the tiny black stripes on the lower coat sleeve which distinguished upperclassmen from Plebes. They thought I was an upperclassman *because* I was looking at my feet. A Firstie approached me one day near Thayer Hall and demanded to know why I was looking at my feet. I told him I felt like looking at my feet. He apologized caustically: "Well, just sew that stripe on your sleeve before the whole year is over." I looked at my feet for two months and that was the worse that happened.

I developed a limp. Not from staring a hole in my feet, but in order to ride the elevators. The elevators were only for officers and for cadets with walking problems. Eight flights of stairs separated me from the Department of E.S. & G.S. (the Engineering Department), and class was at seven thirty in the morning. Going up those crowded stairs that early with a thousand other beanheads was none too pleasant, so I limped—into the elevator with the E.S. & G.S. instructors and the cadet walking wounded. Only I had no bandages, crutches, or cast. One morning a Colonel questioned me during the trip down. "Son, what's the matter with your foot?" "Sir, I have a *limp.* " "Well, don't put too much pressure on it—it could get worse." He courteously held the elevator doors for me as I hobbled past.

I was the birdman of West Point. I took pieces of toast out of the Mess Hall every morning and gave them to the hungry little birdies who lived behind the Slums on the rocky hillside. I put a lot of peanut butter on the toast so the birds could get their vitamins. They loved that peanut butter toast and the birdies loved me for bringing it to them. They ate it up yum yum yum. I gave them as much as they wanted. One little birdie ate so much peanut butter that it couldn't fly any more and had to walk back up the rocky hillside. It never came back again.

So I looked at my feet, and limped, and stole toast for my birdie friends. I had never thought it would come to this. A year before I had been watching Errol Flynn movies and practicing swordmanship with a TV antenna. I'd arrived at West Point expecting to have a valet and a small carriage at my disposal. I had expected to be a Major or a Colonel right away. "You say he's only been in the Army two weeks and he's a Colonel? Well, they must like him." I'd thought I would be shaking hands with the President by now. I had thought I'd meet a treacherous Mata Hari, who would try to sway me to the "other side" with her sultry, feminine mystiques. The secret dagger in my boot. Intercepted plans from the Sultan. Shrapnel in my knee. Lipstick on my crossbelts. But no. Two French cadets came to lunch one day and the table commandant had me translate "French fries." That was it.

There seemed to be no one to talk to. I dropped off to see Rutledge and he said, "Yep." He had his own gloom period to deal with. I spoke to Jerry Drury, who told me I needed to get drunk and contributed to the cause by handing me a half-full half-pint bottle of Seagrams V.O. I drank it in one gulp but it didn't help. I went to see Ted Daisy who had been more or less a comrade back in my nonconformist period. Daisy had lent me his books on Zen. But now Ted Daisy had books on tanks, scale models of tanks, a glossy 8 x 10 of a tank. . . . I stayed mainly in my room confined to quarters, where I heard the glory stories of every Plebe on the floor. They'd find me sitting silently on the radiator and would discuss themselves for half an hour at a time. They came and went and never noticed that I didn't say a word.

The Department of E.S. & G.S., in the fall, had given us "Drafting." The course had been a snoozer. Say a problem had been assigned to connect two parallel lines with a forty-five-degree angle. There were many, many ways to do this. As in most snooze courses, partial credit was given for effort, and you stood a good chance of passing just by putting down three lines, regardless of direction. You could almost pass—and the instructors were very fussy about this—if you properly laid out the paper with your name on one side in neat letters and your instructor's name on the opposite side in very neat letters. If the problem was beyond your ken, the best chance for a good score was to spend your time lettering your name and company and *especially* the instructor's name so neatly that it looked like a professional printing job, then to make several neat, soft pencil lines in the assigned space to show that you had devoted some thought to the problem. A fellow next to me did exactly this on a problem and made a score twice what mine had been. Sure, I might have done the work correctly, but was it really worth it with all my unsightly erasure marks and the hurried, incompetent way I'd lettered the instructor's name? As they said: "Disreputable work is no substitute for clarity."

But our snooze courses had vanished with the football season. The Big Brass felt that if cadets were kept indoors by the bad winter months, then they should have something to keep their minds occupied. In Military Science we had "Tactics"; in foreign languages we had more oral recitation; in English more papers; in math we had logarithm monsters; and in E.S. & G.S. we had COMPUTERS.

The E.S. & G.S. instructors sang a new song. They didn't care how bad your lettering was; their chief concern was that you didn't mix your modes, didn't use Fortran when another computer language was called for. The correct symbolism was required by the computer, not merely by a humble instructor. And this presence of a higher authority made them bark down on us relentlessly. They tended to scream at trifles—neat or messy, it made no difference—which in the eyes of cadets were mere embellishments. We'd just learned that disreputable work was no substitute for clarity, and suddenly it was the other way around. Messy but correct programs would be praised over uncluttered, faulty ones. The cadets didn't like this. They liked the old way of thinking better. Spit-shine it and keep it neat, just so long as it looks spoony. But they were soon conforming to the new order, because it was obvious that Fido was "a tough son of a bitch to put one over on."

My computer "prof" was a TV personality. His name was Schwartzbark, which scarcely fit on his nametag, and his rank was Major, Corps of Engineers. Schwartzbark reminded me of the bored Army psychiatrist who had interviewed me for admission, only with more adrenalin. Major S. was a pencil stacker, but of the most elite variety:

175

his pencils were mark-sense pencils, electromagnetic pencils, not ordinary ones. Schwartzbark was endowed with globular brown eyes, thick regulation eyeglasses, plump rosy cheeks and black hair. For coiffure he had a fuzzy Airborne haircut, or flattop, which was as neat and bristly as a putting green.

On the first day he marched us in, took attendance, rendered a brisk salute to the Section Leader, and positioned himself above us on the classroom dais. For the next five minutes he went through the funniest monologue we'd heard in months; Schwartzbark knocked out one-liners that put us on the verge of hysteria—corny ones, funny ones, dirty ones, and a few offbeat gags which even he didn't seem to grasp. However, once the joke period was over, he began thundering out Fortran truths like a mad dictator. He explained that he, as an instructor, was not a funnyman—he only went through his routine so that *we* could get any giggles out of our system and thereby approach the day's subject matter with a rational sobriety. "You'll find out that computers don't appreciate a sense of humor," he told us.

It is conceivable that Major S. had computer-envy, that he wished he had been born a computer rather than a mere mortal. He spoke of Fido scathingly and even called it a "whore." "I've worked with computers at the Pentagon and Fort Knox which make that thing in Thayer Hall look like a transistor radio," he reminisced with some bitterness, assuming the tone of a man who had lost his fortune. When Major S. referred to his computer pals, he would say he worked "with" the computer, or "the computer and I," to emphasize that teamwork had been involved, that he, Schwartzbark, would never submit to a one-sided love affair.

That cute little computer in Saigon. Ah! The electronic celebrities Schwartzbark had known by their first names, those lovers he had dropped along the wayside! "Now, men, you'll find out that computers are *very* cooperative—*obedient* is the word—and all you have to do for hot potatoes is snap your fingers. But if you make a mistake, the computer will make a mistake, and it's not the computer's fault, it's *your* fault. The computer may not like it—it may spit in your eye—but it will obey. So when you put in a mark-sense card that has 'repeat' when what you really wanted was 'loop,' the computer will repeat. Why? Because it is your *slave*, and the master has spoken. Men, you will also find out in this course that it's the good master who makes the good slave, and never, ever, the other way around."

Major S. had us for slaves three times weekly. His jokes were unquestionably better in the Monday class. Since cadets had no TV, it took us some time to realize that our computer prof wasn't naturally gifted and that he plagiarized the *Laugh-In* comedy show, which was shown on the local network each Sunday night. Apparently Schwartzbark had to improvise his way through the other two classes, and if we didn't laugh, he would become angry, cutting the joke time short and bombarding us with Fortran truths. We quickly learned to laugh at his worst jokes, for survival purposes. On Mondays, when Major S. was brimming, he liked to crack a few in the assembly room so the other computer sections could get a load of his act, and to give himself some practice for the big time—the Pentagon, the Cape, the Elks Club.

One morning Major S. got so carried away with his "original" routines that he went on for half an hour with us. There were some fifteen students in his section—a cozy dinner club atmosphere—and we'd laughed so hard that our eyes watered and our throats were parched. "Well, guess we better get on with today's assignment," he sighed at last, pulling his necktie tight and resting his weight against the lectern. "I guess we really ought to start working, but you've been such a *fine* audience today that I've got *one more* for you!" We applauded. Then

Major S. asked if there were anyone present of Polish ancestry or who might be offended by a Polish joke. Funny he should ask, since Polish jokes were the mainstay of his "original" routines; possibly he was polishing up for the circuit.

"Great! Like they say, where there's one Polack, there's one too many. . . . *Yah, hah, hah, hah.* Now! Now—have any of you ever seen a Polish peeping Tom? . . . NO? Well, here's how they operate." He stepped aside from the lectern and pretended to look down his own pants. We sat in a rocky silence which Major S. couldn't fathom. "A Polish peeping Tom! *Yah, hah, hah, hah.* . . . Don't you get it?"

Schwartzbark's timing wasn't that bad, but the Lieutenant Colonel's timing was perfect. The head of the department had peeked into the section room to drop off a mislaid program at the same instant that Major S. was peeking down his trousers for the punch line. Apparently the Colonel lacked a sense of humor, or was of Polish ancestry; he gravely summoned his comical subordinate out into the assembly room, closing the door. A few minutes later Schwartzbark came back in, embittered. "If you lice had been laughing like you were supposed to, I wouldn't have looked so bad." He never forgave us; the rest of the course was torture. The fickle whim of the public had made a star and then torn him down.

Schwartzbark's most challenging, or *vindictive*, problem assignment was, in the words of our section's stractest computer jock, "A hairy, snotty, gorilla bugger." Major S. had warned us that the problem would "put into use all of what you have learned so far." But if you hadn't learned anything, the problem was a prophecy of disaster.

Owing to my apathetic attitude, I was unperturbed. I could have completed the program in fifteen minutes, but uninclined to show off, I pretended to be hard at work during the three full class sessions he allotted us to work on the problem. I was the only section member who didn't bother to ask Major Schwartzbark for assistance.

"Don't you even have a question?" he asked me, making his rounds through the class.

"No, sir."

He looked at my program, speechless, and crumbled it up in my face. "Start again, Mister. And this time label your variables A, B, and D like the instructions said. Didn't you read the instructions?"

"Yes, sir."

"Then why didn't you label your variables as instructed?"

"Sir, I—"

"Well, read them again! Right now."

Fido was always surrounded by a covey of white-cloaked orderlies, Specialists IV and V. They were computer technicians, Fido's bookies and jockeys, and it was to them, in that white, barren corridor in the basement of Thayer Hall, that we handed our stacks of mark-sense cards for Fido to put to the test. The rule was "Place your bets by 9, get results by 4." If your cards weren't in by 9, you had to come back the next morning to pick up the print-out.

On the morning the problem was due, I made a hasty trip to Thayer Hall to retrieve my print-out, having placed my bets just before the windows had closed the day before. I recognized more than a few cadets from the computer sections who had risen early to do their duties and then "ping" over to Thayer directly after breakfast. They were haggard and happy and had mark-sense pencils stuffed behind their ears. They all looked like they'd just picked a winner.

As class was called to attention at 0735 hours, I felt somewhat ill at ease. Each man had a program before him, and the majority were of a similar thickness, about half an inch, containing roughly ten to fifteen connected

179

print-out sheets. One fellow had a single sheet, and his face was already registering disaster. Major Schwartzbark gave this cadet a curt smile, a farewell toast. My program, however, was the apple of his eye. It was some three inches thick, containing more than fifty sheets. If nothing else, there was plenty of it.

We were given free study time for the period, and Schwartzbark disappeared with his section's stack of programs. He told the Section Leader to make sure everyone studied, but the Section Leader fell asleep—he'd been among the earlybird crew at Thayer. I began writing a letter to my little sister, trying to tell her about the world of apathy in kiddie terms, but I was too apathetic to finish it and fell asleep like everyone else. I think the only person awake in the class was the stractest computer jock, who had begun working on an optional bugger which Schwartzbark had left on the board "for fun."

"A-Tenn-hutt!" The class popped up like a family of jack-in-the-boxes at Schwartzbark's return, ten minutes prior to dismissal. He was cheerful. "Don't worry, Mister Section Leader, I know you were leading the class in a seance. But wish no longer; most of you passed. You're dismissed now, if you choose to go. Except for Cadet Mardis." Major S. closed the door after the class had passed by. He told me to stand up and take it like a man, had me advance in front of the lectern where he'd secured himself in attack position.

"So you don't need any help, eh, Mardis?" he enunciated ghoul-fashion, molding his hands. "*Rot*!!"

"No excuse, sir," I said, to clarify that as soon as possible.

"*Rot!*" he huffed again, his eyes glittering wildly behind his regulation frames. "You are the most apathetic, dull-witted, hound-dog lousy, *incompetent*—" he waved his fingers, searching for the accoutrements. — "the worst student, the most uncompetitive, cowardly, muddle-minded, cockamanie and *disgusting* cadet I've ever had the unfortunate privilege to teach—or even be associated with. Do you know that, Mardis?"

"No comment, sir."

"No comment! No comment! Oh, Holy Jesus, you *better have a comment*! Just look at this—" He spun off the podium with a savage impulse and snatched a satchel off a front desk. He unbolted it furiously, found my program, broke the rubber band with brute strength, and then, at the lectern again, he composed himself. "At least you can stand in *place*," he remarked with a flourish. "No comment—" He held the program above his head and allowed it to unfold over the podium down onto my shoe tops. He immediately reeled it back in and, football style, tossed it across the classroom. The program was longer than the classroom.

Major S. was sputtering disgustedly. He told me that more than half the program was one simple equation, $D=9.4$, and that the computer would still be printing $D=9.4$ if there weren't an automatic shutoff after 750 repeats. He said that I hadn't even looked over the program after it was printed. He said that if he hadn't seen me in class every day, he would guess, just by looking at the program, that I didn't even know what Fortran was. He charged that the idiocy of my program was an insult not only to him but to the department, the standards of the Corps, and my own brain!

"Oh, Mister, Mister," he pleaded. "If you only knew the years, the centuries that mankind has sweated and toiled and *killed* for the sheer purpose of gathering facts and putting together this technology and mathematical genius into what cumulatively gave birth to our first simple computer. That alone was a miracle! That alone took thousands of years of hatred, bloodshed, idea-swapping, stealing secrets, and plain old elbow grease. Just to get to the point of a *simple* computer. And the improvements made since then have been the acts of mentalities as brilliant and innovative as *Pythagoras*!"

181

Major Schwartzbark kicked aside a few feet of my print-out. "And you, you have the audacity, you have the nerve to hand into me a program of some fifty-three sheets that would make a mongoloid idiot look like Einstein! *Rot!*" He walked toward the windows and came back holding the tail end of the sheets. "See this? $3+4=7$, therefore $7=3+4$. You call that intelligence? An earthworm could do that. And that's the final statement of your program—something you could have figured out on your fingers? And you go through fifty-two and a half pages of dick-dribble just to let a multi-million dollar computer verify that $3+4=4+3$? Mister Mardis, you are a disgrace to your classmates. And you are a disgrace to the very spot you're standing on because it is a part of West Point and you are obviously not a part of anything, least of all the Corps of Cadets. My *dog* has more pride than you, Mister Mardis!"

I was wearing a pair of worsted regulation trousers that Carillo had handed down to me for spares. They were too tight for him, and lately had been tight on me due to a new tendency to eat away my troubles. At this very moment, my zipper went *ping!* and then *zip-zip-zip* from the bottom up.

"Wha—what's the meaning of this?" Major S. was dumbfounded.

I glanced down, aware of what had happened, having expected the zipper to bust out sooner or later. Anticipation didn't reduce my embarrassment, though. I chuckled uneasily. "The old Polish peeping Tom, *ta-ha.*"

"Wha-what did you say! Mister, I receive that as a personal affront! Your conduct today has been detestable, unseemly, disgraceful, and now, *insubordinate!*" Fortunately for his health, Major Schwartzbark's circuit breaker went into effect and he shut up. He had talked himself into a frenzy; the veins in his temples had popped out in a brilliant, pulsating blue. He was short of breath. His hands were trembling like the thwarted strangler's. I was unmoved by his abusive language, not because of apathy but because Major S. had stepped out of line by calling me certain names for which he was liable as an officer. I could "dick on him," as it were.

"Just get out," he wheezed. "Get out and take that computer program with you. I've had enough. I'm sick to my stomach. Just get out, and when you come back for the next class, you better be spoony, Mister. You better have a spoony program, and you better have a spoony attitude, Mister. Spoony. Now get out."

I promptly folded the program as Major Schwartzbark padded his brow with a handkerchief; then I left the section room and walked across the assembly room to get my hat and coat. The area was flourishing with early arrivals for the next class, most of whom stood alone, dazed, computer programs under their arms. I hid my busted zipper with the fifty-three pages of Fortran truth, a kind of loincloth which Pythagoras, in all his brilliance, would have never thought possible.

MEMO 16.

America's youthful officer elite were indoctrinated in all things worldly and otherworldly, from the Academy's interpretation of books to the Academy's interpretation of religion, from the Academy's way to escort a date to the Academy's way of swimming the breaststroke. The men of the Corps were so inebriated with their training that on visiting the outside world, they could be right in the middle of it and still be a thousand miles away, like monks forced out of their cells. The consequence of this isolation was either a feeling of inferiority toward civvie life or a bilious contempt, which was the more common reaction. Both reactions sparked a yearning for the gray walls of West Point.

Cadets were instructed to maintain superlative comportment while in civilian circles, and they tried, looking and often behaving like the most aristocratic of Park Avenue doormen. But just cross a cadet and you'd be asking for a haze, regardless of your rank as a civilian.

On my one autumn field trip to New York City, with the Archeological Club, we were given three free hours to roam around the city. I took another Plebe to an East Side pub for an unauthorized drink. He was too "stract," however, to break regulations, so he ordered a cheeseburger and a large glass of milk. The waiters, it seemed, were giggling because the Plebe was sitting in his chair as if nailed to it. The Plebe must have noticed because he immediately made a foul remark.

"The lice in this shitpail aren't too spoony, are they?"

"Relax," I'd said, "have a drink or something."

"I drink milk," he told me stiffly. The Plebe was from a company in the Second Regiment, and I'd only met him on two occasions, the two one-hour sessions that had been called by the Archeological Club to prepare its members for the upcoming field trip. To go on the field trip, you had to attend both sessions. To be a member of the club, all you had to do was sign a sheet and attend one session. After the field trip, the Archeological Club would have extremely few participants in its meetings, because most cadets, like myself, had joined for the privilege of taking the club's one annual field trip. It was the same principle as sending away for your free mail-order trial volume and then never buying the rest of the set.

"You're not so spoony yourself," the Plebe told me as he waited for his cheeseburger. "I'll bet you joined the club so you could come down here and wet your gizzard with liquor."

"That's not true," I said. "I like archeology."

"We'll see if you show next week, Mister."

Some drinking partner! The waiter brought over the cheeseburger about then, but he forgot the milk and had to go back for it. The Plebe wasn't too happy and said the waiter looked like a "second-hand scumbag" to him. The Plebe poured ketchup on his burger and told me he wasn't taking one bite until his milk got there. When it got there, it was a small milk and had a parsley leaf in it.

"*Hey, Mister!*" roared the Plebe. (He could act like an upperclassman in New York and no one would be the wiser.) The waiter halted in his steps and turned around. Customers at neighboring tables now took critical notice of us; I could read their lips: "Oh, they must be from—" The Plebe certainly sensed his audience. "*Oh, Mister,*" he drawled, puffing up his chest. "This milk isn't spoony! This burger isn't spoony! What are you going to do about it, huh Mister? Check out that vegetation in the cow juice, Mister! You call that spoony? You take this away and get me what I ordered or I'll talk to your superior, get it, Mister?"

The waiter cooperated, to keep peace in the crowded club. I had another drink while the Plebe waited, sullen-faced, his eyes jaundiced. Finally he spoke to me. "Gettin' liquored up, are ya? You think that's a good example for these civilians—or do you even care about the image of the Corps?"

"What do you think Officers Clubs are for?"

"I doubt you'll ever be in one," he grunted.

The waiter returned with the cheeseburger, well charred, and a highball glass full of milk. The Plebe muttered to himself as he put fresh ketchup on the burger, "Whadda ya expect from these beanhead civilians, *mumble mumble*." He then took a mighty chomp of his burger, chewing it savagely, his eyes darting around for any well-wishers. He washed down the first bite of burger with a healthy gulp of milk—which came spilling back out of his mouth as soon as he turned up the glass. "Jesus Flipping Christ!" The Plebe fished two fingers down the highball glass and pulled out an iced-tea spoon.

"Hey, *Mister*! Mister!" The Plebe was outraged by a spoon in his milk. He wiped his chin brusquely. "What's with the hardware in the cow juice, huh, Mister? You think you're cute or something?"

The waiter, who really wanted to please, held up his hands helplessly. "Sir, you demanded a spoon in your milk and I gave you one."

"Spoon! Now what would I use a spoon for in my milk?"

"That's what you said, sir."

"I said *spoony*, you beanhead. Don't you know the difference?"

"Sir, we have knives, forks, spoons, salad forks, butter

knives, soup spoons, tea spoons. We have steak knives. . . ."

The Plebe looked to me for support and I turned the other way. He told the waiter to go away, saying, "*Post!*" When the waiter didn't understand that, the frustrated leader stood up and began pointing at the burger and the milk, at spots on the tablecloth, and then pointing at the waiter's haircut and shoe shine. He told the waiter, "Stand at attention when I talk to you!" and it was then I decided to post to the latrine—that is, I conveniently slipped away to the men's room.

The Plebe was gone when I returned, having abandoned his meal and only having paid half his check. The waiter was angry, but I gave him a big tip and he softened up. He asked me, for the sake of politeness, whether the other cadet was "intoxicated." I started to say no, but remembering the image of the Corps, I answered in a loud, clear voice so all could hear, "Yes! The poor fellow was liquored out of his mind!" I couldn't leave these civilians with the impression that a cadet would act like that normally.

The Big Brass provided us with examples of civilian integrity by carefully selecting the staffs of the Academy services. Fido and his prankster research friends had probably done the selecting of these "representative" civilians: The female librarians were butterballs, and the male librarians were so tiny they got a hernia just lifting Webster's Unabridged Dictionary. The Mess Hall waiters had been hired when they got off the ship and could speak no more than ten words of the new tongue. The barbers sang drunken melodies to themselves, and the janitors of the Corps were lovingly referred to as the Werewolf, the Blob, Cyclops, and in our division, the club-footed *Igor.* The representative civilians loved the men of the Corps equally well. The laundry men thoughtfully starched our socks and underwear, the tailors fitted our collars to a strangle hold, the waiters conscientiously covered our food with their hands when they sneezed, and faithful Igor waxed the stairs at least twice a month. The barbers would offer to give you a special regulation haircut—"Like the Beatle, no?"—which turned out to resemble not the mop top, but a carrot too. "Well, *almost* the same, heh heh."

Killer Curly Taylor was one of those open-minded cadets who did not hate civilians so much; he simply liked cadets and Army people better. Killer was a water polo champ who had led the Army squad to the top for several seasons, sending many a civilian foe to the briny bottom with a quick kick in the flipper. Killer was just as fearsome on dry land. On two occasions some peacenik women had staged brief demonstrations on Thayer Road, and both times Killer Curly had demoralized the demonstrators by eating all their flowers.

Killer walked with a paddling motion, and the expression on his kindly, dumb face was like an underwater photograph: mouth agape, eyes slitted, brow drooping. On a Friday morning in early March, Killer Curly was sitting as table commandant when an announcement was made that the entire Corps was "ordered" to attend the Army basketball game that night. The Army team had made it into some kind of playoff, and the Corps was getting a surprise trip to Madison Square Garden to see the game. A few thousand extra boosters wouldn't hurt our chances for victory.

The Mess Hall greeted the news with massive cheering, stomping, shouting, flying ice cubes, and a few lines of "On Brave Old Army Team." Killer had the Plebes at his table stand up on their chairs and give the hat signals for V-I-C-T-O-R-Y. I was only on my C- when I got beaned on the forehead by a low-flying ice cube and fell off my chair. When the confusion was finally over, Killer told us "good job," and then he said "bad job." One of the Plebes, in performing his V-I-C-T-O-R-Y, had thrown up his hat, which had landed in Killer's plate.

"That's *animal*," Killer said. "Really animal." He knew who the culprit was since the name was in the hat, but he said all four Plebes were to blame. He didn't say why, he just said, "All you guys are gonna pay. You wanta be animals? OK. Be animals." He made us pass our utensils to the waiter's table and eat the remainder of our breakfasts with no hands. The other upperclassmen were too excited about getting off the base that night to assist in the haze; they left, and Killer stayed behind to babysit us until Battalions Rise.

The night before, the water polo champion had used the same haze at supper, making us eat dessert without utensils or hands. Killer and the upperclassmen had a big laugh that night as we Plebes slurped up our peach melba in the manner of cats and dogs. (We didn't mind so much, since we got to take bigger bites.) But this morning Killer Curly saw little humor in the haze. The upcoming basketball trip to the "outside" had set him thinking about the civilians.

"All right, you guys. Police your faces and look up here." His elbows were on the table, and he seemed slightly stunned. "When you Plebes get where I am, you're gonna see things different, you know. You're gonna see that some of this diddly-shit stuff like *right now* is actually a test. A *test* of character. I have personally achieved a lot of fame in water polo because I know how to react in a crisis. And knowing how to react in a crisis is the difference between winning and not winning. And it's also the difference between your professional soldier and your stupid contemporary civilian."

Killer paddled his hands modestly. "You'll learn all this before you get out of here." He told us to take a sip of our coffee or juice if we wanted to—but no hands. "Now this's the point. Just this. You put a civilian in the same crisis situation, even this diddly-shit—why, he'd still be sittin' there! A *civvie* would still be trying to figure out how to keep that egg yolk from dripping down his shirt or how to keep it from going up his nose! But *you* guys— you guys didn't even have to think. You just did it! *Bang bang bang*! And that's the difference between you and your contemporary civilian. You guys are trained to react. And a civilian," Killer added wryly, "is trained to be a civilian."

Around six that evening the Corps was loaded into a caravan of buses stretching half a mile around the Parade Plain. The looming bluffs of the Hudson and the hills surrounding the point were a blue gray in the winter dusk. Shortly past seven, the long line of buses was crossing the steel trestles of the George Washington Bridge toward the brightly speckled skyline of Manhattan Island. At a quarter till eight, the long line of buses was still crawling at a fitful snail's pace through the red lights of Manhattan. Three thousand cheerleaders were going to be late for the game. Radio contact was maintained between the buses, and when the first bus reached Madison Square Garden, relay signals were sent back for all busses to pull over and let the cadets out. The cadets were going to "run" the rest of the way in order to be on time.

The whole Corps might have been prompt if the radio commanders hadn't been so fussy about making the busses stay in a uniform military convoy. Each time the first bus hit a stop light, the other seventy-odd buses ground to a halt, with variations. So when the front-runners carrying the First Regiment arrived at Madison Square Garden, way at the back of the line the Fifth Regiment was still in the Theatre District. We disembarked and were told to "follow the leader," single file.

The Long Gray Line was running through the dark

streets of New York City to be on time for the game. They should have implemented this procedure at the George Washington Bridge, because now the traffic was paying due respect—cars and trucks and cabs pulled over to the side of the road to let the Corps go by. They probably thought it was an invasion. The Corps was running, one behind the other, in the far right traffic lane, under the street lamps, alongside the stalled convoy of busses, ignoring traffic signals, splashing through icy puddles.

The cross traffic eventually lost its respect and barged right ahead in flanking movements which severed the Long Gray Line into block-long pieces. As with the convoy, if one party hit a snag, all those following had to halt as well. One resourceful leader, figuring to outflank the cross traffic and double back, made a right turn. He led a hundred men through a fierce campaign in a pit of living hell; he'd accidentally turned off into the red light district.

Golf-5 arrived at Madison Square Garden around five minutes after eight. There was no formation or roll call; cadets were unrecognizably intertwined in a gray mass converging on the Garden entry. Since we were the last of the lot, civilian fans who'd backed off to let the soldiers pass were now pressing forward at the rear of the mob, impatient. I retreated from this onslaught to an out-of-the-way bench. One of my shoes had fallen off en route, and since we'd had to keep running, I held it in my hand.

I wrung the water from my sock, waiting for the crowd to diminish, and was tying my shoe lace when a businessman sat down next to me on the bench. He wore a tailored trench coat, a black hat, and had a briefcase, which he set in his lap. He gave an exasperated sigh, his breath causing an illuminated spear of fog in the cold air. "I'm for Duquesne," he told me.

"I'm a cadet."

"I know you're a cadet and I know you're for Army. I

know you want Army to win. But I flew all the way from Chicago this afternoon to see my son play and I can't even get a ticket."

"Who's Duquesne playing?"

"They're playing Army. Just look at your ticket."

"Right. I thought we were playing Louisville, but that was last week." I began looking for my ticket, in my coat pockets, in the loop in my suspenders, then I thought I remembered putting it in my sock. I slapped my head. It must have fallen out of my sock in the run. I said to the businessman, "Looks like neither of us gets to see the game. I lost my ticket."

"Try looking in the band of your hat."

"Well, there it is."

"I'll give you ten dollars for that ticket, son. I don't care if it is in the Army cheering section. Ten dollars. Twenty dollars. Name your price." He took out his billfold and put twenty dollars on the bench between us. "I didn't fly here from Chicago to sit out in the cold."

"But I have to go. I'm under orders."

"If it wasn't for me you wouldn't have a ticket. I found that ticket for you, didn't I? Orders or not, you can't go in without a ticket, isn't that right?" He pointed to two cadets furtively hailing a cab. "Look at them. They're under orders too. Orders my ass. Go out and have yourself a good time, son. This can buy you any woman in town." He laid a crisp fifty-dollar bill on top of the twenty.

I smiled, and the businessman smiled back, his eyes confident and shining in the crisp outdoor lighting of the Garden entrance. "You'd have a lot of stories to tell the guys back at the company, wouldn't you? So you go out, blow the dough, and get back here by ten thirty. The buses take you back to the Point and nobody's the wiser. If somebody says they didn't see you, you say the ushers seated you in a special section."

192

"But I can't lie."

"So you lose the ticket, like I said. It falls out of your sock, like you said, you look for it, can't find it, try to get in, the usher won't let you, so you have to go out and kill time."

"Or maybe if you *stole* it from me. No, that wouldn't—"

The businessman shot a finger in my face, his eyes narrowing. "Now listen here son. I paid a hundred and seventy-five thousand dollars in taxes last year. And another fifty thousand in property taxes. I *own* you! I paid for your bus trip down here and I pay for the lean meat they put on your table in the Mess Hall. I'm the guy who buys bullets for your gun and I'm the guy who tells your commanding officer where to aim that gun. It's the business community and the bankers of this country who tell you where to point those pop guns, buddy boy, so don't play fresh with me because I'm into you a lot deeper than you'll ever know. You try holding a reception up there for the *taxpayers* of this country and you'll see who steps out front and center on that big red carpet. And just to lay it straight and easy, let me drop a name on you, soldier boy. A very close friend of mine." He flounced his chin at me. "Two stars and he's one notch down from Westmoreland. I had dinner with him last week in Washington."

"A two-star General?"

"Name him, boy. Let's see how much you cadets really know about the Army."

"Is he on Westmoreland's staff?"

"Gettin' close, boy, gettin' close."

"Let's see . . . if he's not on the General's staff but he *is* a General, then, no, that doesn't. . . . *Hey!*"

The businessman had snatched the ticket out of my hat band and was dashing for the Garden entrance, his legs making a rapid, frenzied movement in the tails of his trench coat and his briefcase oddly motionless in one stiff arm. I leaped up, raced a few steps, and then almost fell as I spun around to go back for the money. He was a pretty smart businessman.

The game might have been a sellout, but I wasn't. The ticket was stolen and my honor was in the clear. To make the transaction perfectly "legal," I wandered over to the gate and told the usher my predicament. He said too bad and refused to let me in. "Well, guess I'll just have to kill time till the game's over, won't I?" I asked him. "Frankly," he said, "I don't give a damn what you do."

I grabbed a cab and was back in the Theater District in no time flat. When the Corps was running through the area, I'd noticed the billboards and glittering marquee for the musical *Hair.* I'd also seen the lights of *1776*, the more patriotic choice, but the temptations of civilian disreputability were too powerful. I didn't want to see Alexander Hamilton sing and dance; I wanted to see wild hippie maidens flinging off their clothes in reckless abandon.

I paid for a front row seat, just making the curtain, and was spellbound for the entire first act, at moments becoming so excited I felt dizzy. After three months of confinement to quarters and unmitigated boredom, I was emotionally unprepared to encounter such phenomena. The hippies were singing and dancing and smiling and jumping around and generally comporting themselves with a frivolous demeanor. There was not so much wanton abandonment as I'd anticipated—no one landed in my lap—but I had to admit that this was far more entertaining than any West Point hop!

Understandably, I developed warm-blooded sympathies for the attractive female hippies, and didn't like it one bit when they teamed up with the long-haired pinko-fairies in the leather jock straps to do those intimate numbers. I didn't like it either when the whole cast made fun of the soldier boy, but I could rationalize their rejection of the soldier boy because he made the pinko fairies in the leather jockstraps look like odd ducks indeed.

During intermission, I went to the rest room and threw up. There was too much going on in my mind at once and I felt blurry. My ear drums were pulsating from the loud music on the front row and my heart was palpitating from the romantic proximity of the lovely actresses on stage. I was still angry about their treatment of the soldier, too. I felt like getting up there and giving one of those wise guys the old one-two. Suddenly I felt that I'd made a mistake by coming here, and I felt thankful that the Big Brass kept us protected from these civilians.

The frivolous, lousy civvies. The lousy, disreputable hippies. I'd like to see them in bayonet training. I walked out of the theater lobby, kicking a wastebin on the sidewalk, talking to myself, cursing at pedestrians who bumped by. At an intersection I paused to see which way led to Madison Square Garden. I spotted a bar. Maybe I'd go in and have a gulp of Seagrams V.O. That's what Drury would have done. The bar was on a corner. I put my face to the window and saw two soldiers inside. I saw the stripes on their pants and their regulation shoes. Now this was luck. I'd go in, shoot the scuttlebutt for a while, buy the fellows a drink, and off to the Corps.

I couldn't see the door so I walked around the corner to the other side. The sidewalk was noisy and crowded; I saw what looked like a back door and made a dive. Inside was a narrow carpeted hall which led to a small waiting room. Must be a private club, I thought. I rang a bell that said "Ring" and a heavy-set, middle-aged lady in a shawl appeared through a curtain at one side of the waiting room. She held a candle.

"Is this the club?" I asked her.

She held the candle up to my face. There was a dot of red wax on the lady's forehead and her eyes were dark and mysterious. Maybe she was the owner's wife. Maybe they were Hungarian immigrants. She swept the shawl back on her shoulder, exposing a long braid of black hair.

"The club—" I said. "I tried to find the door but I guess this is the private entrance. I saw a couple of soldiers and figured I'd talk to them. Does it cost money to get in?"

"You're in the right place," she answered in a macabre voice. "How much money do you have?"

"Enough, I suppose." I showed her several ten-dollar bills and she took one. "Well, *wait* a minute. Is that the cover charge?"

The woman could tell that I hadn't been in very many bars in my life; she nodded severely, frowning. "Sit," she said. "I get the cards."

She went back through the curtain again. I'd started to sit down in the leather easy chair but I was too nervous, so I paced. This was quite a nice club, with the private entrance and membership cards and all that—maybe it even catered to soldiers. But I didn't have time. I just wanted a drink. The curtain rustled and the lady waddled out, hands on hips. "All right. I read mind. We no bother with cards." She took my hand in hers. "We get down to business."

"What kind of business? What is this?" I wrenched my hand away. "This ain't no bar!"

"You smart boy," she said.

"Gimme my money back!"

"You want fortune, no? Truth?"

"I just want a drink."

"I know all about you. You cadet. I know girl friend. *Dolores.* Hippie. I see *much*! You walking paranoia trip, *eh*?"

She gave me a shove and I fell back in the leather chair, mesmerized. The lady tightened her shawl and lit another candle. She told me it was a new candle and that if I wanted to find out more I had to give her twenty dollars for the "Madonna."

"Isn't that a little expensive?"

"Not for the Madonna."

I gave her twenty dollars. "Now how did you find out about Dolores?"

"I read mind." It was true, the gypsy could read my mind, and though she could tell me what only I knew, she couldn't tell me what I didn't know, which was what I wanted to know. She went on for about five minutes about Dolores and my Christmas vacation. "Look, gypsy, skip the part about the station wagon and tell me what happened after I took Dolores to the hamburger stand. Hey, this isn't funny! Tell me what happened when Dolores went with that other guy. Did she tell him about me, huh? Well, did she? Anything at all?"

The gypsy set her fingers on her temples in deep concentration, and composing her face, she then told me a very flattering story. Dolores loved me and had always and would always love me until the sun no longer shines, the gypsy said, and the only reason Dolores wasn't writing me letters or sending telegrams and other tokens of her great love such as a lock of hair or a set of cuff links was that Dolores loved me *too much.* "Some people are funny like that," the gypsy said wisely.

The story sounded fine with me, and I wasn't going to insult the fortuneteller by putting her on her honor. I liked the story, and I felt much better now. Then I asked what time it was, and in spite of her extrasensory powers, the gypsy had to walk through the curtain to look at the clock.

The game was just breaking up at Madison Square Garden; cadets were filtering out of the exits, and our buses were waiting in a long line down the avenue. After learning that Army had lost by twenty points, I clustered with other curious cadets around the raucous megaphones of an anti-war demonstration. A crescent of hundreds of cadets had gathered to watch. Most of the demonstrators were women; they shouted slogans, telling us to lay down our arms and bury the dead; they were throwing out flowers and literature and shooting at us with toy machine guns.

The cadets were amused and shouted back at the peaceniks. They took the flowers and put them in the bands of their hats. There was a space of some twenty feet between the cadets and the protestors, and all at once a group of figures came paddling through it. I recognized Killer Curly Taylor and what seemed to be the water polo team. You could tell by the way they walked. Killer's force advanced upon the women radicals, busting up toy guns and scattering their propaganda literature. In a gesture of peace, one of the women made a gift to Killer Curly of a beautiful leafy red budding plant. Killer held it up victoriously toward the cadets, and then he began devouring it like a stem of grapes, plucking the buds with his teeth. But the civvies were no longer so naïve as Killer thought. He'd just eaten a chili pepper plant.

MEMO 17.

The Gloom Period was over. The sky above West Point became a vibrant, cloudless blue, and the Hudson River, free of ice, shimmered radiantly in the warmth of the sun. The grounds sparkled with the melted snow and the first green flush of spring, and on the distant hills dogwoods stood out brightly with early blossoms. The men of the Corps shed their long overcoats for short jackets, put away their overshoes, turned off radiators, and took their time when they walked to class. The chain of command rotated for the third and last time, bringing new cadet leaders and new room assignments. For my part, I had served out my punishment tours and was free to enjoy the nice weather with my privileges restored.

Company G-5 had succeeded in coming in last place in the autumn cadet company competition, and last in the Corps because we had dragged the Fifth Regiment down with us. We'd had one default (Wook's) in the parade season, which wasn't too embarrassing, because other companies had received parade defaults when their men were quarantined with whooping cough. But the autumn had ended with multiple tragedy. We'd had three quick defaults in intramural athletics when the G-5 Athletic Sergeant sent off our athletic uniforms to the laundry on the wrong day. We got another default in an Inspection in Ranks when twenty-seven men couldn't remember their rifle serial numbers. Even then we'd had a whisper of a chance to be something else than last, but in the final

Regimental Inspection Colonel Porterhouse had found a dead pigeon in our company orderly room.

But hope springs eternal. At the onset of the spring competition Major Cutler called his men together in the basement and said, "Men, I have as much confidence in you right now as I ever have! I know we can be first—and it *is* possible." He told us that if B-5, the company which had finished first in the fall, came in *last* in the spring, and if *we*, the company who had finished last, came in first in the spring, and if we had a better parade performance rating than B-5's fall score, then we could actually finish *first* for the year, in the Fifth Regiment anyway, which was good enough for him. It sounded like a probability table.

But in the first Regimental Inspection of the spring competition, Colonel Porterhouse found *another* dead pigeon in the orderly room. That put an end to the probability table right there. Cutler was so furious he put the entire company on their honor to confess or come forward with information leading to the guilty party, but no one came forward and no one confessed to the pigeon caper. Major Cutler jerked the entire company's privileges for the weekend, saying: "On Monday morning I'll be expecting a call—from *someone.*" But no one called him.

Cutler jerked First Class privileges for the next two weekends and left for the Pentagon in a state of disgust. By now, the first week in April, Cutler was more worried about his own glorious future than G-5's, and he began traveling to Washington for top-level hobnobbing. His two-year stint as a Tactical Officer was coming to a close, and if it was any comfort to him, he had done no worse than his predecessors with the men of Golf-5: double zero was par for the course.

My new roommates were Jerry Drury and Ted Daisy, which meant the Big Brass had decoded me as needing the warmth of human friendship. Ted Daisy was a thin, hypertensive fellow with slightly manic eyes and a quick laugh. We'd once been friendly, and I made an effort to renew the terms of our friendship by participating in his new interest—tanks, or "armor," in military talk. I read a book he recommended on "armor field strategy" so that I could listen intelligently to his ideas on how we could defend America with tanks should this country ever be invaded. "We'd set up our command base in good old Omaha, Nebraska," he told me, "and from there, a wedge deployment with aerial cover would be a cinch."

"But what if they landed in California and set up missile bases in the Rocky Mountains?"

"A *very good* question, Mardis. I'd have an auxiliary base in Portland, Oregon, with minimum attack force and a mobile ballistic backup unit. I send this force down the coast and start my men rolling west from Omaha. The old squeeze play, you see, and when I got finished with the strike object, I hate to say it, but there wouldn't be too much left of the Rocky Mountains as we know them. Now, let's imagine that the enemy sets the invasion point in northwestern Canada and deploys advance armor units through the wide-open spaces of Manitoba and Saskatoon. Good old Omaha, Nebraska, is once again the *ideal* place to be."

I asked Ted if he'd ever been to Omaha, and he said, "No, I'm from Pittsburgh, Pennsylvania. Lousiest tank terrain you've ever seen."

My fortunes seemed to be on the increase; to my surprise, I received two letters from two girls, sisters, whom I had met back in the football season. Cadets were never ordered to attend football games because it would have been an insult to the Corps to even consider that we had to be told to go. I only attended one game, however, and even missed the Army-Navy game because I didn't like to stand up the whole game in the time-honored tradition of the ever-ready "thirteenth man." I'd stood up through the first game and that was enough.

Technically, I had been present at another game as an exterior stadium guard. The Guard Commander for the game had warned me and all the other guards that if we abandoned our posts and tried to get in to see the game, it would be a very serious offense, even though he half expected us to try. After the game, the Guard Commander had personally congratulated me for a job well done; he'd spot-checked all the guards throughout the game, and I was the only one who hadn't made an attempt to sneak a peek at the gridiron action. "Or if you *did*, Mister, you were pretty smart about it," he laughed.

My duty had been to keep pedestrian traffic moving through a narrow side gate before and after the game and, during the game, to *protect* that side gate. I wore white gloves and a single white crossbelt and had a special "stadium guard" shield on my hat. I guess I looked fairly impressive. The two sisters, Becky and Belinda Harris, from Boston, had been very much taken by my manner of handling the crowd. They had come over to me after the game and asked if I would escort them around the base that afternoon. They said they'd pay me. I said I'd be delighted to escort them but the tour was going to be "compliments of the Academy." I remember telling them, "Ladies, *please*. It will be an *honor.*"

That afternoon I strolled Becky and Belinda Harris around the grounds, pointing out objects of interest. Grant Hall, the Mess Hall, Cullum Hall, Thayer Hall, Lusk Reservoir, Trophy Point, and the West Point Chapel. They asked me if the Chapel was a landmark and I said it was a great landmark. And then on to the Parade Plain, the Slums of the Corps, the gymnasium, the P.X., and the Hudson River. They asked me if the river was deep, and I said it was very deep. Since they'd admired my comportment as a stadium guard, I didn't want to ruin my act by being overly personal. But the Harris sisters were slightly giddy, this being their first trip to the Point, and they told me all about themselves.

The Harris sisters were nine and a half months apart in age, which, as they put it, made them "two peas in a pod." They had both graduated from the same schools, and were now employed by the same law firm in Greater Boston, Smith & Rung, as paralegal assistants. Belinda worked for J. Thornton Smith, and Becky worked for L. Winston Rung. The Harris sisters were not only sisters, they were best friends. Belinda had once been engaged but had broken it off because Becky didn't like the fiancé. They told me their private joke to this effect, "We'd like to date Siamese twins, but you can't ever tell when they're going to two-time you." They both took down my address at the end of the afternoon and said they would write.

So the Harris sisters had kept their word. One letter was in lavendar ink on tangerine-colored stationary; the other letter was written on a lined, legal-sized yellow sheet and mailed in a Smith & Rung envelope. It didn't matter which one was from which because both letters said the same thing: the Harrises were planning their return to West Point and wished to be escorted. But I preferred the tangerine and lavendar letter.

The Smith & Rung letter sounded too much like a legal statement. I handed it to Jerry Drury and told him he could have a date if he wanted on the coming Saturday. We'd just finished "spring cleaning" the room with aerosol bombs of spray wax, and Drury was surveying the job by flicking the lights off and on. "It shines all right," he said. That decided, he rashly read the legal letter, in no more than five seconds, and looked over at me. "Who's the other one from?"

"They're sisters."

Drury was immediately mistrustful. "Why'd you give me this one, then? Is the other one your girlfriend?" I explained a bit about the Harris sisters, how they did everything together. "Then gimme that orange letter, too, Mardis. If you want me to be in on this, I've got to have a fair choice."

I refused. "It's fair that I'm getting you a date in the first place."

"Yeah, with the dumpling, I'm sure." I told Drury more about the Harrises, that they even looked alike, but he wouldn't believe that I wasn't out to get the better of him. "So tell me this. What happens if you don't come up with a date for this Becky one? They don't show at all, I bet. Then you come up with zilch, right?"

"No, you're wrong. I get two dates."

Drury, who was also in the Advanced English Department, was convinced that man was an aggressive and predatory creature who didn't give his roommate a free date unless there was a catch. Somehow he convinced me to show him the tangerine letter. It began, "Dear Cadet Jaime," instead of "Dear Cadet Mardis," and said, "your white gloves looked like funsy puffs of whipped cream," whereas the legal letter said, "you were strikingly dispossessed in your uniform." Drury put the letters side by side on his desk to scrutinize any hidden meanings; he scratched the top of his ear, reading with an intelligent, analytical look. "This Becky one sounds more educated than the Belinda, and besides, Belinda seems to like you more. But I still say we flip."

We flipped for Belinda's hand and Drury lost. He said it was two out of three so we flipped again and I still won. Drury remained uncomfortable about the setup. "How can I even be certain these are real people, Mardis? How do I know you didn't go down to the cadet store and buy some goofy stationery and write these yourself, just to play a joke on me?" I told him to take a look at the postmarks, and he was *still* suspicious.

"Here's what. Here's how it must be. I agree to go on one condition. If my date doesn't turn out as sharp as yours—or even if I decide I like your date better—then we switch dates, no questions asked. Deal?"

"Now how can I agree to that?"

"Deal or no deal, Mardis? You wouldn't be asking if you didn't want somebody along, and you know it."

Ted Daisy came in the room with a package and I suggested that Daisy wouldn't be so choosy.

"You want a date with a paralegal assistant, Ted?"

"A what?"

"You want a date?"

"Sure. I'm not choosy."

"Then you're sure?"

"Well, as long as she's not built like a tank, har har."

"Wait a minute!" Drury stormed. "What are you, an Indian giver, Mardis!" That sealed the dating arrangement.

Daisy wasn't bothered by his loss. He pulled a box of cigars from the package he carried and then a scale model of a German tank: gifts from home. These days, Daisy liked to puff on a cigar while he constructed models of tanks on the weekends. Unfortunately he had to store his creations in the basement, since we had only one optional display object—his being a prized photograph of a Sherman firing into the night with a great orange flame.

Daisy remarked, "No need to apologize, Mardis. I have my little tankie here to keep me company this Saturday."

On Saturday, Drury and I sat over an optional lunch (in which Plebes were entitled to "fallout") and leisurely sipped our coffee while the minutes ticked away to our rendezvous time with the Harris sisters. I'd telephoned them at a specified hour during the week to confirm. Drury and I were discussing apathy, and how he'd won his own battle with it.

Drury was a dapper cadet; he had dusty hair, a sardonic smile, and liked to talk with his hands. He was three years older than I and had attended a city college in Chicago for a year before applying to the Point. "When I was in college, I was just like you were all winter, Mardis," he said. "I didn't care about anything. The only way I got through my courses was by name-dropping in class, and let me tell you, with my grades I was damn lucky to get in here. It's really tough to get a good score in math or physics just by dropping names." He told me his girlfriend had been pressuring for marriage, and had gone so far as to show him the silver patterns she had in mind for possible bridal gifts. Jerry said that if it weren't for those silver patterns, he might not be a cadet today.

"That thing scared me shitless, all right. It all of the sudden dawned on me what a rotten mess I'd gotten myself in for. West Point looked like the only noble way out, see—because that way, nobody's feelings would get hurt, because everybody knows cadets can't get married. I thought it was pretty clever. I was gonna be drafted sooner or later, so I said to myself, why not go here and get a free education out of it. And sure enough, as soon as I got accepted—guess what? She broke the engagement and married somebody else. She just wanted to get married, that was it, so I was off the hook all the way. But I said to myself, why not go ahead and go through with it, see. I was just wasting my life at some rotten little college, I had no ambition, and I still don't have any ambition. But in the Army you're better off that way—that's the real clever part!"

Jerry poured us more coffee and happily lit a cigarette, a privilege which Plebes could now "get away with" at an optional meal. "Look at it this way. I have my bills paid, insurance, free rent, free food—the works. I get an education, spend a few years pushing pencils in the Army, then get out and get myself a soft job somewhere. I tell you, going to this place was the most sensible thing I ever did in my life, Mardis—if you could have only seen what a mess I was in college. I weighed about fifty more pounds, shaved once a week, and the dishes were always dirty in my apartment. Christ, I hated those dishes! But now— waiters, you dig? And I tell you something else—I can see myself as a happy, retired Colonel, living in a little house on the Potomac. No problems, no worries, got my pension, a wife and a couple of kids." He snapped his fingers. "All I gotta do is put up with this shit for a few years."

We sat at a table in the east wing of the Mess Hall, an older wing which had a massive war mural on one wall, oak panels on the others. The ceiling was some four stories high, and the stone tower stood visible beyond row upon row of white-clothed tables. The atmosphere was that of some grand banquet hall in an ancient fortress. Jerry went on, "You sure had me worried for a couple of months, Jaime. You know, I've been wanting to discuss with you . . . I mean, just look around you, right where we are." He told me to pretend the cadets weren't there, to picture just the hanging banners, the war mural, the stone embellishments.

"It's impossible *not* to go for all this if you just think right, Mardis!" Drury was somehow pleading with me. "All these banners and regalia and stuff, and even the uniforms—it's like being back in the eighteenth century!"

"Like being part of Napoleon's legion, huh?"

"You took the words right out of my mouth. Like we're chowing down before a long campaign."

I was vaguely annoyed with Drury's vision. I had made it through the Gloom Period, maybe not with flying colors, but I had done so without Napoleon, and, for that matter, without having to fight the enemy in Omaha. I told him that I thought the Corps could benefit by a little more of the twentieth century.

"Aw, you're just a spoil sport," he answered. "I had enough of the twentieth century back in Chicago. Every time I think of those dirty dishes—" Jerry glanced his wristwatch and whistled. "We better post or we're gonna be late."

Becky and Belinda were waiting on the steps of Cullum

Hall, the Plebe activities center. They were easy to tell apart since they'd dressed in the same color scheme as their letters. Belinda wore an orange slack outfit with a lavendar jacket. The other Harris had a yellow coat flecked with tiny green pinstripes, which looked a lot like a sheet of legal-sized paper. They had remarkably similar faces: bobbed noses, light freckles, narrow, sparkling eyes, and wide, rosy lips. Belinda, the more petite and impish, was snapping off photographs before Jerry and I were even within speaking distance.

Jerry bowed as I introduced him, and the girls each dropped a coquettish wrist to have their hands kissed. It was the eighteenth century for them, too. Jerry administered a gallant peck to each, which was enough to send the Harris sisters into a pandemonium of giggles.

"Were you an honor guard at the football games, too?" Becky asked him. Belinda added, "Because if we'd seen *you*, we would have snatched you up just like Cadet Private Mardis! . . . Is that correct? Cadet *Private*?"

I said, "You can just call me 'Cadet.' We like to go by our first names around here—haha." They gave me a puzzled look and then asked Jerry what his rank was.

"We're all privates at this stage of the game," Jerry explained. "Jaime didn't tell me he was a stadium guard when he met you."

"Oh, he was a darling guard!"

"You should have seen him giving orders!"

Jerry gave me a sick smile, then said, "Well. Have you young ladies seen Trophy Point?"

"I'm sure we have, but I'd love to see it again!" Belinda chirped, taking Jerry's arm. The afternoon was sunny and pleasant, perfect for a walking tour.

"I recognize it over there!" shouted Becky, the one with the paralegal coat. She pointed to the stalwart obelisk two hundred yards from the steps of Cullum Hall and pranced ahead nimbly along the grassy border of the sidewalk, swinging her bag. Jerry and Belinda followed her path, chatting, and I followed them, sulking.

Trophy Point offered a commanding view of the great bend in the Hudson, which was quite beautiful now, the water glimmering in a lazy sunlight and shadowed by the granite highlands on the far side. The four of us cowered under the majestic, gleaming battle monument, surrounded by the mighty links of chain that had spanned the Hudson River in the American Revolution for the purpose of halting British naval advance inland. There were tarnished cannon, some still pointing across the Hudson from this steep knoll, and one or two, for the sake of uniformity, aimed at the Mess Hall.

The brass plaques affixed to the column had been shined for the upcoming spring ceremonies, so that the inscriptions were visible, and Becky set out to memorize several, jotting them down for future reference. I couldn't think of much to say besides "This is Trophy Point," "That's the Hudson River," and other basics which I'd covered on their first trip. So I stayed quiet and tried to look knowledgeable while Cadet Private Drury delivered an authoritative account of an incident that had occurred in 1779, right where we were standing. At one point in the Revolutionary story, I broke in with an off-color joke about the Freudian properties of the Colonial musketball loaders, but it wasn't appreciated.

Next we trudged around the Parade Plain on Thayer Road, and down the hill, and then across the athletic fields to see the inlet where the great chain had been anchored. The girls had sprinted ahead of us, laughing and excited. Drury tapped me on the arm and asked whether I was upset. I told him I didn't feel wonderful, but it wasn't jealousy. "May the best man win. I just wish I knew more about the Revolutionary War, that's all."

"All right, listen close." As we walked toward the river bank, Jerry quickly gave me the facts on the great chain,

209

the names, the dates, how it was secured, the bleak winter conditions, the poor troop morale, the tactical advantages of the effort, and so forth. We arrived at the river, which was awesomely wide and threatening at eye-level. I stood on a rock above my audience and launched a dramatic tirade about the bravery of the men of 1779, and how they had braved the elements to do service for their brave new land.

"Just take a good long gander at that there river! Really! Can you *imagine* how *dangerous* it was on that cold winter day back in 1779 for Colonel Kosciusko and his small band of faithful, starving men—" I filled in the facts rather hurriedly, since it seemed pointless to give a lecture on the tactical advantages of the chain or the boring engineering problems. I liked the morale problems! "Can you imagine how *desperate*, starving, underpaid, poorly clothed, and sex-crazy those men were? And *lonely*, brother! Just remember, they had no radios or TV! Those soldiers were frustrated, ladies. What's more, they were out of their minds with fear! Ladies, it was living hell! So you tell me: Were those men *courageous*, or were they out of their minds?" I stepped down off the rock.

The Harris sisters were impressed. They asked me where I had learned so much about the men of 1779, and I told them I had an "inner understanding" of the men of 1779.

"Could you recommend a book on the subject?"

"Well, uh . . . the encyclopedias are very informative."

"Didn't anybody get hurt by the chain?"

"Certainly they did. There's always a sacrifice in the games of war, ladies."

Now Jerry Drury was miffed as we started across the athletic fields; Becky and Belinda were on either side of me, bubbling with war questions. I gave them flamboyant answers dealing with the troop morale at the battle in question. But Drury wasn't long in winning back the limelight. We paused before climbing the hill up to the level of the Parade Plain, and Becky asked me an educated question about World War II. "Ah, yes," I replied, "the Battle of Guam. Our men kept their minds busy by reading books. The Commanding General believed this was the best method to get rid of combat fatigue. He came from a fine family. But a hard-nosed fighter. Now the enemy commander, he was a little fat man—"

"But who won? . . . Or do you even know?"

"Who *won*? Is that really the question?"

It was. Regrettably, Becky knew more than I did about World War II because their father had fought in the South Pacific. Jerry fielded her question without effort and was now the exclusive hero. My credibility as a historical commentator had been thrown in question. Becky snapped at me in a nasal, lawyerly voice, "If you, Cadet Mardis, persist in propagating false information, how are we to rely on you as a substantiated source? I'll bet half of the stuff you told us down at the river was *strictly* baloney!"

"Cadets don't lie, do they?" Belinda asked innocently. "Do they?"

"Of course not," said Jerry. "Cadet Mardis just gets his wars mixed up, that's all. It could happen to anyone."

"I wanted to give you a sense of history," I mumbled.

Jerry tactfully shifted their interest to our next destination, the West Point Chapel, and the trio forged ahead of me on the climb to the Plain. I could hear the sisters bombarding Cadet Drury with questions on the legal nature of our Honor Code, and whether a crumb like me was liable for punishment for giving phony information to civilians. Jerry tried to convince them of my good intentions, but the paralegal assistants had lost all respect and told Cadet Drury that he didn't have to bother sticking up for me. But he was certainly a gentleman for doing so.

We walked along the Plain to Old Central Area, our

last point of interest before ascending the incredibly steep hill to the Chapel. I had dropped back about twenty paces. Jerry had the girls wait in the eighteenth century while he came to talk to me.

"What gives, anyway?" he asked me. Are you with the group or not? Look, if you want to make up to the girls I'll give you some new facts and act stupid. Just don't ham it up so much this time. How about it?"

"I don't think I can make it up that hill."

"How else are you planning to get to Chapel? That's the next stop."

"I think I ate the wrong thing at lunch. I don't feel well. Maybe that Martha Washington layer cake—"

"All right, I get the idea. You go back to the room and rest. I'll come by for you before the hop. I think they're staying overnight at the Thayer Hotel. You're probably just sick of this historical bullshit, and I don't blame you. But that's what they're here for, so why knock it? Right? OK—see you around seven."

I walked slowly to the G-5 Company area, like a tired old man, and carefully down the steps to the basement. I wanted a root beer. I didn't feel well at all. It was dark in the basement, silent. I put a tiny, cold dime into the soft drinks machine and heard it go click, click, clack, *strock.* My hand reached over and punched the root beer button and the machine went buzz, buzz, *strock*, ka-bonk, and there was a can of root beer. These machines were amazing devices if you spent enough time alone with them. I took my root beer and set it in the side slot; there was a handle which you brought down with brute force to stab two holes in the top of the can. I brought the handle down with brute force and it didn't even dent the can. My strength seemed to be fading.

I put the root beer back in the side slot and took the handle again, and then I heard something go "*Squawk!*" I thought the can of soda had sprung a carbonation leak. "*Squawk! Squawk!*" I looked over.

212

A lumbering figure had emerged from the black shadows of the lockers . . . a heavy walk, seven feet high, and grumbling under its breath. It was Igor! He had two pigeons in his hand, one bloody dead and one still squawking, and he was holding a huge iron wrench.

"So!—It was you! *Igor.* No. I won't tell anybody!" But he kept coming. . . .

MEMO 18.

Who is the *Surgeon General*? That impressive rascal. His name appeared on the memorandum for "bloodletting day," asking the Corps to donate whole pints of blood. It was the Surgeon General who demanded that we have malaria shots, that we brush our teeth twice daily. The Surgeon General sent his men to teach us techniques to combat the effects of burning cannabis. (If after repeated arbitrary inhalations you suddenly feel wonderful, this is cannabis. Induce vomiting immediately. This might not stop the effects of the cannabis, but it'd sure get cadets kicked out of pot parties.)

Igor had taken me up the stairs on a strong shoulder and tenderly deposited me on the orderly room floor, beside the radiator; then he had disappeared. I was so nauseous that I couldn't stand. The Cadet-in-Charge-of-Quarters came around momentarily and asked, "What is this shit, are you drunk or something?"

"No sir . . . Sir, I'm sick . . . my stomach."

"Well don't sit over there, dang it," he told me, "that's bad luck. That's where all them dang dead pigeons was found."

He arranged for me to be assisted to the hospital for emergency sick call. The orderlies there took one look at my chalk-white face and stiffened limbs and handed me a bottle of Kaopectate. Most cadets were pale from winter, and cadets normally looked sort of stiff, and they go into in the hospital this time of year to get out of midterms. "Drink up and enjoy life, fellah." "Can't I stay here overnight?" "What, and get out of Chapel tomorrow?" So I spent a volcanic night in my bunk at the company.

I had acute appendicitis, but it took them until Monday to find out.

Early Sunday morning I was again assisted to the hospital. This time, I was admitted, but the bureaucratic hospital staff wouldn't waver from the unwritten rule that any case which came in on Saturday or Sunday simply had to wait until Monday morning to be treated. The Army doctors didn't like to be disturbed on weekends, especially now, since the weather permitted speedboat trips on the Hudson River. I was wheeled into a ward and dressed in a hospital gown and placed in a bed next to an ingrown toenail victim.

Sunday morning, Sunday afternoon, Sunday night. I was convulsive, feverish, and in my lighter moments, indignant as I waited for the men of the Surgeon General. Nurse Farge, in charge of the ward, tried to make me go to Chapel with the walking wounded, and I told her to take the Chapel and shove it up her ass. At one point on Sunday afternoon, I overheard a doctor talking in the corridor; he had come by for something in his office. I shouted for mercy and he poked his head in the ward. "Nurse, let me see the temperature chart on this man." He looked at it. "Well, I'll be by in the morning. I've got someone waiting."

I'd cried out, "No! Don't! . . . You son of a bitch!"

". . . and *remind* that man he's still in the Army!"

Nurse Farge came in and hazed me. The ingrown toenail victim, an upperclassman, helped her haze me. Their voices echoed in broken tones. "Don't ever speak like that to an officer." "You may have a bad case of influenza, Mister, but you better learn to remember your rank under all circumstances." I told them to go to hell. Then other voices began screaming at me, and I told them off too. I didn't care who they were.

They said, "You're a disgrace!". . ."Look at him, dribbling and jabbering like a cock-eyed fool!". . ."Shut up while you have the chance, Mister!". . ."Did you hear what he said to Major Kentley?" I told them go kiss the Major's boots, and I told them that I hoped the gooks got the Major and cut out his gizzard and made a bomb out of it. I said I hoped they bombed West Point and I hoped that Nurse Farge felt happy with the Cadet Choir singing up her big flopper. The voices kept threatening and I laughed, slower and slower, slower and slower, and I laughed myself to sleep.

The next voice I heard was a kind voice. Nurse Meadows. The ward was dark now; earlier it had been a gauzy color of yellow. She said my temperature had gone down and I was calmer. She said she hoped I was reacting to the medicines. More blackness. When I woke up I saw the bright white gleam of tile, brilliant aluminum things, a bright white coat. A black technician. He had his hand on my brow. He said, "Just relax, just relax. I'm your friend. No reason to shout now. We're friends. OK?" "OK," I said. It was Monday morning.

They operated, and I was placed in intensive care. My appendix had burst during the night. If this had happened Saturday night, there would have been one heck of a stiff Plebe in the Golf-5 Chapel Formation: ramrod straight and with his chin well to the rear, eyes straight ahead, staring a hole into infinity. The ingrown toenail victim found me in intensive care and shook my limp hand. "I'm sorry I hazed you, Mister. If I'd known you were dying, I wouldn't have taken you so seriously. But now I'm recognizing you, Mister. Tom Scott, Company F-4. Glad you made it, no kidding."

Nurse Meadows—Lieutenant Meadows—visited me. She had stayed with me for part of the critical night. She

216

apologized. She had wanted to declare me an emergency but her superior, Captain Farge, had given direct orders to the contrary, namely, that a doctor had seen my chart and that I was not an emergency, and that even if I were, I was insubordinate and no doctors were going to be bothered on my account. She said she'd volunteered to stay with me till morning but Captain Farge had ordered her to terminate duty at the end of the shift. "I don't know what you did, but it doesn't deserve negligence."

Lieutenant Meadows was angry; she closed the door to speak privately. "I've seen appendicitis more than enough to know that your case was acute. It was terrible. You're very lucky. I tried calling a doctor on my break that night, a personal friend of mine, but I couldn't get through to him. Honestly—" She shook her head, almost in tears. "I'm not going to let this ride, just because you made it by. I'm tired of overlooking these blunders. Foolish, foolish blunders. What did you do, call somebody a *name*, and they're going to kill you for it?"

I was kept in a private room for four days. Nurse Meadows dropped by in spare moments, her soft voice and angelic eyes bringing welcome companionship. I couldn't listen very closely due to my being under sedation. She was trying to tell me of her progress in reporting the incompetent handling of my case. On the third day, she had just come in when she was sternly called away. That afternoon, a talkative officer with Medical Corps insignia visited; he said that we had met the year before, at the qualifying examinations.

His friendliness was disarming, since cadets were seldom on personal terms with officers. He'd recognized my name on a sheet and thought he'd stop in to say hello. The officer said that when he had first seen me, he knew I was West Point material. Then he joked that the rubber duck on my bedside table wasn't very "Army." I told him a nurse had given it to me, so we got onto the subject of pretty nurses, and Lieutenant Meadows. He said, "Yes, I've seen that one—with the pretty blue eyes. She looks real swell. Talk to you much?"

He began browbeating me to tell him what Nurse Meadows and I had talked about, and then he *commanded* me to answer when I couldn't remember. But I couldn't remember; I was, at the moment, very heavily sedated. "Well, don't let me get your goat on this," he chortled. "I'd just like a date with her *myself*. But I guess she likes you better. Mind if I see your incision?" He lifted my hospital gown and folded it on my chest. "Very nice, clean work. Clamp job. Listen, Mardis. If you got sexually aroused over the Lieutenant, d'you think you could remember what you two talked about? Wouldn't that be fun?"

A group passed in the hall and the officer, whose face was a blur, closed the door. He leaned close over my pillow. "What do you like about Nurse Meadows?" I said she was nice. "But don't you like her pretty blue eyes?" "Yes, sir." "And what else do you like?" "Her smile." "*That's it*, now think of her hot little mouth. Now, pretend she's where I am, Mardis, and her breath is warm and smells like perfume, and she's real close, and you can feel her hot little breasts near you, and she's licking her lips and looking right at you, and she has her warm, soft hand behind your neck . . . *Now* what happens?"

"Orange juice."

"No, *that's* not what happens." The officer began describing in vivid detail the sensual treasures hidden under her clean military uniform. He finally whispered in my ear, "Think of all that dirty filth inside her tight skirt, Mardis. Think hard, just what I've told you. Concentrate, Mardis, *concentrate*—" He glanced below the folds of my gown. "You're not concentrating."

The officer sat in a chair. "Well, when you get your brainpower back, tell Dr. Zinner your surgeon, anything Lieutenant Meadows said, anything at all, and you tell him *personally* if the hospital treatment hasn't been up to your standards. Nice room they have you in. So, Mardis, what about West Point? Someone told me you're not too happy here. Why not? Don't you like it? Can't take the pressure, eh? Planning to resign?"

"No, sir."

"But isn't that what you told a lot of the personnel around here, in so many words? Come on, you can tell me what's on your mind. I didn't go to West Point. I won't hold it against you, old buddy. I don't care what they heard you say. But what do you plan to do about it?"

"About what, sir?"

"About resigning. About getting the hell out of here. You don't seem to have much respect for superior officers. Or West Point. You act baffled."

"Sir, I don't remember. I remember . . . I screamed for a doctor. The rest . . . I don't know."

"Thanks—if that's your story. You remember screaming for the doctor and you remember Nurse Meadows' blue eyes, and that's all? And you're staying, right? Good, good. Then you don't have anything to worry about, do you?" The Medical Corps officer left abruptly, and I never saw him again.

When I was well enough to pull myself awkwardly out of bed and wheel the intravenous cart to the rest room, they promoted me to the central ward and took me off intravenous. I was happy because I could no longer hear the brassy voice of Nurse Farge in the corridor; I now had daily chart readings by a regular floor staff, like all the other cadets. My only regret was that Nurse Meadows no longer came to visit.

Five days after surgery, I noticed that my bandaged side was swollen. The following morning, the swelling was the size of a fist, and when the doctors made their rounds, I showed them. The doctor in charge said this was normal and that he would check it the next day when the bandage was changed. A younger doctor suggested they take a look today, to which the higher officer retorted, "You heard me, didn't you?" By the morning of the seventh day, the area around my incision had become distended to the size of two fists. The senior doctor removed the wrappings, mumbled, "*Hm-hm,*" and sent for another doctor. When this man arrived, he took a look and held a conference with the others, who then went away, leaving him alone at my bedside.

"I'm the one who operated on you. You can thank me for saving your life."

"Thank you, sir. It looked all right for a couple of days."

"Of course it was all right. I did a perfect closure on that incision. There'll be no stitch marks."

The surgeon was Major Zinner, a West Pointer, about thirty-five years old, with thinning hair, keen eyes, a healthy complexion, and tight, neat lips. He asked me why I hadn't reported the swelling earlier and I responded that I had. "You're a liar, Mister, because if you had, I would have been told."

"Sir, I did. Yesterday."

"Don't contradict me, Mister, because I know you didn't." He closed the curtains around me bed, unbuttoned the white smock which he wore over his uniform, and sat at the foot of the bed. "Mr. Mardis, I had a nice long talk about you with your company Tactical Officer, Major Cutler. Well, he tells me there are a few people over there in his company who wouldn't mind screwballing his record. In fact, he says for a shitassed Plebe, you've done more than your fair share . . . You know, Mardis, you can only get away with that shit for so long in this man's army."

He spoke in a soft, even voice. His eyes were very bright and strangely relaxed. "I hear you've been having some doubts about the Academy, Mister. You going to call it quits, Mister? That's what you've been saying, isn't it?"

"No, sir, I didn't—"

"*Mister.* You contradict me again and I'll put you up for an honor violation. You ought to know by now that we hate liars around here worse than we do quitters, Mister. But tell me this. If you like this place so much, why'd you tell your buddies you'd like to see it bombed? You think your buddies are gonna put up with that shit, Mister? You think they're gonna let scum like you live with them? And, Mister, do you think you can get away with calling an officer in the United States Army a *son of a bitch*?"

"Sir, I was in pain."

"Oh sure, but if insubordination isn't enough in itself, then you figured you'd like to screwball this hospital, *right*, Mister Quitter?"

Nurse Meadows had apparently reported the hospital's mishandling of my case, and Doctor Zinner, as an administrator, felt that now was the time to intimidate me into silence. But I was frightened, too confused and too fuzzy to immediately grasp this. He stared at me for a while and said, "Mister, you've got an awful sassy jaw."

"No, sir. Sir, I was in pain."

"Pain? What do you mean pain? After an *appendectomy*? I perform a hundred and fifty a year. You think there's any pain from that operation?"

"I mean before, sir."

"Before what?"

"Before the operation. When I had to lie there in the ward."

He waved a scoffing hand. "I guess you think you're a man because of that, do you? If you could have seen yourself in the operating room, sniveling like a little crybaby, even under anesthetics. Well, we'll see."

The doctor made a part in the curtains and went away. I could make out a section of a large, elevated leg cast belonging to a cadet across the way. He'd been injured in basketball, a nurse had informed me, which made me want to laugh. The placard in our gymnasium said:

"Upon these fields of friendly strife are sewn the seeds, which upon other fields, on other days, will grow the fruits of victory." Kill 'em with a smile, in other words.

Major Zinner returned with a scowl, accompanied by Nurse Farge. He instructed her to help me out of bed. Without an intravenous cart to lean on, it was hard for me to lower myself to the floor. She pushed me and I landed with a yelp. Then they spread aside the curtains and dragged me across the ward before I could even step into my official hospital sandals. The doctor led the way with a brisk step, as Nurse Farge pulled me along like their naughty child. I hobbled painfully, with one hand on my side.

In a small treatment room, I was undressed and laid on an examination table. Doctor Zinner told me the wound had become infected and that he was going to open it to drain any fluids and to check the nature of the infection. The bullish Captain Farge pinned my arms back at the shoulders and stuck a tongue depressor sideways in my mouth. "You bite on that when this begins to smart, Mister, because it's going to smart. And if you move, it'll smart even more," he said. "Start biting."

For a split second I thought this a heroic episode from a cowboy movie, and then I realized why they always gave the cowboys sticks to chew on—they had no anesthetics, no pain killers. And Zinner wasn't using any now. I saw the gleam of a scissor-like instrument and the gleam in his eyes, and envisioning brave cowboys, and biting the wooden depressor and under Nurse Farge's strong hands, I managed to withstand the pain for perhaps thirty seconds as the surgeon reopened my incision, clipping through a week of scar tissue. Then I snapped, lost my senses, began kicking, spat out the chewed depressor, cursing. Major Zinner cursed back. The nurse let go and I sat up, weakly. "Go ahead and look," he said. "I've still got halfway to go. So the longer you spend bawling the longer this is going to take. It's your choice, fellow. Now either you act like a man or I'll get some more staff in here to hold you down."

The pain was too much as he began cutting again, jerkily. Each jerk of the scissor blades sent a tremor through my body, made my eyes seem to roll back. I was breathing heavily. Then he hit a snag and I screamed bloody murder. Nurse Farge released one of my arms and quickly stuffed cotton in my mouth. I heard her laughing, deep in her throat. Zinner cut again and hit the same snag. I was flinching and sweating, looking crosswise at the various trays of sterilized objects, trying to tell myself I was only at a visit with the family doctor and that my mother and sister were waiting for me outside. If I looked up, I looked straight into the bulldog nostrils of the nurse. I could see her hard smile as she held me down.

Zinner was muttering in irritation. He said something to the nurse and turned his back for a moment. Then I felt a soft cloth go over my midsection, an absorption pad. I felt warmer. He quickly returned to work, and in one violent thrust, reopened the wound completely. The motion sent a spasm throughout my body, but worse, I was beginning to suffocate from the cotton in my mouth. He had her remove the cotton, and now he was in a joking mood.

"Well, how'd you like that?" he said. "It's not so bad if you've got the guts for it. A little pain never hurt anybody." He stifled a laugh. "A quitter, huh? A quitter. Oh, you don't know what we do to quitters around here. Aren't I right, Nurse?"

"That's right, Doctor."

Doctor Zinner continued his jokes along that line as he swabbed the wound for some five minutes; the smell was wretched. He would dab and dab and then I'd feel a slithering sting, which were the strips of gauze being fished out of the opening. He held one in a pair of clamps over my face, so I could see. "There's the cause of our problem. These drains were left inside when the incision was closed." Considering that it was his oversight, the surgeon hardly sounded apologetic, but on the contrary, amused. "We'll have to probe for some of these," he commented to himself.

On the first probe I screamed so loud that the surgeon removed his instruments and peeked out the door to see if anyone might have heard. He shut it firmly and told the nurse to put the cotton in my mouth. I begged them not to, even bit her hand, but she deftly hooked her thumbs under my jaw and got it in. "Patient *secure,* Doctor." He resumed the probe without replying, hunched over and quite still, shimmying the slender probe deep into the wound to reach for the loose strips of gauze. Sensing that he was successful, I withstood the intermittent bolts of pain as best I could, for around two minutes, three probes. But the instrument went down again, deep and curious, ambitious in the doctor's hands, dancing inside of me. I was counting off the seconds and now I counted ninety. My body was ripping with shooting pains and I wanted to resist, I had to make him stop, but even the slightest tremor of my legs jerked the surgeon's tools and sent a fire running through my midsection. I thought of breaking the nurse's grip, and I tried, twisting my head, and then I tried to scream and swallowed part of the cotton. The nurse reported that I was beginning to turn blue and he said, "All right, all right, I've almost got this one—" But I was choking, and I had to make him stop—and I did, in spite of the flaming pain, by moving my legs. He took out the probe disgustedly, and as soon as she removed the cotton, I cursed the doctor and kicked at him. He was laughing.

"Listen, Mister Quitter. I've already told you that you can make it easy on yourself or you can make it harder on yourself. If you can't take the pain, that's your problem.

So why don't you try to be a man about it? It'll make it that much easier on you. If you keep resisting—" He shrugged his shoulders.

Another session ensued, with another cotton ball. I managed to spit it out and began screaming for help at the top of my voice, also kicked at the doctor so that he had to move back. The nurse tried to cover my mouth with her hand, and when she did I shook loose and tried to escape. She knocked me back down on the table but couldn't cover my mouth, and I went on screaming.

The doctor's attention was diverted by someone entering the room. It was Lieutenant Meadows. He screamed at her to get out; she ignored him and tried to come closer.

"Nurse, you're on report! Get out of here!"

Nurse Farge abandoned me to force Nurse Meadows physically into the corridor. I was still shouting, and Nurse Meadows was shouting too, that they were acting like animals toward me. Zinner screamed for an orderly. An orderly appeared and, on the doctor's instructions, set me back on the table—I'd almost made it to my feet. Blood was trickling all the way down my leg. The doctor then disappeared into the corridor, which was now quiet; he soon returned with a second orderly, whom he instructed to hold down my feet. They taped my mouth. The orderlies, both Hispanic, looked at me as though they knew something was very wrong. Major Zinner coolly forewarned them that he didn't want any backtalk, then he gave them a medical explanation, saying that I was allergic to certain drugs and that this was an emergency procedure.

After Nurse Farge, the faces of the orderlies, concerned, worried, wondering, were the faces of friends. One whispered a word of encouragement to me and the doctor told him to shut up, that they were both under orders to stay shut up. In the silence I heard the distant voice of Nurse Meadows, shrill and accusing, the gutteral voice of Nurse Farge, and two male voices. I waited for footsteps, but they never came.

The operation was completed in fifteen more minutes. Zinner sent one orderly for a wheelchair and had the other one wait outside. I watched him energetically wash his hands. He glanced at me, his lips curling over his healthy white teeth. "It goes without saying you've learned your lesson, Mister." He snatched a towel to dry his hands. "Just looking at you, I can pretty safely say you've learned your lesson."

MEMO 19.

The two orderlies had taken me to my bed, and then
someone came and put a needle in my arm, and I had a
nightmare. I saw Killer Curly Taylor. He was swimming
in a pool and my little sister knelt on the bank with a
flower for him. He ate her leg. I saw Major Zinner
standing at attention with his scalpel under The Flag.
The Vice-President of the United States went by in a
bumper car. Garth U. Tilson was following in another
bumper car; he had a pair of spit-shined shoes draped
around his neck. I was lying on a clean white table in the
Mess Hall. I saw my father whispering secrets to Major
Cutler. I saw Major Cutler look at our family lawn mower
and kick it: "*Incompetent*! He's a bozo and there's only one
cure!" I saw Willie from West Virginia go by in a bumper
car. Willie stood up and said, "I don't speak no chink, but
I think Charlie's saying it hurts to get shot. Hey! See the
one out there with the red spots on his chest. Yeah, he
ain't too happy about it." Dolores landed in a spaceship
which was piloted by a hippie. "You can come, too, Jaime,
if you want to," she called to me, "but are you sure this is
right for you?" The hippie waved, and then he turned
into a gook. I screamed for Dolores to watch out, but the
spaceship flew away. My grandmother came into the
Mess Hall with Major Zinner and put a bag of chocolate
chip cookies where my appendix had been. "Jaime, these
are the good ones, the kind with the little coconut flakes
in them. Doctor Zinner here is such a nice young man.

He won my bet for me. I bet old Mrs. Catalander next door that you would make a *fine* cadet, and here we are! She had to buy me those good bakery cookies and I'm giving them all to you. Please help yourself, Doctor Zinner, we owe *so* much to you." He reached in with his sutures to probe for a nice chocolate chip cookie, and when I screamed he put a scalpel to my throat. "You better leave, Grandma Mardis. We've got a man's work to do here." The orderlies went by in the spaceship and the Corps of Cadets fired at them with their M-14's. Major Cutler went by in a flying lawn mower. I saw Igor crumbling the stone sides of the Mess Hall tower like Samson. But I couldn't move. I could only scream. Nurse Meadows came to the rescue, then told me she'd become engaged to marry a West Point First Classman. The First Classman saw me and said, "We can hide him here." They laid me in a giant spit-shined shoe, where I was safe. Nurse Meadows tied the shoe laces, and the First Classman nervously held his finger for the knot. A flower grew out of the shoe and Killer Curly discovered me. "Mister! What do you think you're *doing*! You've had it, Mister! I guess you figured you'd spit-shine this shoe and try to fool everybody, huh, Mister? But it shows, Mister. Scum always shows." Then I saw Ralph Aberby drive up in an armored alarm clock, and they took me away.

The next day I had visitors: Rutledge, Groovey, Daisy, Drury, and Boyd Royelle. I didn't speak, so they chatted to each other about "Plebe weekend" and left, except for Drury. He wanted to know if I was mad at him over the Harris sisters. "No? Then what's with you, then? You got the goldbrick fever again? I know you're laid up, but, Jesus, you can talk, can't you?"

I told him I was "recovering." Jerry came back again in a few days, and when I still wouldn't talk to him, I began to realize how frightened I was. I found myself wondering whether he and Daisy had been assigned as roommates to spy on me. I wondered whether Major Cutler had been behind the surgeon's butcher-work on me. Maybe Drury had reported that I'd made a mockery of the Corps' principles in front of the Harris sisters.

I didn't care if the Army was the last place left in the world to be a man. I didn't want to "go over the top" any more; I didn't need the enemy's guts hanging on the end of my bayonet. They could go spit-shine their coffins, they could take scalps but I wouldn't be there. Every afternoon, I watched through my foggy window the gray figures below, strutting proudly toward Bartlett Hall. They were going to *Military Science.* I watched them for a week and then I closed the curtains around my bed.

One evening when supper was being served, a cheer swept across the ward, followed by excited arguing. Regi, an upperclassman in the next bed who'd "recognized" me, approached on his crutches. My curtains were parted. "Did you hear that?" Regi asked me. He related the news of the Kent State catastrophe, just broadcast on the television at the other end of the ward. Regi got his tray and sat down in bed.

"Are you going to eat?" I asked him.

"Sure I'm gonna eat," he answered. "I'm hungry."

I started eating, too. Regi was a black fellow, agile, even-tempered. "You didn't cheer, did you?" I asked him.

"Hell, no, I didn't cheer. What do you take me for, anyway?"

"Well, they just killed those students."

"Yeah, but you know and I know that it was going to happen sooner or later. So what do you do?" He buttered his bread and repeated, "Hell, no, I didn't cheer." I watched him eat, and he asked me what I was looking at.

I told him, "I was just thinking. Those students."

Regi grumbled, "And you're wondering how I've still got an appetite. Because I'm hungry, that's why. *Me.*" He cracked a smile. "Be smart, Mardis. Kent State is a

thousand miles away from here, literally and fig-
uratively. I don't like it, but I'll tell you, I accept it. And if
you'd grown up in East Saint Louis, you'd accept it too.
You'd accept all that stuff and just look out for yourself.
That's what I do."

"Accept what stuff?"

"The bad things, man, the bad things." Regi told me
the story of when he was a Plebe. They'd tried to haze
him right out of the Corps. He was on the area marching
off "demerits" every weekend for the entire year. He'd
had to give up Christmas leave to march off demerits. He
said he didn't even mind; he'd expected it. "I kept right
on going 'cause I was thinking of my*self*, Mardis, not
them, Mardis. Just me. You start worrying about the bad
things, brother, then you *do* have worries."

Hearing Regi speak of the Corps in less than beautiful
terms, I decided that he hadn't been sent to spy on me.
Regi wouldn't say much more to me, though, probably
because he felt he'd already confided more than was safe.
I asked him for his opinions on violence and war, and he
answered tersely, "You play tough, somebody gets their
nose busted." But he'd given me something to think
about.

I wanted to resign, and Regi had supplied me with a
legitimate rationale—*I* wanted to resign, me, and that
was enough. So what if they called me a quitter? So what
if I was scum? And if I broke the faith, so what? I'd just
have to endure the consequences, let them rip apart my
guts some more. I'd once seen them spit on a resignee, in
the Boarder's Ward by Central Guard Room. He'd
looked terrified, but now he was out there somewhere,
free.

I formulated my thoughts carefully. I was ill equipped
to be a member of the profession of arms. I was unworthy
of the Point. They'd have to agree with me. A failure as a
cadet, unworthy of my classmates. Came to the Academy
because I thought it would make a man of me. But I'm a

230

natural born bozo. Squeamish and incompetent. I called Cutler several times from the hospital, to tell him I wanted out, but he was unavailable.

On the day of my release, however, Major Cutler and his assistant, a Sergeant, were waiting at the hospital to escort me to the company. The Major was terribly friendly, and his Sergeant shook my hand respectfully. They talked about my "ordeal" and treated me like a hero. In a fluster of vanity, I *felt* like a hero. We walked across the Parade Plain on the diagonal strip used exclusively by officers, and I felt more and more important with every step we took. Perhaps my ordeal *had* been a building block of character!

The sun shone down brightly and the air was warm and soothing. All the trees around the Plain had blossomed; the grounds glowed a magnificent green. It was my first trip outdoors in three weeks, the first time I'd worn my uniform in so long, and it felt good. The Sergeant was calling me "Sir." As we passed through the language sally port under Washington Hall, Major Cutler pointed out my French score to the Sergeant: "This man's been out going on a month, and he's *still* in the top fifty." At the steps of the company, Cutler gave me a sharp salute and said, "Give 'em hell, Mister Mardis!"

The barracks were empty with morning classes in session. In my room, my desk complex was spotless, my bunk meticulously tucked—Drury and Daisy had kept them in inspection order. I was still present and accounted for. A stack of lesson assignments lay in the top desk drawer, and I regretted not keeping up while in the hospital, though I could still easily pass. In the Corps, it was hard not to pass. The Corps was good to its men. I was grateful to be back.

It had only taken one "Sir" from Cutler's Sergeant for my resignation plans to vanish, like the sun melting the morning mist. Maybe Lieutenant Meadows had made a stink. But forgive and forget, as they say. Let bygones be bygones. I felt incredibly foolish now for even thinking of resignation, and I felt incredibly lucky to be able to fit back in. The cadets returned for lunch, and more than a few Plebes and upperclassmen welcomed me home. They'd heard from the Tac that I'd had a tough time of it.

Less than four weeks remained until graduation and June leave for the Corps, yet the current leadership ratings would account for "field" ranks in July summer training, and as a result many cadets were behaving like military madmen. I didn't mind, since my medical excuse permitted me to "fall out" to a degree and be a relative observer. I observed that my fellow cadets were first-rate young men who had every reason to be proud of themselves. It was easy for me to see all their finer qualities, being a hero myself.

On Saturday night, I was on my way to the hop when I ran into Carillo and Hightower in the alley behind the Slums. I was taking the long way to Cullum Hall for a sentimental journey down memory lane. They had a bottle of whiskey. "Tonight's the night," Carillo said. "Tonight's the night we get ourselves kicked out of this dump."

Hightower patted me on the back. "You want a drink, Mardis? We would've come to see you in the hospital but we've been confined to quarters." I told him no thanks.

They were out to break every regulation they could. They were resigning, they said, only it was impossible to resign. "So we have to get kicked out. It's the only way," Carlo said. "That son of a bitch Cutler has been stalling me since Easter. I'm through here. I wanta be a civvie already." He tilted up the bottle for a swig.

Hightower added, "Ol' Clifford baby is figuring to stall us into Second Class year, and that means two years in the Army."

"And, Mardis"—Carillo pointed his finger in my

face—"you know what that bastard Cutler is up to, don't you? You know, he was gonna let Keeng baby quit last year, but Keeng didn't. Nobody did. And nobody resigned this year. And he's not gonna *let* nobody resign. You know why?" Carillo and Hightower laughed in the dark and poked each other in the arm, then they took a sip of whiskey.

I was interested. "No, why?"

"'Cause it's his ace in the hole," Hightower said.

"We got inside information," Carillo nodded. "See this whiskey? You know who we got it from? We got it from this guy in the Tactical Department. Yup, and he's the nicest guy you ever wanta meet, a regular guy. He's a Corporal. We met 'im down at the P.X. one day."

"But Clifford baby ain't going to have not one brownie point left when we get through with him," Chip Hightower said to me. "He thinks he's gonna stall us into Second Class year and get himself a nice little clean spot on his record."

Chip explained that their Corporal friend told them Major Cutler was now competing with two Tactical Officers from the First Regiment for bringing all his men over the finish line: no expulsions, no resignees for his two-year stint. Another indicator of outstanding leadership. Cutler might leave the company in the same dismal condition as he found it, but the record would show that every single one of those bastards had stayed. No deserters.

"But when them rats jump, that shows the old ship is sinkin'!" Hightower slurred. They said good-bye and staggered away, jabbering, "Whoopee! whoopee! whoopee!" in the darkness.

At the hop, I had to keep reminding myself that I *was* a hero. The Plebes were rather outgoing at the hop, mostly discussing their successes during "Plebe weekend," when they'd been theoretical company leaders for a day and a half. I thought of making conversation out of my own recent heroics, and then I fell into a panic. The memories of the hospital, the surgeon butcher, the cadets clapping at the news of Kent State infected my mind with paranoia. I looked at the cadets with their shaved heads——future killers—laughing and eating cookies and drinking fruit punch. I ran out of Cullum Hall. I wasn't a hero, I was a sucker, a neat mark on Cutler's record. But he'd have to let me resign because I could put a big scratch on his buddy Zinner's record if he didn't.

After Chapel the next day I went to talk to Carillo, but he was missing, as was Hightower. Word came down that night that they'd been caught drinking in the bushes Saturday after Taps. In the *Superintendent's* bushes, by the Super's wife when she came out to water her flowers in her bathrobe. Their trunks were packed later in the week by an enlisted man; for all the company knew, they'd been put in an Army brig.

On Monday I called the Tac but couldn't get through to him. I was terrified. If I tried to resign, if I submitted my resignation and it wasn't approved, I'd be trapped in a world of enemies, branded as a quitter. But to commit serious violations, hoping to be kicked out, like Carillo and Hightower—I dreaded that worse. I couldn't be sure what would happen to me then. So I did nothing.

The passing days took a welcome toll; the regimentation and routine drained away my doubts and my will to escape. There was also the great guilt I felt toward my classmates; already I felt like a traitor having to face them every day. But as my thoughts of resignation began subsiding under the busy cadet schedule, I felt a new gratitude for the Point—a gratitude for its traditions and stone walls, for its men, its principles, its honored ground, and especially for *esprit de corps*, almost as if I were experiencing all this for the first time. On Friday I made another unsuccessful phone call to the Tac, but by now I didn't care. The Plebes were excitedly pulling out their combat equipment for inventory, and I was right there with them, polishing the rust off my field bayonet.

Fourth Class Military Science now covered "Squad Tactics." There were nineteen days until June leave. I hobbled into class late, having had to slowly scale the stairs of Bartlett Hall. The instructor acknowledged my excuse and continued with his speech to the class. The United States had invaded Cambodia, and the Major, not long removed from the battlefields of Indochina, was telling us how our tanks were going to roll through those flat lands and squash every gook hiding in every bush in Cambodia. The topic was blood on the tank treads.

"God bless the man who figures out a way to clean those tank treads," he announced vindictively. " 'Cause there's gonna be so much blood flowing on those beautiful flat lands that *some*body's gonna have to do some powerful mopping. This is just the break we've been waiting for in the war. Now we're gonna make this into *our* kind of ball game. Mark my words, we'll have Charlie smoked out *but good* in ninety days—we'll push him back with that big beautiful armor all the way back to the Ho Trail, and *beyond!*, men. And beyond."

The Major's eyes flickered brightly when he mentioned blood, and I became nauseated. I imagined a couple of Oriental kids, my age, enjoying a tidy meal of rice under a fronded bush and all set for a captured Hershey bar when up roars the tank and runs flat over them. I could see the Major riding high on the turret, waving his blood-stained mop for the troops to advance over the squashed foe. I could see Ted Daisy in the next tank, smoking the cigars his Mom always sent him.

The Major asserted his confidence that the war would be ending, now that American tanks were free to roll in Cambodia, but, a sensitive man, he could read the reaction. "Now don't you boys worry," he laughed. "When you get out of here, there'll be a war to fight somewhere. Let's see a show of hands—how many of you going Infantry? Not bad, not bad. And how many going Armor? *Very* good! I'm glad to see we've got some men in this class. . . . Naw, see, when I say the war will be over, that doesn't mean by any manner of speaking that the hostilities will be over. You've always got a cleanup operation, and a few regiments here and there to stay behind and make sure things stay cool. Oh, that can be a lot of fun, just doing that."

He seemed to realize he'd said more than he should, for his eyes stopped dancing, and his face assumed a professional, sober frown. "I've lost good buddies in action. Every one of you in here will lose buddies in action. Those Firsties back in the company—this time next year, a couple of 'em are going to be dead. That is war, men. That's the ugliness of it. Somebody has to pay the price. But don't get me wrong. A good soldier sees to it that the *other* fellow pays the price."

The Major distributed a troop-disbursement quiz to be worked on and then discussed. He'd drawn up the problem himself, and for an entertainment had labeled the objectives to help us pretend we were in the Nam.

1.	Tao-Duk	Charlie Company advances here for reconnaissance.
2.	Kai-Lon	Formerly C.P. #3, evacuated by 1st Platoon.
3.	Gook City	Hill #42—See overlay for height a.s.l.

The class was giving it their all; I noticed, looking around, that I was the only one looking around. The others were too busy fighting the enemy. The Major stood by the windows, lost in a daydream. I reluctantly picked up my pencil to start firing on Tao-Duk and Gook

City, but my pencil felt as heavy as an M-14 rifle. Stealthily, I went to the pencil sharpener, then slipped out the door and pounded down the steps of Bartlett Hall. I was getting out of here, and if Cutler wouldn't help me, I'd go to Colonel Porterhouse.

In the Department of Tactics, high in Washington Hall, I ran into Major Cutler as he came out of his office, leaving for the day. "What are you doing here, Mister?" He held up his watch. "You're in class now." The flinty soldier clinched his face in a sneer.

"I'm here to see Colonel Porterhouse." I was out of breath. "I walked out of class."

"Go in my office."

I refused. He cocked his head, unbelieving.

"Mister, I gave you a direct order. You *move* when I tell you to move. Understand?"

Cutler had backed me up against the corridor wall. "It's my right to see the Colonel, sir. I demand to see him. I'm resigning and you can't stop me."

"*I'll* make that decision, Cadet Mardis. Now walk in that office over there. If I have to say it again, you'll be up for insubordination."

Cutler followed me in and shut the door, fuming. He barked at me for a while about all the leniency which had been extended to me over the year but which I had abused flagrantly. Yet Cutler seemed relieved about something; then it occurred to me that he'd side-stepped all my phone calls because he figured I was out to dick on the hospital, or Zinner, not because I wanted to resign. He brought it up in a roundabout way after citing other "disgusting reports" on me from classroom officers. I thought of Major Wilks, and Schwartzbark. Cutler was lisping craftily. "Mister, I've even received reports from the hospital that you attempted to disrupt morale in the *hospital*, that you even *assaulted* an officer there. Buster, I don't even want to *know* if that's true."

Grinding his teeth, Major Cutler reached in a sliding

file and threw some forms on his desk. "Take those and fill 'em out and give them to your Company Commander. We'll see how far this resignation gets, but in the meantime, Mister"—he smiled, pertly—"I'm gonna make your life miserable."

He warned that if I "pulled any stunts," I'd be liable for detention under the Uniform Code of Military Justice, which was his way of telling me that two of Golfball-5's zeros hadn't been able to jump ship just like that. On my way out I failed to render a salute, and the Major called me back and watched me salute him fifty times, until I had it correct. "You're still a part of the Army, and you're still a part of this institution, Mister, so you better get it through your head. Right now. But you know what bothers me about you? . . ."

Cutler stood up and sarcastically adjusted the tilt of my hat. "It's that you're supposed to be *intelligent.* That's why we—let's make it personal. That's why *I've* had to treat you like a good little boy. If you *only* knew. Well, all I can say is, I wish you could know how sick you make me. You're scum, Mister. I've known it since I opened the file on you back in September. And the worse thing about you is, you're intelligent enough to know what you are and you still don't do a goddamned thing about it. If you had any respect at all for that uniform, you would have resigned long ago. Instead, you *stench* it."

MEMO 20.

The current Golf-5 cadet commanders were leftover
First Classmen, those zeros who had been passed up for
earlier spots in the leadership rotation system. With
graduation around the corner, our zero leaders were
vastly more concerned with goldbrick fever than with the
year-end military fervor. My Platoon Leader was no less
than the clever Firstie who had sneaked out as "rifle-
bearer" in Wook Keeng's parade blackout. In an ironic
turnabout, many of the company's former heros were
now embittered subordinates.

The Golf Company Commander and my Platoon
Leader were sympathetic; they cooperated with my
request for resignation and said they'd try to keep the
matter hushed. But they thought I'd made a mistake.
"I'm not trying to be a neat guy," the Company Commander told me. "I'm not trying to talk you out of it or
threaten you. But these things take months. And with
that flipper Cutler, forget it. You'd be better off easing
through the summer and then processing the resignation with the new Tac, whoever he is. Let's face it, he
couldn't be any worse."

They reasoned with me earnestly, but I felt I couldn't
wait. I was secretly afraid that when I took summer leave
I might desert. As it was, I'd be returning to punishment
tours and confinement to quarters for having walked out
of Squad Tactics class. We talked for several hours, and I

hinted that Cutler might "have to" process the resignation if I went over his head.

"Yeah, he *might*, Mardis, and on the other hand, *you* might just screw yourself over royally. You start monkeying with the powers that be and you'll wind up in front of a Military Tribunal. You break the big rules, like some fellows we know, and they'll pin you down with Regs *and* the Uniform Code, and when that happens, you're stuck. And they can do it."

"That's no shit, neither, Mardis," affirmed my Platoon Leader. "The Big Brass think it's dicking."

They gave me the night to reconsider my strategy before they forwarded the resignation papers. But by the time I returned to my room, I could see no point in reconsidering. A gung-ho First Classman, Bub Hoggins, had been eavesdropping outside the Company Commander's door; he was one of the heros who'd lost rank in the rotation, and he now pounced on the opportunity to rally the good men of the company against a quitter. Hoggins stormed into my room with a handful of duty-minded upperclassmen. They ordered Daisy to go and get every Plebe in the division.

Drury and I were standing at attention by our desks. Hoggins tilted his chin at Drury. "You like living with swine, Mister?"

"Sir, I do not understand."

"I said, do you like living with this swine?"

Jerry repeated,"Sir, I do not understand." Two Third Classmen braced Jerry and started him rattling off poop. Bub Hoggins turned to me, glazing his tiny eyes. "He's a real pretty quitter, ain't he, boys?" The group pushed me up against the wall and began their hazing; they were so close that the saliva spattered in my face.

There were at least five surrounding me.

"You think you're fit to wear that uniform, quitter?"

"Wipe that look off your face, quitter!"

"You think you even deserve to *touch* that uniform, Mister?"

"Let's have an answer—*an*swer us, Mister!"

"No, sir!"

"That's right, quitter—but you sure enjoy disgracing those colors, don't you?"

"Unzip that dress gray, Mister!"

"Take it off before we rip it off you, Mister!"

I unfastened the collar and they ripped the jacket off me. A Second Classman ground his foot down on my shoes. "Look at those shoes, Mister! You call that military?"

I saw one go to my closet to scar the other pairs of shoes; then my uniforms were thrown on the floor and my drawers were emptied. Drury was in the background reciting "The Mission of the United States Military Academy" for the third time. They were hazing him, they said, because he should have smelled me out long ago, living in the same room.

Daisy returned with the Plebes: Puska, Boyd Royelle led a pack of ten. "So *there* he is," Puska boomed. "Let me at him!"

Hoggins cleared the way to let my own classmate haze me. Puska stuck his swarthy mug in my face, hissing, "You figured you'd run out on all us guys, huh? Your very own classmates who put up with your shit all year, you lousy scum. Stand at attention when I talk to you, you hunk of snot."

"Do what he says, Mister! Get that chin in!"

"Hey, *I'm* next!" It was Ted Daisy, my own roommate. He whined out, "You piece of shit, Mardis. I knew you'd never measure up, you punk-faced worm."

I pushed away and told him, "Go to hell, you flipping Nazi." Then I elbowed through them to try to stop Puska from tearing the blankets off my bunk. The laughter roared in my ears:

"You tell him, quitter."

"Listen to the big man talk!"

"Hey, Mister, you think you're *fit* to sleep on a West Point blanket?"

The group eventually broke up, shouting, jeering, kicking at my books and uniforms as they left. Boyd Royelle stayed to help me with my bunk, but when he left he said, "Just remember that I helped you out, Mardis. I wasn't in on this except as a spectator."

I looked at him. "I didn't see you stop anybody, Boyd."

"Why, you ungrateful son of a bitch."

Drury was looking out the window, racing a hand through his fair hair; he was the only one who hadn't gone. He stepped over the debris and took a long look out the door, then he said, hurriedly, "Mardis, I didn't know this was coming, but now that it's here, let me tell you you're going to have to make out on your own. The shit's gonna fly and . . . if I don't talk to you, please don't hold it against me. I got my own ass to cover. I've gotta live with these turds for the next three years, you understand?" I told him I did. We shook hands, and he left the room.

At meals I wasn't allowed to eat until the others had finished, and they finished late. One midday a passing officer asked my table commandant why my plate was empty, and when he found out, the officer leaned behind me and said, "Quitter, officially I'm not allowed to call you the names I'd like to, but since you can't see my name-tag, I'm gonna give it a good try." He hazed me while I stared at the Academy crest on my plate.

Classes were a relative relief until word filtered around. Then the instructors made me sit one desk away from the other cadets. After class, I'd find my books scattered down the hall, my hat on the floor or hidden. This would make me late for the next class or formation:

automatic demerits. I was constantly stopped and reprimanded for damaged shoes and disreputable uniform —more demerits, and more tardies, and more demerits.

Cutler had seen to it that my punishment for leaving class would come down with uncanny promptness: in one day. The medical excuse had expired, so I began marching off my new "tour" every afternoon. Back at the company, I'd find my bunk and desk ripped apart: more demerits. And also, punished with confinement, I had to endure the taunts at night, the doorway comedians—and the bogus room inspections bringing more demerits. I'd received so many demerits in such a short time that technically I should have been kicked out, but because I *wanted* to leave, I couldn't.

A few gung-ho types brought by their friends from different companies and pointed me out: "See this scumbag—he's a quitter. So if you see him again, please give him our best regards." Unless the upperclass were around, the Plebes left me alone, largely; still, I'd walk in the room and find Aberby, or Puska, or even Daisy dumping the waste can on my bed, spraying shaving cream in my drawers. The Plebes had also agreed to "silence" me, which I didn't mind at all.

The G-5 Company Commander hadn't received any word on my papers; Cutler was always "unavailable." I kept waiting for the call from Colonel Porterhouse's office which would mean that the resignation had been processed. So far I was bearing the strain, but my nerves were wearing thin. I decided to go over the Major's head and telephoned the Colonel's office, but when they asked for my name, I froze and hung up.

Final examinations were in progress. Six days remained until June. Like every other Plebe, I had to pack my trunk with fatigue uniforms and field equipment for the transfer to Camp Buckner for July training. I now surrendered myself to the last alternative. I took the money from my cadet bank account. I would desert and go to Canada, with leave or without it.

One of Fido's happiest conclusions was that the United States Military Academy has the lowest attrition rate of any college in America. According to the brochure, the print-outs, the officers, and legend, nobody wants to leave. *Esprit de Corps* and all that. Plebe year supposedly "weeds out" the ones who don't belong. So I asked myself why they didn't come after me with a garden hoe.

I might as well have joined the Mafia after graduating from prep school. "Join us and you'll have no bills to pay. The going will be tough but the tough get going. In the Mafia, you will feel the great camaraderie that has been a tradition for hundreds of years. If you don't measure up, you don't got nothing to lose except a few teeth. Unless you're a *welsher*."

Piper, a timid G-5 Plebe, found me alone one morning and handed me a note, returning in ten minutes for my response. Piper had been entertaining "confidential" thoughts of resigning, the note said, and wanted to know whether my resignation was being processed. He was afraid to talk to me, afraid someone might put him on his honor. I went along with the "silence" game and wrote down my answer—I said that if he wanted to know, he could ask me aloud.

In a last act of despair, I phoned the Colonel's office and gave them my name. "Your company?" "Company G-5." The call was transferred to another line. I heard, "Who is this?" and when I identified myself, Cutler laughed back, "Mister, you're cooking your own goose. My stint here may be up, but you can rest assured that everybody else knows about you, Mardis. You'll rot in here, Mister. You'll rot until you can't take it, and then you'll screw up so bad that we'll have you right where we want you, you insubordinate little bastard." He asked me if I was standing at attention while he talked to me.

Two days until June. The Company Commander brought word that I would be detained during June leave for an excess of demerits. I was on the roster of men from all classes, who were assigned to a wing of Washington Hall for summer session, some to serve out punishment tours, the remainder to redeem failing marks with "crash courses." He remarked that I didn't seem surprised, then said, "Oh, yeah, you got a call from Regimental Staff. Go up there and see Hopalong Haroldson."

I took it for granted that I'd been requisitioned for their personal hazing pleasure. After supper, I reported to Regimental Headquarters, a floor-through network in one of the units of the Slums. Haroldson, the autumn G-5 Company Commander, was now on the Fifth Regimental Cadet Staff. As soon as I walked in, a Firstie began hazing me for a scratch on my hat bill, but Haroldson appeared and called him off. "Hi, Mardis." He shook my hand, giving me a boyish grin. Hopalong wore a track warm-up jacket, slippers on his feet. He took me to the vacant conference room.

"Mardis, I saw your name on the bozo list. What's the story?"

"Sir, there is no story."

"Look—fall out." He wrung his hands, then bit his nails. "I know you're resigning and that they're hazing the hell out of you. Have you seen the Colonel yet?"

"No, sir."

"That's what I thought. Did you know that six Plebes are resigning from other companies in the Regiment? Well, two reneged, but the four have already had their resignations processed. They're in the Boarder's Ward right now." He furrowed his brow and asked, "What did you do over in the hospital? I got a friend, he's on Second Regiment Staff, and he knows a nurse there. He's engaged to her. Lieutenant Meadows is her name."

I shook my head yes; I vaguely remembered that she'd mentioned it to me. Haroldson continued. He said he liked me, but he was also doing this for his friend, as a favor to his fiancée. She wanted to know what had happened to me. "Anyway," he said, "you're damn lucky that someone's giving this thing a shove. The Colonel's been gone off and on all month, but the chances are, your resignation—which *was* late, Mardis—hasn't even gotten to him." He told me to be at the Colonel's office at nine the next morning and he would fix it with the company.

We stood. "One more thing. The Colonel's a fair man, and I'm sure he'll set this thing straight. But, Mardis, do yourself a favor. Don't knock West Point."

Mark Rutledge, a General's son, once told me "the story" behind Colonel "Tips" Porterhouse. Porterhouse had been much decorated in World War II as a young officer; he had become a Lieutenant Colonel in Korea and was expected to be a young General. But he never made that grade. Something in him changed; they said it was from seeing too much action too soon. After Korea, the Colonel had owned a dog, and one day the dog didn't obey him and Porterhouse had beaten it to death. The Colonel had changed after that, the story went.

He was a staunch, sawed-off old warrior of perhaps fifty-five, with a snow-white flattop, a thick scarred nose, and a raucous bourbon voice. He snickered and sucked on a dead cigar as he leafed through my file. He showed me a type-set sheet bearing a Freedom Foundation of America emblem: my essay.

"You expressed determination in your essay, son."

"Thank you, sir—Colonel."

"It's not 'Sir Colonel,' Mister. This isn't the German army. Sir will suffice." Porterhouse spun around in his swivel chair to gaze out his window at the sunny morning rooftops of the Slums, his regiment's barracks.

"Determination . . . and intelligence." He spun back around to look at me across his desk. The Colonel's leathery jowls hung down to where his tight, starched officer's collar neatly nipped them off. He absently tried to light the cigar, then asked, "Have you ever been to Poughkeepsie, Cadet Mardis?"

"No, sir." To calm myself I was eying a set of bronzed hand grenades which Porterhouse kept on his uncluttered desk. He tapped them.

"Those are from North Africa. A gift from a dead . . . colleague." He clicked his cheeks. "They aren't American grenades, either."

"Yes, sir. Foreign."

The Colonel cleared his throat and frowned. He was skimming the FFA essay, and now waved it off. "Well. Do you know the way to Poughkeepsie?"

"No, sir." To show I was alert, I mentioned the travel service.

"No, that's not the point. You young people are inclined toward music. Do you recall the old song— maybe you've heard it—"It's a long, long way to Tipperary'?"

I nodded; he went on, "Well, this is the same thing. You see, you've got to know the road to Poughkeepsie in order to get to Poughkeepsie. The town of Poughkeepsie, population zebra charlie, isn't going to do you a tol-darned bit of good unless you know how to get there. Now, the personal indicators in this file—some naïve, some downright stupid, some out*standing* . . ." The Colonel finally got his cigar lit. "This says to me that you want to get to Poughkeepsie, if you know what I mean, but you don't know how to get there. But the point I'm making is that you do know that Poughkeepsie is a real, honest-to-goodness place, if you know what I mean, which is a lot, lot more than many young men your age are aware of, cadets or civilians. And I find that commendable."

He briefed me on the disadvantages of being a civilian. If I left the Academy, the road to Poughkeepsie was still going to be the same length, but getting to Poughkeepsie was going to be that much harder because I'd no longer have good directions. "They'll have you going every which-way looking for your destination, but in the Army, you get that map. It's a good map and it's a free map. And the West Point map is the best the Army has. Do you want that map, son?"

"No, sir."

"But you do want to get to Poughkeepsie?"

"Yes, sir."

Colonel Porterhouse next went over, systematically, the tribulations of a cadet going to the "greener grass" of civilian society. You'd have things stolen because you were used to trusting people. You'd find yourself sitting alone in your room, since no civilian friend could ever live up to a classmate. He said I'd find no better college campus than the one I had. I might even fall in with a bunch of hippies and forget all about Poughkeepsie. "In all sincerity, Mister Mardis, I've seen men leave the Point and a year later come begging to get back in. But they can't. I've seen West Point graduates call it quits with the Army, and five years later, back again, and a rank lower than when they left. That's because you don't just walk through that gate and it ends there. It stays. It'll stay with you and eat your guts apart. For the rest of your life it'll claw your insides out, day and night, because when you make a wrong decision, Mister, you're the one who pays the price. By the same token, if you think you know what you're doing, then, brother, you *do* it. If you don't, or if you *can't*, that's when you hang up your cleats. I don't care who you are."

As he talked, the Colonel's eyes were flashing a bright brown, his bottom lip flattening against his teeth. Over his shoulder, hanging on the wall, were pictures of his commands, the men he'd fought with—platoons of smiling GI's, trios of officers, a staff saluting by an airplane. I looked at the Colonel's pictures and told myself they must have been proud to fight under this officer. Then I

248

noticed the light death X over a GI's face, then another X, and another, and the X's on the officers' faces, and X's on the men beside the plane. The Colonel looked at me, silent, pondering.

"Well, one more resignation isn't going to make or break our current, glorious war effort," he sighed vacantly. An hour later I was in the Boarder's Ward, by six that night, on a bus to New York City.

MEMO 21.

Five Years Later.

Another hard run, I told myself, but I'd made it once again through the living hell of the New York City afternoon rush hour. My Checker Medallion was happily clacking across the corrugated side lane of the Queensboro Bridge. Night lights were just flashing on in the November dusk, and I could see the luminescent skyline tracing hazily down the East River all the way to Brooklyn Heights. This was the great moment of peace for a cab driver.

I wheeled into Myrtle's, tires flinging gravel. I'd found Myrtle's by luck. Got lost in Queens one day trying to find my way to the bridge and wound up under the bridge. Myrtle's is the only restaurant under the Queensboro bridge, and it was designed for people just like me. The Big Boys ate here—kind of an exclusive joint, the kind you have to be told about. The Big Boys had asked me who'd told *me* about it and I said: "I heard." I parked my Checker between a silver-blue Pederbilt semi-diesel cab and a fire-engine-red Mack IV tandem rig. This was a class joint.

"The usual, Jimmie?"

"Ditto."

It was Myrtle. She came in around five and hung around till maybe seven. The receipts and stuff. I took off my newsboy cap and aviator shades and took a gander. A few of the Big Boys grunted hello. Busy watching the sports report. Myrtle splashed a hot cup down and did her thing with the towel. "We're outta cutlets. Had a big lunch crowd today."

"Yeah? Make it a chopped steak."

"Still want carrots and peas?"

"Ditto."

"M.P. or F.F.'s?"

"The *usual*, already, Myrtle."

She called the order to the cook, then she gave one of the Big Boys a free refill. Myrtle put on some lipstick and high-heeled over in front of me, clapping her compact shut and slipping it neatly into her apron pocket. Sometimes I thought Myrtle only came in between five and seven to show off. She didn't have to come in and count the receipts. With all her dough, she could hire an accountant to come in and count the receipts.

Myrtle set down a glass of water, fork, knife, even a napkin. "Hey—Jimmie. You look like you swallowed a tire tool. You *agitated* about something?"

"What's that mean?"

"Aw, come on, honey. Myrtle knows when her boys have got something on their mind. West Point again?"

She said it softly. I'd spilled the story to Myrtle one night around seven, on my third beer. Even the Big Boys hadn't been to West Point. Cookie rang the bell and Myrtle brought over the platter. Now I remembered why I never ordered chopped steak. Myrtle looked at me crossly. "So what are you so agitated about?"

"I've had a hard day, Myrtle. I've had it tougher than any joker in here."

"So get out of the rat race. That's what it is. New York is one big rat race. Move to Queens."

I shoved my coffee at her. "Make it a beer, Myrtle." She nodded quietly and drew it off the tap; I started eating.

251

She put on some more lipstick. "Queens is a community," she told me. "We got people over here. Take Joey there, and Hank. Both married men, home owners. Over here we do things right. Where you live, it's a . . . it's a . . . a what-ya-macallit. A filthy human jungle."

"Amen."

"You like that?"

"I can't change it."

"But you can better yourself. I think you're in a *rut*. You say you want to be a truck driver. Why, I'll bet a nickle on the donut you could be something better than that. If you want to be. This is America. You're free to go as high as you want to go."

"From thirty floors up I should make a good splat."

"Oh . . . now. That's a horrible thought."

"I'm just kiddin'. But no kiddin', this cab-driver stuff is getting to me. Yes sir, no sir, yes ma'am, no ma'am. Don't get me wrong, I like being polite to people. But ask yourself this: Do they deserve it? And here's the clincher, Myrtle. Last Saturday, I drove around for six hours and I didn't pick up *one* customer. Nobody." I finished what I wanted of the platter and shook my head.

"Is business that bad?"

"No, not bad. I didn't want to pick anybody up. I felt better just passing them by, even in the rain. Let 'em run a little bit and then boom, off I go. Or maybe the puddle treatment. Mess up their nice clothes, their nice Saks Fifth Avenue clothes."

"Don't tell me you're one of *those*." Myrtle cleared my place angrily. I felt guilty, tried to say I gave the dry cleaners business. She went away. I finished the beer.

Myrtle returned with the check. I said, "Really, I only splashed one or two people. And they had raincoats on. It wasn't even a dirty puddle. It was on Fifth Avenue, Myrtle."

I slid over a tip and Myrtle slid it back, saying, "It troubles me to think a West Pointer would do something that *low.*" I started away sullenly, and she called to me, feigning cheer. "You know the coffee's always hot at Myrtle's!"

A few hours later I was at the cab company. Lousy night, very competitive. Almost got in two accidents on Third Avenue. First another driver cut me off for a fare, and then, using the same trick, I cut another guy off and he did a sideways screech and just missed me by inches. The fare didn't even appreciate my eagerness to serve. Almost got my tail-side swiped for a 35¢ tip. "Go buy yourself a chocolate malted," she said, both of us knowing chocolate malteds cost more than that.

Very cutthroat. My last fare of the night was some blonde on York Avenue. Another Checker was one light up, heading toward me—two-way street—and I'm at this light facing her but she's on the other side of the street. So as soon as the lights change I pull a U-turn and get to her first. He comes peeling up from his light but she gets in my cab after a hesitation. The cabbie is some Armenian who likes blondes; he hops out of his cab and tries to get in my cab—why, I don't know. But I lock the doors as soon as she's in and the Armenian climbs on top of my cab. He gets a free ride until I shove on the breaks for the next light. The blonde thinks it's funny and I get a dollar tip out of the escapade. The Armenian gets a free nose job off the cobblestone of York Avenue.

The guys are sitting around at the cab company telling yak stories. Yak yak yak. Ha ha ha. I'm too tired to participate and even turn down an invite to go to Cleo's, the local topless setup. When I handed in my chart, big shot didn't like it. I'd been putting too many miles on his vehicle without enough money to show for it. I get a percentage of the meter and tips. He figures with all the miles, I'm doing it off the meter and putting it in my pocket. "This is your last warning, bubs." "Yeah, yeah," I tell him.

High-wheeling cab driver that I am, I have to walk

home. I can't afford a cab. Fifteen blocks through the Lower East Side—not so bad, as long as it isn't past midnight. So I walk along, thinking of matters far and wide, of odds and ends, of the kind of soup I'll have tomorrow, peering into barred-up shoestores, glancing at a darkened doorway, admiring a neon sign or two. I pause at a pet store on Fourteenth Street and recall Beanhead, my spider monkey. Beanhead ran away.

I guess I ran away, too. Mom and Dad and Sis, they didn't like it too much when I dropped out. Dad had to explain to the guys at the office; Mom was hurt that I hadn't brought her my Full Dress Hat so she could make a lamp out of it. To Sis, I was just another drab civilian. The gallant warrior, the youthful Bengal Lancer, had turned coward and fled the battlefield.

Two colleges, three cities, a year of ulcer traces from sweating out my draft lottery number. Night school, pawn shops, bicycle messenger, cheap hotels, Local Ship Scalers & Painters Union, file clerking, hitchhiking, so what. Cry in my beer and cry some more, I had to answer to the Big Soldier in the sky for what I had become, or what I hadn't become. No excuse, sir.

Mrs. Bernstein revealed one eye through the slit of her door on the first floor. "Psst! Jimmie." One eye and half her face. "Mister Bernstein stuck in basement again. Bad leg, you know. You know. You go help, yes? He went to fix fuse." The Bernstein's pet chihuahua and my little Beanhead had been excellent friends. "Made for each other," Mrs. Bernstein used to say. I assisted her husband up from the basement and they thanked me profusely.

I didn't mind; doing good turns made me feel like a good boy scout—-like a good *cadet*. Five years and here I was, still cringing when I saw a scuff on my shoe. Still negotiating staircases with my arms held in right angles for the correct double-time position. My desk, a closet door nailed onto an old wooden bedstead, was always in Special Inspection Order.

My mother occasionally asked in her letters: Why don't you *please* go back to West Point and finish? Quite prophetic, because I had frequent nightmares in which the men of the Corps sought me out and invited me back. Once a cadet, always a cadet. You can take the boy out of West Point, but you can't take West Point out of the boy. Old Colonel Porterhouse was right.

My prep school mates were somewhere in America in three-piece suits, or in law school, or medical school. My West Point classmates were scattered over the world on military bases—young Lieutenants, bouncing quarters off beds. *Who am I?* An American! *What am I?* Nothing. *What is this?* The East Village, and I'm propped back in a leatherette easy chair, staring a hole into the TIRE TUBES UNLIMITED sign across the street.

Why did that lousy spider monkey run out on me? I kept asking myself. I couldn't get over it. I'd traded a chest of drawers—good condition—to an acquaintance for the young monster and then spent valuable weeks training him to be a good cadet. Do your duty in the right place. No swinging on the chandeliers because he'd short-circuit the whole building. I went to the fun shop and bought him a little outfit with brass buttons. That monkey had the best.

I suppose I did exploit the monkey for my own reasons, a therapy of some kind. If Beanhead didn't obey orders, I would confine him to quarters. When Beanhead exhibited faulty table manners, he had to eat K-rations, monkey-chow. I forced him to accompany me on the cab route, since he doubled my tips: "*Here's for the monkey.*" But when we two soldiers got home from combat duty in the cab, Beanhead was rewarded; he got a saucer of beer and his choice on TV. Usually a Tarzan movie or a safari adventure.

Then one night Beanhead made me mad and I hazed him. It was over some trifle. I can't even remember what it was, maybe just the expression on his face, but I was saying, "After all I've done for you and look! You're a disgrace to that monkey outfit! You're got to work just like everybody else, fellah, and if you don't like panhandling from the front seat of a yellow Checker, then go find yourself a skid-row organ grinder! And if you think you're so great, why did Elwood and his wife want to get rid of you—huh?" I ripped the little epaulettes off his shoulders. "You're on monkey ration for the next week!"

Beanhead threw a temper tantrum. He was dashing off the walls, screaming in a high voice, trying to break plastic dishes, totally disrupting the living room inspection order, and in general behaving like an impudent, uneducated monkey. He hopped out an open window and went down the fire escape, crossed the street, and the last I saw of him he was waving farewell from the TIRE TUBES UNLIMITED sign.

Where was I? In the East Village. And where was Beanhead? Probably in some posh uptown high rise, a rich lady's pet, having his nails painted and sucking on a piece of store-bought pastrami. I suppose Mrs. Bernstein's wasn't good enough for him. I guess he's dating a toy poodle now. It just didn't figure. But maybe Beanhead was trying to tell me something.

I reported to work early the next morning and did the day shift. A fast Saturday. I hung out at the Statler and did a lot of short runs—some convention or other. I was booking good all morning. The conventioneers were young execs from the Midwest and the South. I kept my yak shut and did OK.

They'd lean forward and read the hack license: "Say, uh, Mardis, buddy. Where the action at around here?"

"Blonde or brunette, sir?"

"Hey Marvin—our driver's got a sense of humor."

Over comes a fiver. "Brunette and no surprises to take home to the wife. I'm a decent guy, you know." Ten o'clock in the morning and the junior executives are hot

256

to prove their manhood on the streets of New York. Fine with me. Ring the buzzer twice and ask for Madame Fogarty.

I've decided today, once and for all, for now and forever, in spite of overwhelming odds, to stop feeling sorry for myself and get ahead in life. I may be driving a cab, I'm thinking, but this job was going to get me back on my feet. Save money, enroll in night school, begin looking for a better job, buy nice clothes, buy Mom a birthday gift, move out of my slum neighborhood. I was going to spring through the open window of hope just like Beanhead. There was a time for everything and my time had come. This was it. The big showdown. Today was the beginning of the rest of your life. The power of positive thinking. "Poughkeepsie."

"Huh?"

"Poughkeepsie, please. Do you know how to get there?" I'd picked up a couple at Seventy-Sixth and West End. Kinda fancy. Young like.

"I'll have to call this one in to the company, you know."

"Go right ahead," the man said. "We'll wait. My car's in the shop."

"Well—it'll cost you an extra dime, you know. It's upstate, right? So you pay the tolls, too, you know."

"Fine, fine."

I answered, "OK, you wanta go to Poughkeepsie, you hailed the right cab. Yes, sir, this cab will go to Poughkeepsie like you never seen."

"*All* right, here's your dime."

I called in to the company, as was the procedure on long rides, to get the flat rate. My boss said I'd better not do any joyriding because he knew how many miles it was to Poughkeepsie and how many miles back and if I didn't have fifty cents to the mile on the penny when I got back tonight I could take my driving abilities elsewhere.

The couple gave me directions and chatted merrily,

and in forty-five minutes we were approaching that burgh. They asked me why I drove a cab and I said, "Somebody has to drive a cab." They argued about someone named "Raoul" for a moment and then we arrived at a crossroads where they said to take a right. I dropped them off in front of the Lower Hudson Valley Real Estate Corporation, a smalltown building.

"All right, don't get lost going back!" the man said cheerfully. "Take the left fork and don't take the right fork."

The woman put in, "Be *sure* and take the left fork and *don't* take the right fork because that road leads to West Point and I don't think they like long-haired people like you up there at *all*!"

"Huh?" I'd made it to Poughkeepsie, hadn't I? The cab peeled out with me at the helm, veering for the fork that led to West Point. In the rearview mirror I could see the couple frantically waving their arms. In my gut was a daring feeling such as Errol Flynn must have known in *The Charge of the Light Brigade*! The yellow Checker flew by traffic, ignored warning signs, passed on curves, and soon sped through the high stone gates of West Point. The guards didn't stop me, since on Saturday afternoons the Point catered to tourists.

I was awe-stricken, slowing my pace to "gawk." West Point! The United States Military Academy of America! Jumping catfish! Cadets and stuff. The carefully groomed grounds, the ancient austere halls, the vast sweep of the mighty Hudson, and here and there on escorting privileges were the hand-carved men of the Corps. The new men of the Corps. But they looked like the old men of the Corps. And they looked like each other. I beeped my horn at them.

I shook my fist at them, leisurely cruising along Thayer Road in my battlefield-dusty Checker. I saw a Firstie walking along with his date—right toward a puddle—

and I sped up. To my glee, he turned and saw me speeding toward him and stepped out in the road to flag me
down in the manner of a hostile traffic cop. I'm sure I
looked like one powerful commie infiltrator with my
aviator shades and newsboy cap. Such joy! The Firstie
marched up to the naughty vehicle, scowling severely.
His date, who wore a corsage, remained on the sidewalk
beside Thayer Road, clasping her hands, watching the
movements of her masculine maestro with an obvious
quiver of stark admiration.

The First Classman told me to roll the window *all* the
way down. "Okay, *wise* guy," he enunciated, gangster
style.

"You got somethin' to say, buster?"

He shot his head down closer. "Mis*ter*! You play the
game when you're on *these* premises. Get it?"

I took off my aviator shades, glanced down at his feet,
then put the shades back on. "You talk pretty fancy for a
bozo, you know what I mean? You call those shoes military, Mister Cadet?"

The Firstie removed his hat and stuck his face in the
window. "All right, you. You got a smart lip, learn this
one. We don't like your type around here, *get* it? And if
you don't get it, you will get it. What's your mission
here?"

"My mission? An excellent point, my friend." I gave
him a raspberry and screeched away, tires smoking. The
Firstie would just have to explain to his lady-in-waiting
that everybody has a tough time hazing a cab driver from
New York City! After that, I calmed down, parked the
cab, and strolled over to the newly constructed activities
center for a soft drink and some closer observations.

Amazingly, their faces, amidst the sea of gray
uniforms, looked strikingly similar, not only to each
other, but to the men of the Corps whom I had known.
Perhaps it was the saltpeter in the mashed potatoes,

259

possibly the regimentation. Give these bozos a Plebe year in the Lower East Side and they'd come up with a few lines of character. I gawked and analyzed and felt so deliriously wonderful after arbitrary whiffs of free air in this old environment that I thought I should induce vomiting. . . . Here I was, in a private paradise of gawking and general disreputable delight, high as a kite, my shoes unshined, not having seen a slide rule or an officer in five years, and my grudges and misconceptions were evaporating like fog off the morning turnpike. A repeat and well-known performance of the grand but exceedingly monotonous West Point Production. First Sergeant, First Classman, first man on the totem pole—those scary stripes on the sleeve were now the emblems of so much child's play in a playpen of preposterous proportions! I had to laugh out loud, which brought me to the attention of two cadet guards posted in the snack bar of the activities center.

"On my honor," I told them, "a cadet friend of mine is supposed to meet me here."

Unescorted, I wasn't allowed here. The guards didn't fall for my story; no doubt my smile was too diabolically wide. "Sorry," one said snobbishly, "but you'll have to proceed elsewhere."

"Can't I even buy a root beer?"

The other guard pointed the way out and huffed, "*Post!* You civilians can't just walk in here." Which was the most fundamentally *nice* thing a cadet ever told me.

West Point did get one last lash of vengeance on its turncoat that night, at 10:00 P.M., 2200 hours, when the Chelsea Checker Medallion Company fired the nogood, boondoggling—and champagne silly—joyrider with too, too many miles. However, my distraught soul could now relax into the leatherette easy chair of a man with no misgivings. The Point, I had concluded, was not a menace, not a manhood machine, maybe a masterful masquerade, but not a hardline proving grounds for the

260

good pure blood of America. I didn't really know what *exactly* it was, but I was just as proud and free and bold and courageously innovative as I could ever hope to be. I was myself. But not without a sense of heritage:

As history will bear out, I was the first West Pointer to ever stand in an unemployment line.